# International Social Work
## of All People in the Whole World
## A New Construction
### Second Edition

Edited By Masateru Higashida, Tatsuru Akimoto
and Kana Matsuo

ARIISW-Shukutoku

Junposha

Published by Junposha
544 Waseda Tsurumakicho, Shinjuku-ku, Tokyo 162-0041, Japan

Copyright ©2024 Editorial and selection matter: Masateru Higashida,
Tatsuru Akimoto and Kana Matsuo,
Individual chapters: The contributors
Asian Research Institute for International Social Work,
Shukutoku University
Printed in Japan

Book design by welle design

ISBN978-4-8451-1955-4

All rights reserved. No part of this book may be reproduced or utilized in
any form or by any means, electronic or mechanical, including photocopying,
recording, or by any information storage and retrieval system, without permission.

For information, address
Asian Research Institute for International Social Work, Shukutoku University,
200Daiganji-cho, Chuo-ku, Chiba City, Chiba 260-0812, Japan
Tel: +81-(0)43-265-9879
Email: asiainst@soc.shukutoku.ac.jp

# Contents

*Contributors* ................................................................................................ 8

*Preface* ......................................................................................................... 9

## Part I:
## A New Construction

*Prologue* ...................................................................................................... 15

*Glossary* ....................................................................................................... 19

## Chapter One:

A Review of the Conceptual Development of International
Social Work in Western-Rooted Social Work—Understandings
of the Term, Concept, and Definition— .................................................... 22

1.  The Conceptual Development of International Social Work
    by Period ........................................................................................... 24

1.1 Up to the 1920s to the Early 40s: Birth and Beginning ............... 24

1.2 The Late 40s to the 80s: The Transfer and the Assistance from
    the North to the South, and the Leap from "International"
    Social Work to "International Social Work" .................................. 27

1.3 The 1990s to the Early 21st Century: Maturity of Definition
    and International Social Work in Globalization ........................... 31

2.  Roundup and Limitations ................................................................ 42

## Chapter Two:

Another Understanding of International Social Work—
Not Categories of Activities but a Way of Viewing Matters— .............. 58
To Create 'the International Social Work'—Practice and Research
and the Norms of International Social Work— ....................................... 61

1.  To do What is International Social Work?—Practice and
    Research Conducted Under the Name of International
    Social Work ....................................................................................... 62

2.  This Is Not Necessarily International Social Work ......................... 67

3.  What Is International Social Work? ................................................. 71

4.  Not to See and Think from the Perspective of One's Own
    Country—A tentative definition and 'the way of viewing
    matters' of international social work— ........................................... 75

5.  Where Are We Now? ......................................................................... 77

3

6.   Summary ⋯⋯⋯⋯⋯⋯⋯⋯⋯⋯⋯⋯⋯⋯⋯⋯⋯⋯⋯⋯⋯ 80

## Chapter Three:

A New Construction of International Social Work ⋯⋯⋯⋯⋯⋯⋯⋯ 86

1.   Two Models of Conceptual Development of International Social Work and Questions on the Achievement of International Social Work of Western-rooted (Professional) Social Work ⋯⋯⋯⋯⋯⋯⋯⋯⋯⋯⋯⋯⋯⋯⋯⋯⋯⋯⋯⋯⋯⋯⋯⋯⋯⋯87

1.1  Simplified Models of the Conceptual Development of International Social Work ⋯⋯⋯⋯⋯⋯⋯⋯⋯⋯⋯⋯⋯⋯⋯⋯87

1.2  Brief Discussion on the Achievements of the International Social Work of Western-rooted (Professional) Social Work—Questions Raised at the End of Chapter 1 ⋯⋯⋯⋯⋯⋯95

2.   A New Construction of 'International Social Work' ⋯⋯⋯⋯⋯⋯ 98

2.1  Groundwork ⋯⋯⋯⋯⋯⋯⋯⋯⋯⋯⋯⋯⋯⋯⋯⋯⋯⋯⋯⋯ 99

2.2  Framework ⋯⋯⋯⋯⋯⋯⋯⋯⋯⋯⋯⋯⋯⋯⋯⋯⋯⋯⋯⋯ 104

2.3  Core elements of International Social Work ⋯⋯⋯⋯⋯⋯⋯ 108

2.4  Birth of International Social Work and the Historical Development of its Relation with 'National' Social Work and Social Work as a Whole ⋯⋯⋯⋯⋯⋯⋯⋯⋯⋯⋯⋯⋯⋯⋯ 112

2.5  The *Idealtypus* and the 'Actual Being': International Social Work and International Social Work (dash) ⋯⋯⋯⋯⋯ 114

2.6  Environmental Factors: Internationalization and Globalization ⋯⋯⋯⋯⋯⋯⋯⋯⋯⋯⋯⋯⋯⋯⋯⋯⋯⋯⋯⋯ 116

2.7  The Future: Unsolved Questions ⋯⋯⋯⋯⋯⋯⋯⋯⋯⋯⋯ 121

3.   A Newly Constructed Definition and Conclusive Summary ⋯⋯ 125

## Chapter Four:

The Essence of International Social Work and Nine World Maps—How to Induct Students Into the Secrets of International Social Work— ⋯ 137

1.   What Is International Social Work? ⋯⋯⋯⋯⋯⋯⋯⋯⋯⋯⋯ 137

2.   How to Convey the Essence of International Social Work ⋯⋯⋯ 139

Appendix ⋯⋯⋯⋯⋯⋯⋯⋯⋯⋯⋯⋯⋯⋯⋯⋯⋯⋯⋯⋯⋯⋯⋯⋯⋯⋯ 153

*Epilogue* ⋯⋯⋯⋯⋯⋯⋯⋯⋯⋯⋯⋯⋯⋯⋯⋯⋯⋯⋯⋯⋯⋯⋯⋯⋯⋯ 161

# Part II:
## The Foundations Underpinning the Construction

## Chapter Five:
Birth, Growth and Transformation of Borders and Nation-states ········168
1.  What is a Border? ·················································································· 168
2.  Some Aspects of Borders ································································· 169
3.  The History of Borders: Their Birth, Development, Change and
    Disappearance? ·················································································· 171
4.  Problems and Issues Related to Borders ································· 175
5.  Summary and Implications ···························································· 176

## Chapter Six:
Nationalism, Internationalism and Cosmopolitanism: A Comparative
Analysis of the Concepts ··········································································· 179
1.  The Meaning of Each Term ··························································· 180
1.1 Nationalism ························································································· 180
1.2 Internationalism ················································································ 182
1.3 Cosmopolitanism ·············································································· 184
2.  The History of Each Term ····························································· 185
2.1 The history of nationalism ···························································· 185
2.2 The history of internationalism ··················································· 187
2.3 The history of cosmopolitanism ················································· 189
3.  Comparing Nationalism, Internationalism and Cosmopolitanism
    in the Context of Contemporary Geopolitics ······················· 190
4.  Conclusion ··························································································· 194

## Chapter Seven:
A World Behind and Beyond "Nationality" ······································· 196
1.  The Three Meanings of Nationality ············································ 198
1.1 Nationality as a fundamental human right ······························ 198
1.2 Nationality as proof of identity ·················································· 201
1.3 Nationality as a tool for achieving a better life ···················· 203
2.  The Dilemmas of Migrants' Social Integration and the Refugee
    Protection System ·············································································· 204

2.1 Complex structures of exclusion that transcend the dichotomy
of "foreigners" and "nationals" ⋯⋯⋯⋯⋯⋯⋯⋯⋯⋯⋯⋯⋯⋯⋯ 204

2.2 Refugee protection systems: Nationality and border control ⋯ 205

3. Intersectionality, or Deconstructing Categories ⋯⋯⋯⋯⋯⋯ 208

4. Beyond Nationality and Categorizations ⋯⋯⋯⋯⋯⋯⋯⋯ 210

# Chapter Eight:
## Foreign Aid and the National Interest ⋯⋯⋯⋯⋯⋯⋯⋯⋯⋯ 215

1. What Motivates Countries to Provide Aid? ⋯⋯⋯⋯⋯⋯⋯ 215

1.1 Overview of Official Development Assistance ⋯⋯⋯⋯⋯⋯ 215

1.2 Linking foreign aid to national interest
in the past and present ⋯⋯⋯⋯⋯⋯⋯⋯⋯⋯⋯⋯⋯⋯⋯⋯ 219

1.3 Foreign aid and national interest: The case of Japan ⋯⋯⋯ 220

1.4 Free and Open Indo-Pacific (FOIP) Initiative and
the Abe Doctrine ⋯⋯⋯⋯⋯⋯⋯⋯⋯⋯⋯⋯⋯⋯⋯⋯⋯⋯ 221

2. Foreign Aid Competition and Cooperation ⋯⋯⋯⋯⋯⋯⋯ 222

2.1 Recipient perspectives ⋯⋯⋯⋯⋯⋯⋯⋯⋯⋯⋯⋯⋯⋯⋯ 222

2.2 China's cooperation on international development ⋯⋯⋯⋯ 223

2.3 The aid complementarity hypothesis ⋯⋯⋯⋯⋯⋯⋯⋯⋯ 224

2.4 Aid complementarity in practice ⋯⋯⋯⋯⋯⋯⋯⋯⋯⋯⋯ 225

3. The Post-COVID-19 Development Paradigm ⋯⋯⋯⋯⋯⋯ 226

3.1 The collapse of liberal capitalism and the search for
a new form of capitalism ⋯⋯⋯⋯⋯⋯⋯⋯⋯⋯⋯⋯⋯⋯ 226

3.2 Platform capitalism ⋯⋯⋯⋯⋯⋯⋯⋯⋯⋯⋯⋯⋯⋯⋯⋯ 228

3.3 SDGs reexamined ⋯⋯⋯⋯⋯⋯⋯⋯⋯⋯⋯⋯⋯⋯⋯⋯⋯ 229

4. Concluding Remarks ⋯⋯⋯⋯⋯⋯⋯⋯⋯⋯⋯⋯⋯⋯⋯⋯ 230

# Chapter Nine:
## Mapping the Distribution of Social Workers and Social Work Schools ⋯ 234

1. Number and Distribution of Social Workers ⋯⋯⋯⋯⋯⋯ 235

2. Number and Distribution of Social Work Schools/Programs
Identified by the International Association of Schools of Social
Work ⋯⋯⋯⋯⋯⋯⋯⋯⋯⋯⋯⋯⋯⋯⋯⋯⋯⋯⋯⋯⋯⋯⋯ 240

3. Example: Relationship between Mental Health Social Workers
and Social Work Schools ⋯⋯⋯⋯⋯⋯⋯⋯⋯⋯⋯⋯⋯⋯⋯ 241

4. Conclusions ⋯⋯⋯⋯⋯⋯⋯⋯⋯⋯⋯⋯⋯⋯⋯⋯⋯⋯⋯ 242

## Chapter Ten:
Buddhist Social Work ⋯⋯⋯⋯⋯⋯⋯⋯⋯⋯⋯⋯⋯⋯⋯⋯ 244

    1.   A Brief History of Research Activities on
          Buddhist Social Work ⋯⋯⋯⋯⋯⋯⋯⋯⋯⋯⋯⋯⋯ 245

    2.   Characteristics of Buddhist Social Work ⋯⋯⋯⋯⋯ 246

    3.   Conceptualization ⋯⋯⋯⋯⋯⋯⋯⋯⋯⋯⋯⋯⋯⋯⋯ 248

    4.   Conclusion ⋯⋯⋯⋯⋯⋯⋯⋯⋯⋯⋯⋯⋯⋯⋯⋯⋯⋯ 250


*Postface* ⋯⋯⋯⋯⋯⋯⋯⋯⋯⋯⋯⋯⋯⋯⋯⋯⋯⋯⋯⋯⋯⋯⋯ 254

*Index* ⋯⋯⋯⋯⋯⋯⋯⋯⋯⋯⋯⋯⋯⋯⋯⋯⋯⋯⋯⋯⋯⋯⋯⋯ 256

# Contributors

**Tatsuru Akimoto, DSW**
Honorary Director, Asian Research Institute for International Social Work, Shukutoku University; Professor Emeritus, Japan Women's University

**Josef Gohori, PhD**
Professor, Graduate School of Integrated Human and Social Welfare Studies, Shukutoku University

**Masateru Higashida, PhD**
Head Researcher, Asian Research Institute for International Social Work, Shukutoku University

**Kana Matsuo**
Senior Researcher, Asian Research Institute for International Social Work, Shukutoku University

**Ayako Sasaki, PhD**
Associate Professor, Graduate School of Global and Transdisciplinary Studies, Chiba University

**Takeshi Sato-Daimon, PhD**
Professor, School of International Liberal Studies, Waseda University

**Hiromi Satoh**
Lecturer, Faculty of Global Studies, Reitaku University

**Taichi Uchio, PhD**
Associate Professor, Faculty of Cultural Policy and Management, Shizuoka University of Art and Culture (SUAC)

The affiliations and titles are accurate as of March 31, 2024

# Preface

What is international social work? What perspectives are required for it? A century has passed since international social work came to be, but these fundamental questions remain important. This book approaches these very basic questions that are arguably the most important ones for international social work. To become acquainted with the main arguments of this book, please refer to the prologue of Part I (equivalent to the preface of the first edition). In this preface, I introduce the background and structure of the book.

The original version of this book, a four-chapter monograph by Dr. Tatsuru Akimoto, Honorary Director of the Asian Research Institute for International Social Work (ARIISW) at Shukutoku University, was published in February 2024 by Junpo-sha. Following Dr. Akimoto's proposal, this book is here being republished in an expanded edition, with the addition of new chapters to support the discussion of the first edition. The new, significantly updated edition of the book includes the original Chapters 1–4 of the first edition as Part I, and Chapters 5–10, written by other researchers, have been added to form Part II. This second edition was compiled to make the arguments of Part I stronger and clearer while maintaining them as the core of the book.

The structure of the chapters is as follows. Chapter 1 of Part I provides an overview of the historical context and achievements of international social work based on Western-rooted professional social work (WPSW). Chapter 2 discusses the similarities and differences between WPSW and international social work in the non-Western region of the Far East, drawing on the results of a survey of international social work, international social welfare, and related concepts. In Chapter 3, using the findings in Chapters 1 and 2, a new definition of international social work is presented after the Theory of the State is conceptualized. Chapter 4 portrays how the essence of international social work can be conveyed to those who are entering this field, using different world maps as an educational tool.

In Part II, each chapter is written by an author from a different academic background to supplement the discussion of international social work in Part I. With the exception of certain chapters, points supporting the new theory of international social work in Part I were introduced without requiring discussion of international social work itself, and points were delved into in a way that beginners could understand. It was also requested by the editors that the authors not set the discussion in any one home country or a specific country with which they had an exclusive relationship. This was done to ensure that special value not be placed on specific countries or regions as emphasized and clarified in the new definition of international social work, shown in Chapter 3. Under these conditions, each chapter of Part II was reviewed by the editors and then revised by the authors.

Chapter 5 briefly outlines the complex relationships among borders and states, which are important elements in the new theory of international social work. This chapter introduces the nature of the borders and boundaries and the process of their formation in historical and geopolitical contexts, among others. Chapter 6 outlines the content and historical background of nationalism, internationalism, and cosmopolitanism systematically and clearly while untangling the threads between them. This view of these concepts and their relationships promotes an understanding based on a more comprehensive and multifaceted perspective. Chapter 7 examines nationality, citizenship, and identity from multiple angles. It challenges the limits to discussions of nationality and categorization and discusses them in the light of the author's own thoughts and experiences. Chapter 8 provides an overview for foreign aid and the national interest, based on the latest findings. This chapter scrutinizes the dynamics of foreign aid and its intersection with the national interest, shedding light on the complexity picture of international aid in the real world. Chapter 9 visualizes the distribution or imbalance of social work professionals and social work schools worldwide, adopting the use of the geographic information systems with open public data as a source. Chapter 10 outlines the findings of Buddhist social work research conducted by ARIISW as an example of non-WPSW. The description of Buddhist social work in this chapter gives the author's own understanding, adding the author's own perspective to ARIISW's findings.

In this new exploration of international social work, each chapter forms a contribution to the development of a comprehensive discussion, drawing on multiple perspectives. However, some other candidate chapters that were considered in the plan for the expanded edition of this book did not come to fruition (see the epilogue of Part I). They may be included in the future, along with the further development of the second edition's discussions.

This book is significantly different from previous work on international social work. As Dr. Akimoto writes in the prologue to Part I, the uniqueness of this book is outstanding, and even its form or type is hard to classify. We hope that it will not only be read by scholars around the world who specialize in international social work but will also provide stimulus to readers who have never even heard the term international social work.

On behalf of the editors
Masateru Higashida

# Acknowledgements

We would like to express our deepest gratitude to everyone who has been involved in the creation of this second edition of the book, whether directly or indirectly. First, we are grateful to all the pioneers who have contributed to the development of international social work, and to those who have engaged in discussions and exchanges of opinion at forums and study groups with the Asian Research Institute for International Social Work. We believe that without the give and take of knowledge and experience with all of you, we would not have been able to conceive the ideas in this extended book.

In addition, we extend our heartfelt thanks to all of the authors and everyone who was directly involved in the creation of this book. We are also deeply grateful to those who supported this process, including Prof Noriko Totsuka, Director of the ARIISW, Prof Yosuke Fujimori, Director of the Asian Centre for Buddhist Social Work Research Exchange, and Mr. Kazuya Ejima, Ms. Kana Nonaka, Ms. Yuki Someya, and Ms. Takako Nose at ARIISW's office.

Finally, we express our utmost gratitude to Mr. Hiroyasu Kiuchi, President and CEO of Junpo-sha, who recognized the significance of publishing this book and supported the entire process.

Tatsuru Akimoto, Kana Matsuo, and Masateru Higashida

Part I

# A NEW CONSTRUCTION

Tatsuru Akimoto

# Prologue

What is international social work? Is it work that concerns other countries? To do social work in a colony to make it easier to rule, or to be engaged in missionary work or an ODA project as a herald for one's own country's political aggression or economic expansion—is this international social work? Is it international social work to research and introduce to the rest of the world the social welfare situation of any country? Is it to learn from other nations about the solution to problems that immigrants from other countries have, or the improvement of policies and programs of child welfare in one's own country? (Or would this be more national social work?) Is it international social work to be involved with global social issues such as climate change and pandemics, to discuss multiculturalism, or to make international comparisons? Is it international social work to strive for the globalization of Western-rooted social work in the name of a global profession? All of these are not necessarily international social work.

Nearly 100 years have passed since the foundations of international social work were laid. Since then, it has grown into a grand "architecture" due to our predecessors' formidable efforts. These we unconditionally respect and appreciate, and pray that this advancement continues.

These efforts and achievements have been mainly those of the English-medium and/or the Western world. This book is a contribution from the non-English-speaking, non-Western world, which has been neglected. Something new and unique may come out of it.

Part I of this book will introduce a new approach to international social work which will be different from prevailing mainstream international social work approaches. This is conceptually to construct a new international social work. It is not to deny, redefine, and reconstruct mainstream international social work.

We think that international social work centres not on certain categories of activities but on a certain "way of viewing matters," which sees things from a perspective outside a nation state (a sovereign nation) including one's own country and/or with "compound eyes" (multiple points of view). The antonym of international social work is national (domestic or local) social work.

The constituency of international social work includes all people(s) of all countries and regions on the Earth. It sees and serves all people equally. To make it a reality, international social work cannot take the equation "Social work = Western-rooted professional social work" for granted. Other types of social work must be also borne in mind if international social work is discussed at all. Western-rooted professional social work has not served, and cannot serve all or the overwhelming majority of the constituency today or in the near future, both in terms of its quantity and quality. International social work must be conformable to all kinds of social work.

International social work does not stop, for example, at the levels of human rights and the United Nations. It further questions their substance. Human rights is not a single-meaning concept. It is also not a peculiar value of international social work but of social work as a whole. The United Nations' organizations, activities, and products are the outcomes of strife among sovereign countries.

The new international social work shows other features. For example:
1. International social work is born twice. Firstly when national borders are drawn up, and secondly, when nation states mature.
2. When nation states mature, there are two ways to overcome their limits or their national borders. One is to have international-related activities of national social work in a sovereign nation, and the other to have activities (including a view) from the outside of a sovereign nation. Only the latter has been adopted as international social work in our new definition.
3. International social work, which has spun off from (national) social work to be an independent entity out of the sovereignty of nation states and remaining within the framework of social work, reminds us that the element of "being out of the sovereignty of nation states" is inevitable in social work from its birth—as if it were in its genes.
4. International social work is defined not from the "professional (or

occupational) social worker" side but from the "social work" side.

5. International social work does not simply aim for the globalization of Western-rooted (professional) social work.

(Readers who wish to jump straight to the final definition of the new international social work may refer to Chapter 3.3)

Chapter 1 reviews the achievements of international social work as part of Western-rooted professional social work. Chapter 2 concerns the findings from a study made in a non-English-medium country in the Far East. And based on both chapters, Chapter 3 constructs a new international social work. Chapter 4 gives an example of how the essence of international social work could be conveyed to incoming participants in this field.

Part I is composed of four rather independent chapters whose original manuscripts were written in different years over three decades. Chapter 1 mainly in 2021; Chapter 2 in the early 1990s (published in 1995 and 1997); Chapter 3 in 2021-22; and Chapter 4 in the early 2000s (published in 2005). Some out-of-date and inconsistent descriptions among the chapters may be found, but we have kept them to respect and record the original achievements in each year.

The reader may start at any chapter. The repetitive descriptions that occur throughout Part I have been retained intentionally for this reason.

Should this book be classified as a textbook, an architectural design, an investigative report, a scholastic academic book, or an essay telling of one man's dream? It does not matter. The author hopes that veteran international social work professors and practitioners enjoy this book with critical sentiment, and anyone who may be interested in international social work will find this book to be the first one their hands alight upon.

## Acknowledgements for Part I

I am indebted to all my predecessors who dedicated themselves to the development of international social work, particularly, the authors of two specific subsections of the two Handbooks of International Social Work, which were published in 2012, Lynne Healy and Nathalie Huegler, Karen Lyons, and Mahohar Pawar. Without their work, this book, particularly its Chapter 1, could never have been realized.

I am also indebted to all the students who attended my international social work classes at various universities in Japan and responded to my assignment in classrooms. Without their contributions, this book, particularly Chapter 4, could not have been possible.

I thank Emily Shibata-Sato and John Burton for their editorial help and support.

## Note to readers

Part I follows the Hepburn system of romanization.

Long vowels are indicated by macrons (with some exceptions).

Spelling and the use of commas follow the Oxford style, in principle.

On the other hand, the numbering of chapters, sections, and subsections and the use of double and single quotation marks are based on the author's own rules.

# Glossary

1 **Activities** (of social workers or those who are engaged in social work): Mainly in Chapter 1, functions, practices, actions, and acts have been interchangeably used in replacement of activities, without strict definitions and discussion on difference and commonality and the relation among them. To excuse the fluidity in the use of terms, the word is enclosed in single quotation marks, as in 'activities.'

2 **Final products**: Definitions. Regarding the use of single quotation marks as in 'a/the final product' see 1 (**Activities**) above.

3 **Functions** (of social workers; mainly in Chapter 1): See 1.

4 **Idea** (*idee*) (Chapter 3): The meaning here is close to one in philosophy rather than one in daily life—a "thought or suggestion as to a possible course of action." (*Oxford* Dictionary of English, 2nd Ed. Revised, Oxford University Press, 2005)] "The idea (*rinen*) which transcends experiences. The fundamental thought of how the matter is to be." (*Japanese Language Dictionary*, Shōgakukan, 2006) "It is used as the purpose for decision and interpretation without the ontological implication." (*Kōjien*, ver.6, Iwanami Shoten, 2008, 2014). The idea (*idee*) is used in the chapter as a rounding-up concept including a certain way of viewing matters, historical perspective for the future, and dreams (See (a) to (d) on pp.108-110). When used in this meaning, the word is enclosed in single quotation marks as '**Idea** (*idee*).'

5 **International social work**: A general term for social work related to other countries. It can include both international social work (A) (See 6) and international social work (B) (See 7).

6 **International social work (A)** (mainly Chapter 3): International social work as part of national social work. Social work related to other countries or beyond national borders for one's own country. See 7. Cf. Chapter 3 p.105.

7 **International social work (B)** (mainly Chapter 3): International social work positioned outside national social work or nation states. Social work

that works equally for all people in all countries and regions in the world. See 6. Cf. Chapter 3 p.105.

8  **International Social Work** (mainly Chapter 3): International social work (B) in the above 7 is replaced with International Social Work (capitalized) to show its authenticity as the international social work we name as such in Part I.

9  **International Social Work'** (dash) (Chapter 3, p.114): It is International Social Work in real in an actual society, which is the actual being. A (dash) has been attached to avoid readers' oversight of " ' " a dash.

10  **Local** (mainly Chapter 1): In most cases in Part I, it could be replaced with national, domestic, state, or country by country. In some cases, it of course means a particular area within a nation or a country.

11  **Local social work** (mainly Chapter 1): In most cases in Part I, it could be replaced with **'national'** social work (mainly Chapter 3); domestic social work; state social work; or social work country by country (See 10 and 15). Regarding the use of single quotation marks as in **'local'** social work or **'state'** social work, see 1 (**Activities**).

12  **Nation** (mainly Chapter 3): It is used as the synonym with state, country, nation state, or sometimes government mostly without strict definition and the discussion on difference and commonality and the relation among them in Part I.

13  **National borders** (mainly Chapter 3): It replaces **national boundaries** in Chapter 2 without difference in meaning.

14  **National boundaries** (mainly Chapter 2): See 13. It has been kept respecting the usage in the original article reprinted as a chapter of Part I.

15  **National social work** (mainly Chapter 3): Local social work in Chapter 1 is replaced with national social work in Chapter 3 to avoid confusion with the local within a country (See 10) and to clarify the contrast with the international social work outside a country. National social work is also replaceable with domestic social work, state social work, or country-by-country social work. Regarding the use of single quotation marks as in **'national social work,' 'national'** social work, or national **'social work,'** see 1 (**Activities**).

16  **Norm:** See 22. Regarding the use of single quotation marks as in **'norm/s,'** see 1 (**Activities**).

17 **Period** (mainly Chapter 1): The word period is used as a division of historical time sequence (cf. See 18).

18 **Phase** (mainly Chapter 3): The word phase is used as a division of developmental stage in a model (cf. See 17).

19 **Theory of the State** (Chapter 3): It is a nickname given to a model which has a focus on a nation, the birth and development of a nation state, the orientation from welfare state to the welfare world, and does not mean the reference to such grand theories as those of Platōn, Bodin, Spinoza, Rousseau, and Marx. Regarding the use of single quotation marks as in **'a/ the theory of the state,'** see 1 (**Activities**).

20 **TA**: The initial of Tatsuru Akimoto (the current author). It is inserted to indicate his original idea or interpretation input by him (mainly Chapter 1).

21 **Value** (mainly Chapter 1): It could be replaceable for purpose; aim; standard; or ethics in the chapter. Regarding the use of single quotation marks as in **'value,'** see 1 (**Activities**). The content of the value in mainstream social work is defined as e.g., human rights, social justice, democracy, or the promotion of the profession mainly in Chapter 1.

22 **The way of viewing matters**: In Chapters 2 and 3, the value (see 21) in Chapter 1 is replaced by the way of viewing matters, which may be interchangeably replaced for the way of looking at things; perception; perspective; yardstick; standard; and norm. Regarding the use of single quotation marks as in **'the way of viewing matters,'** see 1 (**Activities**). The content of 'the way of viewing matters' in International Social Work in this book is the view from the outside, not from one's own country, or with multiple views ("compound eyes").

23 **Yardstick**: See 22. Regarding the use of single quotation marks as in **'yardstick,'** see 1 (**Activities**).

# Chapter One

## A Review of the Conceptual Development of International Social Work in Western-Rooted Social Work
### —Understandings of the Term, Concept, and Definition—

This chapter is devoted to the review and interpretation of the conceptual development of understanding of the term, the concept, and definitions of international social work in Western-rooted social work, from its birth to the present day. The purpose of this chapter is to share with readers the common basic knowledge and understanding of the foundation for the discussion on a new construction of international social work in the following chapters. How has the authentic mainstream of international social work been understood throughout its own history? Without this knowledge, no one who would study and/or discuss international social work could move forward.

International social work research seems to have reached a high degree of perfection. Many great works have been amassed. In the last few decades in particular, several extensive volumes have been published, including two books with the same title of *Handbook of International Social Work*, edited by Lyons, K., et al. (Sage Publications, 2012)[1] and by Healy, L. and Link, R. (Oxford University Press, 2012)[2]. Other books in English with the title of *International Social Work* (or with the title including the same words) were written or edited by Hokenstad, M. C. et al. (1992) (1997), Lyons, K. (1999), Healy, L. (2001; 2008; 2021 coauthored by Thomas, R.), Cox, D. and Pawar, M. (2006; 2013), Xu, Q. (2006), Payne, M. and Askeland, G.A. (2008), Hugman, R. (2010) and other authors. Many outstanding journal articles have also been published.

The literature review of this chapter is thanks mainly to the above two *Handbooks* and also Lynne M. Healy's *International Social Work: Professional Action in an Interdependent World* (2001; 2020 coauthored by Thomas, R.,

---

1 Particularly, the section "1 Setting the Scene" by Huegler, N., Lyons, K. & Pawar, M., pp.5-13.

2 Particularly, the section "2 Defining International Social Work" by Healy, L. pp.9-15.

Oxford University Press[3] listed in the same above paragraph. These works have thoroughly reviewed the earlier literature and succinctly introduced how the term has been used, the concepts, and the representative definitions of international social work. The description of the following sections in this chapter is mostly composed of cited sentences and paragraphs from those books and literature by which they were guided. In that sense, the credit of the literature review in this chapter goes to the original authors of those *Handbooks*, not to the current author.

Cited sentences and paragraphs are dealt with as if they were raw data in field research, and have been edited and interpreted. The editing and interpretation are the current author's. The original data have been assumed to be accurate, appropriate, and sufficient with respect and such a way of treatment would be sufficient and justifiable[4] to achieve the aim of this book which is a new construction of international social work. Carrying out an extensive, complete bibliographical review in itself is not the aim.

Input by the current author (Tatsuru Akimoto) has been intentionally minimized in this chapter to record the authentic history as it is. Exceptions to this have been indicated by the initials, (TA). Examples are the division of periods, the leap from "international" social work to "international social work," the attention to social work at the regional level, the three steps of internationalization/globalization (problems, standards, and practices), and the reference to social background and context.

The development will be basically described along a chronological sequence divided into three periods. The main indices for the divisions are the North-South relationship, the incorporation of a value factor, and globalization. The divisions are "1. Up to the 1920s to the Early 40s: Birth and Beginning," "2. The Late 40s to the 80s: Transfer and Assistance from the North to the South," and "3. The 90s to the Early 21st century: Maturity of Definition and International Social Work in Globalization."

---

3    Particularly, the section "What Is International Social Work?" pp.5-13 (2001); pp.5-15 2020).

4    A few citations may even be open to the charge of being requotations. The excuse is the accessibility to resources and the lack of availability of time and capacity of the current author, in a non-English medium.

# 1. The Conceptual Development of International Social Work by Period

## 1.1 Up to the 1920s to the Early 40s: Birth and Beginning

(1) The first usage of the term—the 1928 conference

As far as the current author knows, the first occasion for the term 'international social work' to be used[5] was in 1928 in a presentation by Eglantyne Jebb[6] in the first international social work conference in Paris (Jebb, 1929: 637-657).

Jebb used the term 'international social work' several times in the presentation. The meaning of her international social work was basically international cooperation, particularly through international social institutions such as Save the Children, The Red Cross, and The International Migration Service. She also emphasized[7] the importance of the exchange of intellectual research for efficiency, experience, ideas, and suggestions, as well as special education [for international social work] and constant contact between the international workers (pp. 651-2, 657). She recognized that the conference itself was one form of such exchanges (p.652)[8]. At the conference, there were "approximately 2,500 [participants] from 42 countries of six continents," including those from the South such as Latin America and Asia (Healy, 2012: 9). Huegler, Lyon, and Pawar (2012) recognize the conference as adding momentum to the strengthening of the internationalization of social work by these representatives. The present three major international professional organizations, that is, IASSW (International Association of Schools of Social Work), ICSW (International Council on Social Welfare), and

---

5　Huegler, Lyons and Pawar write, "the term 'international social work' was first used in 1943 by Georg Warren" citing (Xu, 2006) (p.10). However, the first use of the term was by Jebb in the 1928 conference and Warren's first use in writing was in 1937 (See 1.1 (3) p.25).

6　"[S]he was unable personally to present her report" due to her illness. "[H]er death occurred soon after the Conference was over." (A footnote of Jebb, 1929: 637; cf. 655-657).

7　She also emphasized their organization and management including the financial aspect (pp. 647-8), and its relationship with national agencies (Jebb, 1929: e.g. 652).

8　She also discussed nationalism, internationalism, and cosmopolitanism as background ideas (pp.637-640, 656).

IFSW (International Federation of Social Workers) have their roots in this conference. "Subsequently (from the 1920s to the 1940s), social work knowledge and models were also transferred from the North to the South" (Huegler, Lyon & Pawar, 2012: 10).

## (2) Before the 1920s

Even before this period, the exchange of information, ideas, and physical visits had been made although the term 'international social work' was not used. International activities "in the form of exchange or transfer of knowledge and practices [were] present in social work from its earliest days. Until the 1920s or so, emerging social work knowledge was mainly shared within the North" (Huegler, Lyon & Pawar, 2012: 10).

Not only 'exchange' within the North but also 'transfer of knowledge and models' and 'support and assistance' from the North to the South, which would be largely seen in the following years (see the next subsection (3) below), had been already seen much earlier. Although sections of the books on which we are relying in this chapter have not referred much to the activities at the regional level, there was much individual and organizational involvement from the North in the South. The expression 'missionary work'—not necessarily being in the religious sense—might often better fit. For example, "Social work was first introduced to Asia before the turn of the 20th century, and some social work programs/schools were established in the second and third decades of the new century" (APASWE, 2013: 1) (TA).

Jebb also attested to "a rapid and surprising increase in actual international social work," which meant international cooperation through international social organizations, as described in the previous subsection (1), "since the Great War[9]...organization after organization has sprung into being under the pressure of hard necessity" (Jebb, 1929: 650).

## (3) The first article—*Social Work Yearbook*, 1937

Russell Sage Foundation's *Social Work Yearbook*, the forerunner of the current NASW *Encyclopedia of Social Work*, had the entry words "International Social Work" for the first time in its Vol.4 in 1937. In previous volumes of the series,

---

9    WWI

there were entries carrying the word "international," namely "International Conferences of Social Work" (Vol. 1, 1929: 229), "International Institutes" (Vol. 2, 1933: 253), and "International Social Case Work" (Vol. 3, 1935: 214), but no entry word "International social work." The content of the latter two (Vols. 2 and 3) pertained to immigrants. The entry word "International Institutes" directed readers to "See Immigrants and Foreign Communities," without any text. "International Social Case Work" (Vol. 3) stated "problems arise in public and private welfare agencies because of the migration of individuals and families to and from the United States" with three subsections: "Nature of problems," "Cooperating agencies," and "The International Migration Services," which had nine offices in European cities and New York (Vol. 3, 1935: 214)[10]. In Vol. 4, under the first entry word of "International Social Work", George Warren wrote that international social work is composed of the following three activities (Warren, 1937: 224).

(a) international social case work; (b) international conferences on social work subjects; (c) international cooperation by governments and private bodies under the auspices of the League of Nations, the International Labour Organization and the League's Health Organization in the world-wide efforts to combat disease, improve conditions of labor, and to protect women and children (Warren, 1937).

The next Vol. 5 (1939: 192) had four activities instead of the previous three, adding, between (a) and (b) above, "(b) International assistance, public and private, to disaster or war sufferers and distressed minority groups." The earlier (c) above was rewritten as "(d) the international cooperation by governments and private bodies through the medium of the League of Nations. The International Labour Organization and the Health Organization of the League, in combatting disease and securing social and political peace and harmony throughout the world."

---

10    It is composed of three subsections, "Nature of problems," "Cooperating agencies," and "The International Migration Services" which had nine offices in European cities and New York (Vol. 3, 1935: 214-216).

In this period or even in the earlier years, most kinds of international social work activities which would be seen in later periods were already presented: exchange and transfer; service and assistance to migration, war, and disaster suffers and distressed minority groups; international cooperation through intergovernmental organizations such as the League of Nations and the ILO (International Labour Organization), and INGOs (international nongovernmental organizations) work, including professional social work organizations. Their main activities seemed to focus on activities within the North (and cases, incidents, and challenges related to their own countries), but some involvement in and of the South was already observable.

## 1.2 The Late 40s to the 80s: The Transfer and the Assistance from the North to the South, and the Leap from "International" Social Work to "International Social Work" (TA)

**(1) The immediate postwar period and following decades, and the North-South problem with the East-West relationship behind (TA)**
"During the 1940s and 1960s, and particularly following the Second World War, a particular kind of international social work peaked, in terms of transfer of education, practice and welfare models and skills..." It was "mostly from the North to the South," the "linear flow," "with support from UN organizations and INGOs, and respective governments of new nation states" (Huegler, Lyons & Pawar, 2012: 11). The Asian and Pacific Association for Social Work Education (APASWE)'s history publication begins with the following sentences (TA):

[V]arious social work-related activities were carried out and workshops, training seminars, and conferences were organized in the Region by non-Asian agencies, most typically from the United Nations and United States. Some other international organizations along with the United Kingdom, a previous colonial power, were involved as well as people from other Western countries. These same entities and individuals initiated new schools and supported them in many countries (APASWE, 2013: 1).

In the Asian region, the first schools of social work were established in 1944 in

Thailand, in 1946 in Indonesia, in 1950 in The Philippines, in 1952 in Malaysia and Sri Lanka, although in India its first school had been established in 1936 (Matsuo, 2015: 74).

As far as this particular period and the following few decades are concerned, it is worth looking at the social situation of those years to understand international social work at that time. Just after World War II, the United States was active (directly and through the United Nations and NGOs), in aid in political, economic, and social arenas for postwar rehabilitation in the broad region, first including Europe.

By the 1970s, more than 80 new countries had gained their independence, mainly in Asia and Africa, and some in Latin America. This independence was the denial of the rule of previous colonial suzerain states such as the United Kingdom, France, and some other mainly European countries, and the liberation from the old imperialism. Independence did not eliminate all problems. The mass poverty and other serious political, economic, and social problems continued and sometimes even worsened. The North-South problems co-existed with the East-West or socialism vs. capitalism issue. Competition intensified between the West and the East and among the new Western or Northern powers (new imperialism). ODA (Official Development Assistance) was one of its representative examples. (TA) Under these conditions, on one hand, social work spread all over the world due to the profession's own efforts. Social work regional associations were born from within IASSW, firstly in Latin America in 1967, secondly in Africa in 1971, and thirdly in Asia in 1974 (APASWE, 2013: 1). On the other hand, the dissemination of social work was limited to a certain level, due to the negative reaction against the reformist approach offered by the West or the North. 'Placation measures by American imperialism,' or 'preventive measures against socialist revolution,' were words sometimes hurled against social work among "undeveloped" countries as well as within some "developed" countries (TA).

This period stands out as the time of transfer and assistance from the North to the South, not only knowledge and skills but also models of social work itself. The North's social work was involved in various direct practices, consultative and advocacy roles in policy and program development, and program and curriculum development in social work education in the South.

**(2) The leap from "international" social work to "international social work," and narrow definitions and broad definitions**

Phase II was years of the leap from "international" social work to "international social work." "International" social work, which comprised of two terms, 'international' and 'social work', turned into "international social work," which was one independent term or concept, at some point during this Period.

In the 1950s and later, the territory of international social work, or what international social work was, was more consciously discussed. Some preferred a narrow/specific territory or definition and some others a broad/general territory or definition. The working committee of the Council on Social Work Education (CSWE) of the United States (1956), and Sanders and Pederson (1984) were deemed to be the two poles. The former chose a narrow definition and the latter a broad one. The former confined itself to programs by the United Nations, governmental or non-governmental agencies. The latter opted for "social work activities and concerns that transcend national and cultural boundaries" (Sanders and Pederson, 1984: xiv). Healy introduces citations to support each position as well as those in between.

For the former:

[CSWE's] working committee members wrestled with the question of narrow versus broad interpretation and examined six different usages of the term…, "ranging from social workers working in other countries to refugee services to common professional concerns with social workers in other parts of the world" (Healy, 1995: 423).

The committee opted for a narrow definition…"[T]he term 'international social work' should properly be confined to programs of social work of international scope, such as those carried on by intergovernmental agencies, chiefly those of the U.N.; governmental; or non-governmental agencies with international programs (Stein, 1957: 3)" (Healy, 2001: 5-6).

For the latter:

> At the most general level, international social work can be defined as any aspect of the profession that involves more than one country. This draws on the dictionary definition of *international* as meaning 'of, relating to or affecting two or more nations' and 'active, known or reaching beyond national boundaries' (Marriam-Webster, 2011) (Healy, 2012: 10).

> Kimberly (1984) argued that international social work, as a relatively new field, should be left open for broad interpretation rather than prematurely limiting its scope (Healy, 2001: 6).

There could be various definitions with different widths between these two. At the very end of the 1980s, Healy conducted a study of the International Association of Schools of Social Work (IASSW) member schools, yielding 200 responses from all 5 regions (1989/90) to "identify the component concepts...essential to the definition of international social work." (Healy, 2001: 6) It listed various presumable international social work activities for schools' selection:

> Respondents...selected the following concepts as essential, in descending order: cross-cultural understanding, comparative social policy, concerns with global issues, a general worldwide view, knowledge of a common profession worldwide, international practice, intergovernmental social welfare, and a sense of collegiality with social workers in other countries (Healy, 1990)...[C]ross-cultural understanding [collected the biggest votes] (Healy, 2001: 6-7).

## (3) Four points to keep in mind for further discussion

While "[l]ittle was written about practice roles during this period [the 1970s and 1980s]" (Healy, 2012: 10), there are four points to be kept in mind in this period for future discussion. (TA)

The first one is Goldman's idea in the early 1960s and unique "to define international social work as the fourth major practice method to complement casework, group work, and community organization." Goldman (1962) proposed as a logical step in expanding social work attention beyond the community level to seek 'international solutions to international problems' (pp.1-2), much as a caseworker seeks individual solutions to problems of individuals" (Healy, 2012: 11). There was no progress on this idea in later periods.

The second and the third points are the attention paid to the general ideas of the importance of an international perspective, and partly related to this, the importance of comparative study. Both will be the focus of the interest of more disputants (e.g. Lyons, 1999: 12). In this period, "Boehm (1976) loosely defined international social work as including the obvious work of international agencies but also comparative analysis and its contribution to the transnational exchange of ideas and innovations" (Healy, 2012: 10).

The fourth is criticism of the "unidirectional," "linear flow," transfer and support (aid and assistance) from the North to the South: "professional imperialism"[11] (Midgley, 1981). To some social workers, the word "imperialism" might sound abrupt, but was nothing peculiar outside of the social work field in the social context of that time, as seen in the above subsection (1.2 (1) p.27). We, however, read this criticism as an impetus having an important effect on international social work (See the next section 1.3 (2) p. 35, 2 (1) (ii) pp.46-48) (TA).

## 1.3 The 1990s to the Early 21st Century: Maturity of Definition and International Social Work in Globalization

Two points feature in this period. On one hand, the reference and discussion on 'what international social work is' became active in the form of a definition. While definitions based on activities, acts, practices, or functions (hereinafter to be referred to as either 'activities' or 'functions' in this section) had come close to maturity, definitions based on values, purposes, aims, goals, standards, or ethics (hereinafter to be referred as mainly 'value' in this

---

11    Cf. "cultural imperialism"(Lyons, 1999; Midgley, 1983). The warning of social work colonialism was also repeatedly sent to the chorus of professionalization, internationalization, and globalization in "developing countries" in these few decades on various occasions including international conferences and workshops (e.g., Akimoto, in Indonesia (2013), Vietnam (2014), and Thailand (2015)).

section) emerged and became popular.

On the other hand, in the 1990s, the term 'globalization' emerged and gradually replaced 'internationalization' although the two terms significantly differ in meaning.

The reference and discussion on international social work's relation to 'local' (or domestic, national, state; hereinafter to be referred to as 'local' in this section) social work became unavoidable.

## (1) Towards the maturity of functional definitions

### (1-1) Falk and Nagy's survey: 12 classifications of international social work knowledge and activities

Falk and Nagy conducted a survey in 1995/96 to give "rise to a wide range of ideas about the 'meaning' of international social work" (Huegler, Lyons & Pawar, 2012: 11). The subjects were 800 schools of social work in 20 countries in Europe, North America, and Australia. The response rate was 50 percent. "The following is a summary of their classification of international social work knowledge and activities (derived from respondents' views)" (Lyons, 1999: 26) (cf. Falk & Nagy, 1997):

1. International events and social forces that generate the problems faced by the world's peoples
2. The implications of the increasing interdependence of nations
3. The role of international governments and NGOs
4. The increasing influence of multinationals and global financial organizations
5. Comparative social policies, structures, values, and cultural assumptions
6. Practice approaches, programmes, and methods used in other cultures
7. The range of international practice opportunities
8. Struggles for a more just world and support for human rights
9. Working with immigrants and refugees in one's own country
10. Educational exchanges for educators, students, and practitioners
11. International consultation projects
12. International seminars and conferences.

Items 1 to 6 pertain to "knowledge" which international social work should be equipped with while items 7 to 12 to "activities" which international social work would be engaged in.

## (1-2) Healy's definition: A representative functional definition

In 2001, Healy gave a representative definition of international social work which was based on the review of the various works including ones cited above, particularly ones providing categories of practice activities. She named it the functional or practice-based definition. This was consistent with the trend since 1937 Warren's Year Book article, which continued in the early decades of the twenty-first century. A feature of Healy's definition here was the reference to "international policy development and advocacy," and not only direct practice.

> International professional action and the capacity for international action by social work profession and its members.[12] International action has four dimensions: (a) internationally related domestic practice and advocacy, (b) professional exchange, (c) international practice, and (d) international policy development and advocacy (Healy 2001: 7). (The letters (a) to (d) are the insertion by the current author.)

The definition comprises "four dimensions of action" ((a) to (d)) by the profession and professional social workers (Healy, 2012: 10). She gives these with the following examples for each dimension (Healy 2001: 7-13):

(a) Internationally related domestic practice and advocacy: "Refugee settlement, work with other international populations, international adoption work, and social work in border areas." (p.7)
(b) Professional exchange: "To exchange social work information and experiences internationally, and to use the knowledge and experience to improve social work practice and social welfare policy at home."

---

12    The phrase "to promote human dignity and human rights and enhance human well-being" was inserted later in the third version of her same book (Healy, 2020: 8). See (2-2) pp.36-37.

"Reading foreign periodicals and books in one's field, corresponding with professionals in other countries or hosting visitors, participating in professional interchange at international meetings, and identifying and adapting social welfare innovations in other countries to one's own settings." (p.9)

(c) International practice: "To contribute directly to international development work through employment and volunteer work in international development agencies." (p.10)

(d) International policy development and advocacy: "A worldwide movement to formulate and promulgate positions on important social issues and make a contribution to resolution of important global problems related to its sphere of experience." (p.12) (e.g. domestic violence, women's status; "The goal of the educational effort was to influence UN policy deliberations.") (p.13)

## (1-3) Hugman's classification of practices of international social work

Reviewing definitions that had been proposed, Hugman neatly presented international social work practice and work in the form of five categories made from the combination of the locations of social workers and clients and the problems they are engaged in (Hugman, 2010: 18-20):

(1) The practice of social work in a country other than the home country of the social work;

(2) Working with individuals, families and communities whose origins are in a country other than that where the social worker is practicing;

(3) Working in international organizations;

(4) Collaborations between countries in which social workers exchange ideas or work together on projects that cross national borders; and

(5) Practices that address locally issues that originate in a globalized social system.

Items (1) to (4) are often commonly found in definitions we cited in previous sections, but item (5) is not. Noting the globalization of social issues and problems as a connecting factor between social work providers and beneficiaries, Hugman gives the following definition:

34

'International social work' refers to practice and policy concerning situations in which professionals, those who benefit from their services or [sic] the causes of the problems that bring these two actors together, have travelled in some way across the borders between nations (Hugman, 2010: 20).[13]

## (2) Incorporation of the value factor

Up until this period, international social work was mainly defined around the kinds or the categories of activities or functions by social workers, broadly or narrowly, but some authors focused on 'value' in their definitions.

## (2-1) Haug's definition: A value-focused definition

Item 5 of Falk and Nagy's (1997) 12 classifications above ((1-1) p. 32) had the word 'value' in it. "Ahmadi (2003) called for focusing or refocusing international social work on promotion of human rights, democracy, social justice, conflict prevention, and peace" (Healy, 2012: 11). Haug (2005) also "focus[ed] on common goals and values such as a clear commitment to human rights and social justice" (p.132) in her definition:

> International social work includes any social work activity anywhere in the world, directed toward global social justice and human rights, in which local practice is dialectically linked to the global context (Haug, 2005: 133).

Instead of 'value,' each writer does and could use a different term—aim, purpose, goal, standard, perspective, or ethics. The content of 'value' could be also of a verity. The 'value' in Haug's definition is social justice and human rights, but Ahmadi above, for example, adds democracy, conflict prevention, and peace, while Cox and Pawar added ecology and social development under the name of perspective (Cox & Pawar, 2013: 29-30; (2-2) pp.36-37).

Haug's short definition implies a few important points. First, it begins with the clause "International social work includes any social work activity anywhere in the world." This statement seems not to limit the subject, or the

---

13    "and"?

player, of international social work merely to professional social workers as far as we can see in these three lines above, although it is not clear if it limits the subject to social workers. Most of the definitions cited in this chapter define international social work as some categories of activities by professional social workers and/or as those to promote social work profession, including Healy's definition above and Cox and Pawar's definition below.[14] Haug's clause also clarifies the object, or the target population, of international social work, to be all people anywhere in the world. Most other definitions would share the same idea but their expression is less clear and direct. Cox and Pawar's in the next subsection reads "(the wellbeing of) large sections of the world's population" and Healy's and Hugman's definitions above partly start with the social worker's own people.

Secondly, Haug's definition ends with the clause "local practice is dialectically linked to the global context." It has shown the interest in the relation of local practice under globalization, which will be discussed in the next subsection (3) below.

Thirdly, are "social justice and human rights" appropriate as the 'value' of international social work even if she inserts "global" in front of them? They are core elements of the typical Western-rooted professional social work,[15] which the author of the same article was critical about. She argued this point extensively in the first half of the same article including her definition above (Haug, 2005). It is difficult to "get out of the hands of Western-rooted professional social work."

These discussions, however, mostly pertain to the understanding and definition of social work itself, not those of international social work, strictly speaking.

## (2-2) Cox and Pawar's definition and Healy's revised definition: Combined (functional and value-focused) definition

---

14    Their inclusion of professional building is in keeping with developments by the international professional associations to promulgate a global definition, ethical guidelines, and an action agenda for social work from local to global levels, the Global Agenda for Social Work and Social Development (Healy, 2020:7).

15    cf. IASSW/IFSW Global Definition of Social Work Profession.

Cox and Pawar give a long definition emphasizing "the promotion of social work education and practice" and aims at "building a truly integrated international profession."

International social work is the promotion of social work education and practice globally and locally, with the purpose of building a truly integrated international profession that reflects social work's capacity to respond appropriately and effectively, in education and practice terms, to the various global challenges that are having a significant impact on the wellbeing of large sections of the world's population. This global and local promotion of social work education and practice is based on an integrated-perspectives approach that synthesizes global, human rights, ecological, and social development perspectives of international situations and responses to them (Cox & Pawar, 2013: 29-30; cf. 2006: 20).

This definition seems to be between Healy's functional definition and Haug's value-focused definition. Healy reads this definition to fit "within the category of a functional definition" "with its action and practice emphasis," "but it also includes...value dimensions," "with the purpose of building a truly integrated international profession" (Healy, 2012: 11). The 'value' has been replaced with perspectives which integrate not only human rights but also ecology and social development.

The discussion on the subject, the object, and the 'value' in subsection (2-1) (pp.35-37) under Haug's definition is also applicable to Pawar's. Pawar pointed out the "Northern contexts reflecting Northern concerns" in those definitions discussed above (Pawar, 2010) (cf. Huegler, Lyons & Pawar, 2012: 12).

Functions and value factors are combined in definitions of international social work. Healy, for example, inserted a phrase in her definition, a phrase "to promote human dignity and human rights and enhance human well-being," at the end of the first sentence of her definition above in the third version of her book (See the above (1-2) p.33). "[I]nternational social work is value-driven action aimed at promoting human rights and human well-being globally" (Healy, 2020: 15).

## (3) Globalization and social work: International social work's relation with 'local' social work

The literature review pages of the books which we have been relying on have mostly a focus on the 'globalization.'[16]

### (3-1) Social work under globalization

Everything comes under globalization. Social work alone cannot be exempted. "All social work is enmeshed in global processes of change" (Lorenz, 1997:2). The globalization of social work seems to be in three layers: (a) The globalization of the realities; (b) the globalization of standards; and (c) the globalization of practice[17] (TA) (cf. Akimoto, 1992).

(a) Globalization of realities: "Globalization has led to new social problems and increased awareness of others that have long existed; increasingly, these problems are experienced in most or even all countries." Payne and Askeland (2008) discuss "the growing inequality and injustice [as] the result from globalization" from their postmodern point of view (Healy, 2012: 10, 11).

(b) Globalization of standards: "Standards in human rights are increasingly negotiated at the global level and social provisions and programs are modelled and emulated across borders." (Healy, 2008). Haug (2005) also specified social justice and human rights as standards (1.3 (2-1) p.35). "Human rights" is also found in the above-cited Ahmadi (2003) and Cox and Pawar (2013). (1.3 (2-1) p.35 and (2-2) p.37).

(c) Globalization of practice: "[G]lobal trends in every sphere of life— economy, security, health, environment, and culture—affect social work practice, practitioners, and clients of social work interventions" (Healy, 2012: 10).

---

16　The conscious discussion on the difference of 'globalization' from 'internationalization' is not cited. Questions and discussions parallel to those raised here in this subsection must be also made on 'internationalization' (TA).

17　"Theory," not "practice," in the original article (Akimoto, 1992: title, etc.).

All social problems or social work needs are in the global context and are affected by the element of 'globalization.' Standards are also the same. Both clients[18] who have faced problems and social workers who work for them must have recognized and understood these facts and also the fact that their cases or practices themselves are under the same globalization.

### (3-2) 'Local' social work under globalization

All social work comes under globalization. 'Local' social work cannot be exempted and is in the same three layers immediately above. In other words, the element of 'being in the global context' penetrates all aspects and every corner of 'local' social work. 'Local' practice must be seen through an international lens.

> [I]ncreasing numbers will find it necessary to develop their comparative knowledge of welfare systems and social work services if they are to engage in transnational activities in specialist areas of work which might previously have been seen as restricted to the national scene, e.g. transnational fostering (Lyons, 2006) (Huegler, Lyons & Pawar, 2012: 12).

In not only the transnational cases but also 'purer domestic' cases, more generally, "applications of international perspectives to local practice" become requisite (Akimoto, 2020: 42).

> Lyons et al. (2006) and Lawrence et al. (2009)...suggest that local practices can—and should—be viewed through an international lens or that knowledge about international events and different cultures should inform local practices (Huegler, Lyons & Pawar, 2012: 12).

"[L]ocal and national borders are no longer sufficient limits for our information sources and ethical practice" (Link & Ramanathan, 2011: 1). "These shared social problems and the movement of people across borders challenges the very notion of a domestic social work practice" (Healy, 2012:

---

18   The term 'client' is not acceptable for many social workers. We will, however, use it for the easier understanding of the line of thought.

10). "[L]ocal practice is dialectically linked to the global context" (Haug, 2005: 133; (2-1) pp.35-36). The word 'dialectic' would promise the 'local practice' which is rather different from the existing 'local practice'—synthesis on thesis and antithesis (TA).

### (3-3) Discussing not '(local) social work under globalization' but 'international social work under globalization' (TA)—Will international social work disappear?

These discussions in this subsection, however, all seem to pertain to ('local') social work, or ('local') social work in the global context, and not to what international social work is, which we have been examining. It is similar to the discussions on professional social work, Western social work bias, and the equation of the 'value' = 'human rights and social justice' in the previous subsection ((2-1) pp.35-36). We will have to focus on international social work under globalization.

1) Will international social work disappear? If the answer is "no," what, then, will it look like?

On one hand, it could be said that ('local') social work absorbs international social work into it. If the element of 'global' penetrates all aspects and every corner of 'local social work,' and all social workers need to understand and have the view of international social work, how do we distinguish international social work from globalized 'local social work'? According to this logic, will the field of practice/research of international social work become unnecessary and cease to exist? The following citation has supposed that international social work will, in practice, remain.

[W]hile not all social workers will choose to engage in 'international social work' as a specialist activity...the internationalization of social problems will require increasing numbers of social professionals [sic][19] to have knowledge about international conditions and current affairs in order to understand the concerns of the service users and respond appropriately (Huegler, Lyons & Pawar, 2012: 12).

---

19    "social work professions"?

At least two out of four areas in Healy's definition ((1-2) p.33), that is, "(c) international practice, and (d) international policy formulation and advocacy" might be kept for international social work.

Not all social workers will become international social workers and be equipped with knowledge about international conditions and current affairs at the same level as international social workers. The lens mentioned above ((3-2) p.39) is one of 'globalization' or 'global context,' and not one of international social workers.

What will the roles and functions of international social work be? What will the meaning, concept, and definition of international social work look like? The discussion has not proceeded beyond these questions yet.

2) What will it be like if the answer is "yes", that is, if international social work disappears?

On the other hand, there are a few ideas questioning the retention of 'international social work' in the future. Lyons wrote that international social work "is a nebulous concept" while mentioning "elements of cross-national comparison and applications of international perspectives to local practice, as well as participation in policy and practice activities which are more overtly cross-national or supra-national in character" (Lyons, 1999:12). Huegler, Lyons, and Pawar, (2012: 12) noted:

> There are also those within the North who question the appropriateness of the term 'international social work' and argue for more work to develop a theory and practice that examine processes and the diverse ways in which the global and the local interact (e.g. Dominelli, 2010)[20] or who advocate the notion of social work internationalism, rather than international social work (Lavalette & Ioakimidis, 2011).

It may be worth remembering, lastly, Webb's argument to "reject the validity

---

20    Being invited to a forum (The Fourth ARIISW-Shukutoku-University International Academic Forum, February, 2021, at Chiba, Japan) to discuss the future of international social work, she focused on the increase and the importance of global social issues such as climate change and COVID 19 pandemics.

of an international or global social work."

"[S]ocial work is inherently local and requires deep understanding of local culture," therefore social work "has no clearly identified or legitimate mandate in relation to globalization" and "'global social work' is a practical impossibility" (p.193) and no more than a vanity for the profession (Webb, 2003: Huegler, Lyons & Pawar, 2012:11).

We wonder if Webb would keep the same insistence if replacing "globalization" and "global social work" with "internationalization" and "international social work." Unfortunately, he did not distinguish between international social work and global social work as far as his quoted lines above are concerned.

Meanwhile, in this period, various forms of international social work activities—starting with 'exchange'—have continued to increase. Healy comments, "Communication technologies facilitate rapid and frequent exchange of ideas across the globe and access to information about local and global developments." "The profession is continuing to mature and develop in a highly globalized context" (Healy, 2012: 10).

## 2. Roundup and Limitations

### (1) A summary of the conceptual development of international social work by period

We have reviewed the entire development of meanings, concepts, and definitions of international social work from its birth to today, chronologically dividing it into three periods in the previous section. These will be summarized in Table 1-1 below with some current author's analytic interpretation added.

The first column is the division of those periods: Period I (Up to the end of the 20s to the early 40s), Period II (the second half of the 40s to the 80s), and Period III (the 90s to the early 21st century). The second column is the developmental stage of the term/concept/definition of international social work: Birth-Growth-Mutuality (and Re-examination). The third column is 'Events' (publication and social background). The fourth column contains representative activities practiced under the name of international social work and some explanatory remarks. The last column on the right is the North-South relation and the main supposed beneficiaries which characterize each period.

### (i) Period I: Birth and infancy

Period I refers to the birth and infancy of the term 'international social work.' This was from the end of the 1920s to the early 1940s, but virtually to the end of the 30s due to the World War.

The term international social work made its appearance in Jebb's paper for the 1928 Paris international social work conference, and Warren's article in the 1937 *Social Work Year Book* Vol.4. These authors referred to activities in several categories under the name of international social work.

These categories can be summarized as follows: 1. international cooperation among governments, (e.g. the League of Nations and ILO) and non-governmental agencies (e.g. Save the Children and Red Cross); 2. the exchange of information, knowledge, skills, experiences, and ideas including international conferences; and 3. the casework and assistance to migrants, war and disaster victims, and distressed minority groups.

These activities were mostly carried out in and among the Northern, social work-developed countries. The main motivation was in learning and benefiting themselves as individuals or agencies in their own countries, and/ or in providing good services and assistance to people relating mainly to their own countries. Some interest was also shown in helping people and disseminating social work in non-North regions.

In the years (from the 19th century to the 1920s) before Period I, some of these activities were carried out in the North and/or non-North out of "goodwill" and as "missionary work" (not necessarily a religious sense) without being called international social work. It was the period of prehistory.

During this period, the term international social work was mostly used as "international" social work, which meant social work related to or concerning

Table 1-1. The historical development of the understanding, concept, and

| Period | The development of term/concept/definition | Events [Publication and social background] |
|---|---|---|
| (Prehistory) 19c-the end of the 1920s | No terms, no concepts | |
| I The end of the 1920s- the early 40s | The Birth of the term and Infancy *"International" social work (SW related to "international")* | 1928 Paris Conference (Jebb)<br><br>1937 SW Year Book Vol. 4 (Warren) |
| II The 2nd half of the 40s-the 80s | Growth *"International" social work* ⇩ *"International social work" (An independent concept)* | [Immediate postwar; Independence of previous colonies] [North-South problems] [East-West relations] [Internationalization] |
| III The 90s- the early 21c | III-A Maturity towards the final product *Incorporation of value factor* | 2001 Healy<br><br>2005 Haug 2020 Healy; 2006 Cox & Pawar |
| | III-B Reexamination of the concept ISW Prosperity or dissolution | [Globalization] |

## definition of international social work by period

| Representative ISW activities/explanatory remarks | North-South relation [For whom] |
|---|---|
| Virtual international social work activities following the nomenclature in the later periods (from e.g. "Goodwill"; "Missionary obligation"; Intellectual/practical interest) | North→Non-North [others] |
| Exchange (intellectual ideas; conferences); Organizational cooperation (INGO, UL, ILO, etc.); International research; Case work (immigrants), Assistance to war, disaster victims, and depressed minority people, etc. | Within the North [Self/own country] |
| by social workers | |
| Assistance/Aids (relief and development); Transfer of models<br>    The criticism of the North-South (unidirectional; power differential; unequal) relations; imperialism<br>The exploration of the concept/definition<br>The extraction and combination of various categorized activities (functions)<br>→International perspective; Comparative studies; Cross cultural perspective | Within the North North→South [others; South]<br><br>(South-South) |
| Pursuing the final definition—"What is ISW?"<br>    Correction of unidirectional→Bidirectional; equal→<br>    *Value in general→Filling its content* (e.g. human rights, social justice, democracy, and the promotion of professional social work)<br>• Functional definition (Certain categorized functions/ activities by professional social workers)<br>• Value-focused definition (purpose; aim; standard)<br>• Combined function-and value-focused definithon | North=South (Bidirectional; equal) [Both North and South] At least in theory |
| →Social work is globalized. The whole 'local' social work is put in the global context. →All 'local' social works must be seen through lens of "global".<br>ISW will be more prosperous. Or will disappear? | Centre→Peripheries (North→South) [All or uni-polar] |

45

matters "international."

## (ii) Period II: Growth

Period II runs between the latter half of the 40s and the 1980s, which includes the immediate postwar period (when rehabilitation aid was given to the North as well as the South, by the North); the decades of the independence of former colonies; and the emergence of the Third World and North-South problems. The transfer of knowledge, skills, and models of social work was made from the North to the South, and the financial and technological assistance and support in practice, policy formulation, and education were given in and for the South by the North. These became the major forms of international social work activities in this period. In the background, there were East-West relations.

In the face of this unidirectional move, criticism of imperialism and colonialism was raised. Towards the end of this period, the international social work side made some responses to this criticism.

Period II was also the time when "international" social work leaped to "international social work" and the concept of "what 'international social work' is," or its core elements and definitions began to be explored. The major trend was the extraction of the elements and the combination of various categorized activities (functions, acts, practices; hereinafter to be referred to as activities in this section).

Internationalization, which became a popular word worldwide, brought to social work the international perspective, international comparative perspective, and cultural perspective. International comparative studies and cross-cultural counselling, for example, became popular subjects in international social work research and practice.

However, the conceptual or definitional development of international social work was slow during this period, except for the leap from "international" social work to "international social work," while there was much cross-national activity and growth in terms of social work practice and education.

## (iii) Period III: Maturity to the final definition and self reexamination

Period III (The 1990s to the early 21st century) is characterized by two features: firstly, (A) the maturity of the definition of international social work, and (B) the re-examination of the understanding of international social work due to globalization.

(A) Looking at (A), Period III was the succession of Period II in terms of North and South relations, but the unidirectional relationship from North to South in the previous period was gradually corrected into a two-directional or horizontal relationship—the recognition of mutual relation, interdependence, mutual learning and sharing, and the acquisition of the eyes of parity—between the two, in theory. In reality, however, the power difference certainly remained. A historical background event in this period was the mitigation of East-West relations.[21*]

The conceptual pursuit of 'what international social work is' continued towards and approached its final form. There were two trends—one conventional and one new.

The conventional trend was the exploration of the elements and categories of activities/functions of international social work which succeeded from Phase II, even some from Period I. Over them, definitions basically developed—from Warran to Healy ('functional definitions').

The new trend which replaced 'function' with 'value' (purpose aim, standards, and ethics; hereinafter to be referred as 'value'), emerged in the middle of the first decade of the 21st century (e.g. Haug). The 'value' most representatively meant human rights and social justice, sometimes democracy, the promotion of professional social work, development, ecology, and others ('value-focused definitions').

In later years, both the functional definition and the value-focused definition merged, in some definitions. Healy's (revised) (2010) was a representative model. Cox and Powar's (2006) was interpreted as one of these definitions.

The criticism of professional imperialism raised in Phase II to the reality of international social work was from the outside of these definitions. It turned to a necessary definitional component to be international social work. It is

---

21*　In around the 2020s, a new China and Russian-Western relationship is emerging.

not the international social work unless the component is included (cf. Box 1-1).

Period III was a time of the correction of the 'unidirectional' and the incorporation of the 'value' judgement factor, and the finalization of the product (definition).

(B) Looking at (B), Period III was also the time of globalization. The above discussion in (A) and the following discussion in this (B) proceeded at a time, not in sequence, in Period III.

Society was globalized and social work was globalized. All 'local' (national, state, or domestic) social works were put in the global context. The 'global' element penetrated every corner of 'local' social work. As a result, everything in social work had to be seen with "global" eyes or lenses—with the understanding that everything is in such a global world. Problems, standards, and practices are all globalized. International social work will increase its own importance more and more. Or international social work will conceptually disappear, being absorbed and swallowed by 'local' social work. The concept of international social work itself is requestioned.

The features of each Period sometimes overlap. Some characters and elements of a Period may appear in earlier Periods, and characters and elements of earlier Periods continue appearing in later Periods.

## Digression for the intellectually curious

### Box 1-1. Hypothetical logical progress from a criticism to a value

The criticism of professional imperialism and social work colonialism, which were born in Phase II, is one of the driving forces that led to the incorporation of a value factor into the concept and definition of international social work. It was hypothetically developed as follows:

1. It criticized the unidirectional North-South relationship and power differential.
2. This meant that a value judgemental factor was brought into the international social work discussion.
3. In the later years of Period II, criticism sought a correction to the bidirectional relationship between North and South, and extended the interest to the broader, general issues, e.g., interdependency, mutual benefit, and mutual sharing, that is, to the concept of equality in general.
4. These qualities are common in social work in general, but not particularly so to international social work. Particular to international social work is that the subjects of equality are between and among countries, peoples, and individuals beyond national borders.
5. Once equality becomes a general term, it is easily expanded to become a value, which is a more extensive general concept.
6. In the process from 1. to 3. and from 3. to 5., the original interest and focus of the criticism of power differences and mass poverty (the North-South relationship) becomes diluted in a sense. The coverage becomes broader, and the aim becomes diluted and euphemistic.

There is no factual and historical connection between the criticism of professional imperialism in Period II and the incorporated 'value' factor in Period III. However, it would be possible to trace a logical and hypothetical connection, from the criticism to the 'value.'

**(2) The final definitions of international social work**

(i) Basic structure: Categorical activities × Professional social workers (a
  function-focused definition)

Almost all these understandings of the concept including definitions seem to
be the aggregation or partial combination of categorized activities, which
professional social workers have been engaged in. Those activities range
from (a) the exchange and transfer of information, knowledge, ideas, skills,
and models, including mutual visits and conferences, (b) practices related to
overseas at home countries, (c) practices in other countries, (d) assistance by
the North to the South, including the development of social welfare policies
and programs, (e) the work for international organizations, (f) collaboration
among professional social workers, to (g) the engagement in other social
work activities crossing national borders.

There are a few deviating ideas on each term of the formula (multiplication)
above in the title of this subsection. They remove restrictions of "categorical
function" and "professional social workers" to replace them with "social
work in general" and "social workers" respectively.

(ii) The incorporation of the value element (a value-focused definition and
  combined definition)

In the early 21st century, the factor of 'value' (purpose, aim, standard, or
ethic) became a definitional element. For many authors, this value most
typically meant human rights and social justice, but for others, it could mean
the correction of "unidirectional" and power differentials, the achievement
of an equal North-South relation, and the promotion of the social work
profession, for example. Some definitions have both elements of the
functional definition and the value-focused definition to become combined
definitions.

(iii) The disappearance of international social work?— "Globalization"

Under globalization, 'local' social work has been globalized. Social problems
on which it works, standards with which it works, and practices in which it is
engaged, have been all in the globalized context. The global elements have
penetrated every aspect of 'local' social work. If we suppose that

international social work has been completely absorbed by it, would there still be a place for international social work to exist? If there could be, what would the relationship with 'local' social work be, and what would the roles and functions of international social work be, and what would the definition of international social work be?

**(3) Some questions to come**
Over Period III, some questions would come to 'the final products' and 'international social work under globalization.'

1) As soon as 'the final products' (definitions) are reported, three questions would be spontaneously raised about their content: (a) Is it appropriate for those activities/'functions' which were raised in functional definitions to be said to be those of international social work?; (b) Is it appropriate to include the 'value' elements with the specific content such as human rights which were mentioned in "value-focused definitions" and "combined definitions" under international social work?; and (c) must those activities of international social work in "functional definitions" and "combined definitions" be carried out by professional social workers?

2) The second category of questions pertains to "international social work under globalization." They are more theoretical questions on international social work. (d) The first is the question of subsection (2)(iii) just above (on this page) —if the 'local' practice is put in the global context, is the globalized 'local' practice still 'local' social work, or is it international social work? Will international social work continue to exist? If so, what are the roles and functions of international social work while such globalized 'local' social work coexists? What will it look like? (e) How does international social work deal with the globalization of social work itself? Is it the role of international social work to globalize Western-rooted professional social work to the world? And (f) What is the contribution of international social work to the development of 'local' social work and social work itself to its third stage? (e.g. Akimoto, 2017: 1-5).

Item (a) will be answered in the next Chapter 2, and items (b) to (f) will be followed up in Chapter 3.

## (4) Two additional remarks

(i) A different usage of the term 'International social work'

One is a different usage of the term 'international social work' in meaning. In some "social-work-less developed countries" such as Bhutan, Sri Lanka, and Vietnam, the term is often used to refer to the social work outside their own countries, particularly the Western-rooted professional social work of Europe, North America, Australia, New Zealand, and International social work-related organizations such as the United Nations (most typically UNICEF) and NGOs (Red Cross, Save the Children, IASSW, IFSW, etc.). 'International social work' means the social work of 'social work-developed countries,' or sometimes of any other countries including neighbouring countries.[22*] The aim of this book should allow us to put this usage aside in our following discussion.

(ii) The review of English-medium literature mainly limited to English-
      speaking countries

The second remark concerns the limitation of this study which has been based on limited literature reviews. The books on which we have relied dealt with only English-medium literature, mostly from English-speaking countries. Non-English books and articles, i.e., the discussions in non-English speaking countries, even those from French, Spanish, and Portuguese speaking countries which comprise the majority worldwide,[23] have been totally or largely neglected. It is detrimental, particularly in a serious inquiry on the topic of 'what international social work is.' In addition, Russia, China, and the Middle East have been seldom discussed in the

---

22* There is another usage in "less-developed countries." It could be named as international social work for schools to provide knowledge and skills to students to find and get social work jobs in other countries (cf. Vasudevan, 2023).

23  In addition to the United States, the United Kingdom, Ireland, Canada, Australia, New Zealand, and South Africa, a third of the world's countries and regions have English as their official language.

literature we reviewed.[24]

Chapter 2 is a reprint of a non-English-medium article that was written in a non-English-speaking country in the East in 1995 and explored almost the same subject in this chapter—what international social work is. In Chapter 3, the results of Chapters 1 and 2 will lead to the construction of a new definition of international social work which will hopefully be acceptable to the whole world today.

---

24 There may not be many publications in their languages, and if any, the content of the discussion in those non-English-speaking countries may be identical to those in English countries due to the latter's learning from the former (cf. Ch.2 Box2-1). In that sense, the neglect may be justifiable.

# References

Ahmadi, N. (2003). Globalisation of consciousness and new challenges for international social work. *International Journal of Social Welfare*, 12(1): 14-23.

Akimoto, T. (1992). Kokusaika to rōdō sōsharu wāku: Genjitsu no kokusaika, shiten no kokusaika, gainen no kokusaika [Internationalization and Labor Social Work: Internationalization of Realities, Internationalization of 'the way of viewing matters,' and Internationalization of the Concept]. In S. Sato, (Ed.). *Kokusaika Jidai no Fukushi Kadai to Tenbō* [Welfare Issues and Perspectives in Days of Internationalization] (pp.233-249). Tokyo: Ichiryūsha.

Akimoto, T. (1995). 'Kokusai shakaifukushi' wo tsukuru: Kokusai Shakaifukushi no jissen/kenkyū to kijun [To Create "the International Social Welfare/ Social Work": Practice/Research of International Social Welfare/work and its Norms] (pp.97-101). *Jurist*. Yūhikaku.

Akimoto, T. (1997). A voice from Japan—Requestioning International Social Work/Welfare: Where are we now? Welfare world and national interest. *Japanese Journal of Social Services*, 1, 23-34. Translated and revised version of Akimoto (1995) above. ARIISW-Shukutoku.

Akimoto, T. (2017). The globalization of Western-rooted professional social work and exploration of Buddhist social work. In Gohori, J. (Ed.). *From Western-rooted Professional Social Work to Buddhist Social Work—Exploring Buddhist Social Work*. Gakubunsha.

Akimoto, T. (2020). Dai 1 shō: Kokusai sōsharu wōku no mokuteki to rinen [Chapter 1: The Purpose and Idea of International Social Work]. In Oka, S. & H. Harashima (Eds.). *Sekai no Shakaifukushi 12: Kokusai Shakaifukushi* [Global Social Welfare 12: International Social Welfare] (pp.22-50). Tokyo: Junposha.

APASWE (Asian and Pacific Association for Social Work Education). (2013). *The Birth and Development of the APASWE—Its Forty Years of History: Rebellion, Dissemination, and Contribution*. (Booklet). Asian and Pacific Association for Social Work Education.

Boehm, W. (1976). Editorial. *International Social Work*, 19(3), 1.

Cox, D. & Pawar, M. (2006). *International Social Work—Issues, Strategies, and*

*Programs.* Thousand Oaks, London and New Delhi: Sage Publications.

CSWE (Council on Social Work Education of the United States) (1956). The working committee.

Dominelli, L. (2010). *Social Work in a Globalising World.* Cambridge: Policy Press.

Falk, D. & Nagy, G. (1997). Teaching international and cross-cultural social work. IASSW Newsletter, Issue 5.

Goldman, B.W. (1962). International social work as a professional function. *International Social Work,* 5(3), 1-8.

Haug, E. (2005). Critical reflections on the emerging discourse on international social work. *International Social Work,* 48(2), 126-135.

Healy, L. M. (1990). [International content in social work educational programs world-wide]. Unpublished raw data. (Cited in Healy, 2001 below.)

Healy, L. M. (1995). Comprehensive and international overview. In T. D. Watts, D. Elliott, & N. S. Mayadas (Eds.). *International Handbook on Social Work Education* (pp.421-439). Westport, CT: Greenwood Press.

Healy, L. M. (2001; 2008; 2020). What Is International Social Work? In L. M. Healy (2001; 2008). and L. M. Healy & L. Thomas (Eds.) (2020), *International Social Work: Professional Action in an Interdependent World.* Oxford University Press, 5-13, 5-15, and 5-15 respectively.

Healy, L. M. (2012). Defining International Social Work. In L. M. Healy & R. J. Link (Eds.). *Handbook of International Social Work: Human Rights, Development, and The Global Profession* (pp.9-15). New York: Oxford University Press.

Hokenstad, M.C., Khinduka, S.K. & Midgley, J. (Eds.) (1992; 1997). *Profiles in International Social Work.* Washington, D.C.: National Association of Social Workers Press.

Huegler, N.,Lyons, K. & Pawar, M. (2012). Setting the Scene. In Lyons, K., et al. (Eds). *Handbook of International Social Work* (pp.5-13). Sage Publications.

Hugman, R. (2010). *Understanding International Social Work: A Critical Analysis.* Basingstoke, Hampshire: Palgrave Macmillan.

IASSW (International Association of Schools of Social Work), (1989/90)

Jebb, E. (1929). International social service. In *International Conference of Social Work: Proceedings, Volume 1.* First Conference, Paris, July 8-13, 1928, 637-

657.

Kimberly, M. D. (Ed.) (1984). *Beyond National Boundaries: Canadian Contributions to International Social Work and Social Welfare.* Ottawa: Canadian Association of Schools of Social Work.

Lavalette, M. & Ioakimdis, V. (2011). International social work or social work internationalism? Radical social work in global perspective. In M. Lavalette (Ed.). *Radical Social Work Today: Social Work at the Crossroads* (pp. 135-52*).* Bristol/Portland, OR: The Policy Press.

Lawrence, S., Lyons, K., Simpson, G. & Huegler, N. (2009). *Introducing International Social Work.* Exeter: Learning Matters.

Link, R. J. & Ramanathan, C. S. (2011). *Human Behavior in a Just World: Reaching for Common Ground.* London, MD: Rowman & Littlefield.

Lorenz, W. (1997, August). Social Work in a Changing Europe. Paper presented at the Joint European Regional Seminar of IFSW and EASSW on Culture and Identity. Dublin, Ireland, August 24, 1997.

Lyons, K. (1999). *International Social Work: Themes and Perspectives.* Aldershot: Ashgate.

Lyons, K., Manion K. & Carlsen, M. (2006). *International Perspectives on Social Work.* Basingstoke: Palgrave Macmillan.

Lyons, K., Hokenstad, T., Pawar, M., Huegler, N. & Hall, N. (Eds.). (2012). The *SAGE Handbook of International Social Work.* Sage Publications.

Marriam-Webster. (2011). Online dictionary London: Heinemann.

Nagy, G. & Falk, D. (2000). Dilemmas in international and cross-cultural social work education. *International Social Work,* 43(1), 49-60.

Payne, M. & Askeland, G. A. (2008). *Globalization and International Social Work: Postmodern Change and Challenge.* Aldershot, Hampshire: Ashgate.

Pawar, M. (2010). Looking outwards: teaching international social work in Asia.*International Journal of Social Work Education,* 29(8), 896-909.

Sanders, D. S. & Pederson, P. (Eds.) (1984). *Education for International Social Welfare.* Manoa: University of Hawaii and Council on social Work Education.

*Social Work Yearbook.* Russell Sage Foundation. (Predecessor of NASW *Encyclopedia of Social Work*). Vol. 1, (1929) 229; Vol. 2, (1933) 253; Vol. 3, (1935) 214; Vol.4, (1937); Vol. 5, (1939) 192.

Stein, H. (1957, January). An international perspective in the social work curriculum. Paper presented at the Annual Program Meeting of the Council on Social Work Education, Los Angeles, January 1957.

Warren, G. (1937). International social work. In R. Kurtz (Ed.). *Social Work Yearbook.* Vol.4 (pp.224-227). New York: Russell Sage Foundation.

Webb, S. A. (2003). Local orders and global chaos in social work. *European Journal of Social Work,* 6(2), 191-204.

Xu, Q. (2006). Defining international social work: A social service agency perspective. *International Social Work,* 49(6), 679-692.

Conference, Lectures, Speeches, Presentations

Akimoto, T. 23 October 2013. "Social work education programs, professionalization and dilemmas." In the Bandung University Social Work Conference, "Strengthening the development of social work in Indonesia." Bandung, Indonesia.

Akimoto, T. 10 November 2014. "Human resource policy framework: Is professionalization the way we take? Rejection of 'social work = professional social work." In the 17th Vietnam Social Work Day International Conference. Hanoi, Vietnam.

Akimoto, T. 23 October 2015, "Proposals to professional social work: Prepare for global crisis, rejecting IA/IF global definition. In the panel discussion, "Social work and policy in response to global crisis." APASWE/IFSW(AP) Social Work Regional Conference. Bangkok, Thailand.

Vasudevan, V. 9 February 2023. "International collaborative research project on "international social work" curricula in the Asia-Pacific region. In The 7th ARIISW-Shukutoku International Academic Forum, online, Chiba Japan.

# Chapter Two

## Another Understanding of International Social Work
### —Not Categories of Activities but a Way of Viewing Matters—

This chapter (pp.58-85) is a translated reprint [25] of a non-English language article written in an Eastern non-English-speaking country on the same subject as one of the cited articles in Chapter 1—the exploration of what international social work is. Keeping some distance from the mainstream could lead to different views, ideas, perspectives, and a proposal of a new definition without being fully swallowed up by the mainstream. [26] The original article was written in the early 1990s.

The first section out of six presents a holistic list of activities (acts, functions, practices or research; hereinafter to be referred as 'activities') being conducted under the name of international social work. [27] The findings by Western writers in Chapter 1 were almost identical to this list. [cf. Box 2-1, p.60]

In the next section, however, the author argues that these 'activities' are not necessarily international social work, and leads us to conclude that international social work is not simply fields (categories) of 'activities' but rather a norm or 'a way of viewing matters' (perception, perspective, norms, the point of reference, approach; hereinafter to be referred as 'a way of viewing matters') at the beginning of Section 3 below. With a ten-year time-lag, in the middle of the 2000s, Western literature discussed this similar point, using the terms 'value,' 'standard' and 'purpose' (cf. Chapter 1).

---

25  With revision and re-editing. See the footnote 4 for details.

26  This piece of work does not lead to the accomplishment of the current author's ambition to understand and construct international social work acceptable to the whole world. But looking at even one country outside the English sphere would somehow contribute to this ultimate goal (cf. Ch. 1, 2.(1-2)).

27  The original term of "social work" in their language was "*shakaifukushi,*" which could be translated into English as "social welfare," "social policies and programs," "social work," "social development," and "(social) well-being" depending on the context. It is mostly translated as "social welfare" in the country, but in this chapter, it has been translated as "social work," neglecting the difference between these two terms.

The section 3 reviews the development of such background thoughts and theories to extract a core 'way of viewing matters' or the norms, such as those regarding the significance and limitation of the United Nations and its conventions; modern Western thought and fundamental human rights; the welfare state and the welfare world; the concept of a national, a world citizen, "being a human being," and an "Earthian"; the relationships of nationalism, internationalism and cosmopolitanism to each other; and a theory of the State and the nation state.

The section 4 presents a skeleton of a tentative definition of international social work, considering today's stage of development of international society. The following the section 5 measures where we are now in the course of the development of international social work in reality and in theory, and the author calls the readers' attention to the future direction of international social work.

Sections 1 and 2 answer question (a) raised in the summary section of Chapter 1 (2.(3)), sections 3 and 4 to question (b) to some extent, and the section 5 would be beneficial to a discussion of question (d), although there is a difference in the core words 'internationalization' and 'globalization.'

In this article, "a non-English country" is Japan and a "non-English" language is Japanese. As far as the content is concerned, however, that discussed is not specifically about Japan but about all countries. Readers of this chapter may still find some skew towards Japan and Asia in the cited country names and cited case examples, which may be an eyesore. This happened simply because the original article was written in Japanese assuming Japanese readers. Current readers could and should replace these cited country names and case examples with the reader's own, to understand the author's real intention. The aim of this article and its reprint is to contribute to the construction of an internationally acceptable concept of international social work while utilizing the recent discussion in a specific country and in its language.

## Digression for the intellectually curious

### Box 2-1. Why did meanings in the Western world and in Japan tend to become identical?

While Chapter 1 reviewed literature written in English mostly in the Western world and Chapter 2 reviewed literature written in Japanese in the Far East, why is the product extracted identical? Social work is supposed to be based on the culture, tradition, and life, and political, economic, and social conditions of the society. These two societies are very different.

The reason may be because Japanese social work had simply learned and copied the Western-rooted (mainly United States') social work in content. If it is the case with other non-Western, non-English countries, the author's anxiety at the very end of Chapter 1 (2.(4)(ii))—the limitation of the literature review of the books and articles on which we relied (while discussing 'international social work,' we have not seen other language and cultural spheres) —would be in vain, wouldn't it?

# To Create 'the International Social Work'
## —Practice and Research and Norms
## of International Social Work [28*] —

In the past decade [the 1980s to the early 1990s], interest in international social work[29] has heightened in Japan. In the remaining years of the 20th century [sic] and in the first few decades of the 21st century, this interest will increase further. International social work seems to have been accepted as a field of social work, but what international social work actually is has not yet been agreed upon at all. This paper aims to contribute to the construction of an internationally acceptable concept of international social work through a review of recent discussions in Japan on this topic.

The article was written based on the extensive literature review of all representative books and journal articles related to international social work which was published during the 1970s to the early 1990s in Japanese in

---

28* [* indicates not original but newly-added footnotes for this reprint: hereinafter to be same.] The original article is Akimoto (1995b). "To create 'the international social work'—Practice/research and the way of viewing matters of international social work—['Kokusai-shakai-fukushi' wo tsukuru—Kokusai-shakaifukushi no jissen/kenkyu to kijun—],' Jurist, Special Issue, November 1995 (in Japanese), which was based on a presentation at the Japanese Society for Social Welfare Studies' annual conference held at Doshisha University on October 8, 1994. The article was translated into English and published with some revisions in the Journal of the Japanese Society of Social Welfare Studies, 1 (1997), 23-34, with the revised title "Requestioning international social work/welfare: Where are we now?—Welfare world and national interest." This chapter is basically the translation of the original article with some revision and editing (for the publication of the above English journal and this book). The English is mostly based on the 1997 translated version.

29 See footnote 3.

Japan[30] [31], and on some brief surveys and interviews.

# 1. To do What is International Social Work?
## —Practice and Research Conducted Under the Name of International Social Work—

The understanding, or misunderstanding, of international social work has been confusing in various ways. What are students expecting when they register for courses named as such, and what are practitioners and researchers doing when they believe they are practicing or conducting research on international social work? The table below provides the answers obtained from the literature review and our small informal surveys and interviews. [References in Japanese on each item are mostly omitted below in this section. Readers who are interested in, see Miki and Akimoto (1998).]

What do people call international social work? Our interest in this section is not the definition but the content or the constituent elements of what international social work is.[32] Eleven major and 18 minor concepts were identified (Table 2-1).

Some people think that "1. studying or researching about other countries" falls into the category of international social work. This includes two sub-

---

30 Seventy-five (75) works were covered. The literature was "limited to those by the authors known as 'researchers' and practitioners in the 'social work field' and those with the term 'international social welfare/social work' or 'international welfare' as a principle." Much literature from other disciplines should have been included but has been excluded from the examination including "Development Economics, International Relations, Anthropologies, Sociology, and Psychology." Documents from the government (e.g., the Annual Report on Health and Welfare [White Paper]) and vast volumes of publications by JICA (Japan International Cooperation Agency) must also be reviewed (Miki & Akimoto, 1998).

31 The literature review itself was made a few years earlier by the current author (T. Akimoto), but published later under a co-authorship with Miki, K. (Miki & Akimoto, 1998).

32 Re issues and problems which international social work deals with, see e.g., Figure 2 on p.301 of Kojima, 1992.

## Table 2-1. Practices/Researches Conducted Under the Name of the International Social Work

1. Study/research about other countries
   a) Study/research on the social welfare situation (in general or on specific subjects) in other countries
   b) Field study/research in other countries

2. Practice of social work in other countries

3. International comparative research

4. Practice/research on issues and problems which arise in the bi-lateral or multi-lateral relationships
   a) Practice/research on issues and problems which arise at the individual level
   b) Practice/research on the effects of nature or society

5. Practice/research on issues and problems which arise on a global scale
   a) Practice/research on issues and problems which arise at the individual level
   b) Practice/research on the effects of nature or society

6. Practice/research on cross-cultural contact

7. Practice/research on "internationalisation at home"

8. "Foreign affairs" (communication; the promotion of colleagueship and friendship)

9. International exchange
   a) Friendship promotional activities
   b) Exchange of information, experience, ideas, people (students, teachers, practitioners, [and citizens]) and research
   c) Holding/participating in international conferences

10. International cooperation/collaboration
    a) Activities by the United Nations, other intergovernmental, governmental and non-governmental organisations
    b) Joint practice/research projects with practitioners, organisations or researchers in other countries

11. Practice/research on North-South relations including relief and development aid to the "Two-Thirds World"

ideas: One is "a) studying or researching the social welfare situation in other countries," such as Swedish nursing homes for the aged (sic), United States ADA (Americans with Disabilities Act), and the social welfare situation in general in various countries (e.g., Kojima & Okada, 1994; Ogiwara, 1995). The other is "b) field research in other countries," or research conducted physically putting self in the research subject country, such as research in the slums of Dhaka or in rural villages in Peru (Numerous examples of this 1. b), as well as ones of 2. to 5. and 10. b) below, are found in journals of various universities of social work, Japanese Society of Social Welfare Studies (1994), and many issues of International Social Work (Sage Publications).

The simplest and most common usage of the term is to "2. practice (any) social work in other countries" than his/her own home country, not limited to "field research."

A large number of people conduct "3. International comparative research." Themes could cover the whole range of social welfare policies, programs, and problems, for example, comparison among Malaysian, Indonesian, and Vietnamese child welfare, or between British and Japanese social security systems (e.g., *Encyclopaedia of Social Work* (Vol. 16 (1971) and thereafter), Mohan (1987: 957-969); Furukawa (1994)).

Many of them think that conducting these forms part of international social work. Taking the word "international" literally, international social work should mean "4. practice or research on issues and problems which arise in a bi-lateral or multi-lateral relationship." Included are two types of practice or research on: "a) issues and problems which arise at the individual level" such as those of Japanese-Filipino children[33*] and "b) effects of nature or of society," that is, effects due to activities by a nation or some of its potent components, such as acid rain in neighbouring countries because of thermal power generation in Country A, or floods in Country B caused due to deforestation in an area in Country C. The cause or background of the former, a), is of course social, and the result of the latter, b), concerns individuals' lives.

---

33*   Children who were born in and out of wedlock between Filipino women, who worked in
      Japan mainly since the 1980s, and Japanese men. Many of these children had various eco-
      nomic, mental, and legal problems.

Interpreting "international" as "global," international social work would be practice or research on "5. issues and problems which arise on a global scale." Poverty, the destruction of environments and ecosystems, refugees, and AIDS are examples (e.g. Kendall, 1994: 11).

Some people understand cross-cultural social work and international social work to be interchangeable. "6.Practice/Research on cross-cultural contact," covers the understanding of different cultures, the conflict between them, and the efforts to solve such conflict if it occurs (cf. e.g., Sitaram, 1976). Cross-cultural counselling may be an important field within international social work practice. "Foreigners" may have many difficulties in any country.

Quite a few people turn their attention to their own countries with an "international" perspective after they have looked at other countries for a while. They question "7. internationalization at home" as being an indispensable component of international social work. In the case of Japan, some questions raised are the treatment of foreign workers, refugees, Koreans in Japan, and Japanese war orphans who returned from China.

Some people perceive the engagement in "8. foreign affairs" of organizations they belong to as being the practice of international social work. Just like the Ministry of Foreign Affairs in a state, most organizations that constitute today's society have a foreign affairs section or business with other countries. The Japan Association of Schools of Social Work [the present Japanese Association for Social Work Education], for instance, has the Special Committee of International Relations [dissolved in 2019] to contact its counterparts in other countries.

Three types of activities are included in "9. international exchange" which is executed at individual, group, organizational, and local and national government levels. The first is "a) the promotion of international friendship activities." In addition to friendship promotion at the individual level (e.g., Okada, 1985:185 emphasizes its importance), various international friendship programs have been implemented, including personnel exchange programs for members and non-members at the group and organizational levels. Being asked what sorts of international social welfare policies and programs they run, many local governments mention sister city programs, citizen exchange programs, as well as others. The second pertains to "b) exchange of information, experience, ideas, people (students, teachers, practitioners, [and citizens]) and research." The third is the "c) holding of international conferences," which is a form of b). Numerous international meetings, symposiums, and conferences have been held. They have been the central activities of international social work since the early days of its development (e.g., Each volume of *Social Work Year Book* (Russell Sage Foundation) and *Encyclopedia of Social Work* (NASW (National Association of Social Workers)); Nemoto (1989)).

Central activities of "10. international cooperation/collaboration" today are those of "a) the United Nations and other international organizations." Included are both the United Nations organizations such as ILO (International Labour Organization), WHO (World Health Organization), and UNICEF (United Nations Children's Fund), and voluntary international organizations such as the International Red Cross. Activities by respective states are, however, also important. Examples are ones by the United States Children's Bureau and the Japan International Cooperation Agency (JICA). Activities by NGOs (non-governmental organizations), e.g., CARE (The Cooperative for Assistance and Relief Everywhere) International and Médecins sans Frontières, have been increasing in importance recently. International social work organizations such as IASSW (International Association of Schools of Social Work), IFSW (International Federation of Social Workers), and ICSW (International Council on Social Welfare) fall into this category. Some people understand that the engagement in "b) joint practice/research projects with practitioners, organizations or researchers of other countries" is equivalent to the practice of international social work.

Some people regard international social work as the engagement in "11. practice/research in emergency relief activities in case of wars and natural disasters and developmental assistance activities to "Two-Thirds World" with a long-term perspective. Typical activities are ones by the United Nations and other international organizations. They could be included in the sub-item "a." of "10. International cooperation and collaboration", but are put under a separate item 11. as many people associate "developing" country assistance with the term 'international social work.' John M. Romanyshyn says, "international social welfare [is] the redress of inequalities between the 'have' and 'have-not' nations." (Romanyshyn, 1971:12, cf. Ashikaga, 1985: 187) (cf.

66

Sanders & Pedersen, 1983, cf. Okada, 1993: 16; Many publications by JICA).

The items above are not mutually exclusive. In particular, items 7. to 11. are continuous and overlapping. These items are not definitions of international social work. Each contender does not necessarily insist on any specific single item. They simply name any combination of items as international social work. For example, early versions of the *Social Work Year Book* (Russell Sage Foundation) combine "4. a) Practice/research on issues and problems which arise at the individual level," "9. c) Holding/participating in international conferences," and "10. a) Activities of the United Nations', other intergovernmental, governmental and non-governmental organizations" (e.g. Warren, 1937: 224). Recent versions of *Encyclopaedia of Social Work* add to them "3. International comparative research," "9. a) Friendship promotion activities," "11. Aid to developing countries," and others (e.g. NASW, 18th ed., 1987). Y. Kojima and L. Healy (1993) include "3. International comparative research," "5. Practice/research on issues and problems which arise on the global scale," "9. a) Friendship promotion activities," "6. Practice/research concerning cross-cultural contact," and others (cf. e.g., Tani, 1993: 54).

## 2. This Is Not Necessarily International Social Work

Scanning the list above, it seems as if anything that concerns "other countries" is considered international social work. The author's understanding is different. It might not be international social work to carry out any one item in the list or a combination of several items. Why is this not necessarily international social work? There are two reasons: Firstly, simple and plain questions arise on each item, and secondly historical development should not be neglected. We will discuss the first point in this section, and the second point in the next section.

Simple and plain questions arise on each activity item in the list. Here we cannot describe all items in detail, but in a word, it is not necessarily international social work if we do something related to foreign countries. Let's cover the points on our list in Table 2-1 above.

Firstly, to "study/research other countries" (1.) or "the social welfare problem and situation (in general or on a specific topic) of other countries" (1. a)) is not necessarily international social work. To study and describe the history or the present state of social welfare in other countries would be something that could be called "overseas information" or "the situation abroad." Once we start this kind of thing, it becomes endless.

Studying Swedish nursing homes, the United States' Americans with Disabilities Act (ADA), child labour in Bolivia and Bangkok urban slums might not be international social work. They may be part of domestic social work. Because of the internationalization of society, each field of social work, such as social work for the aged, people with disabilities, children, and the poor, could not be completed unless it deals with issues and problems beyond its national boundary.

To conduct a "Field study/research in other countries" (1. b)) may not be necessarily international social work (Akimoto, 1995a). "Field research" here means the research that is conducted in the field or country of the research subjects. The meaning is broader than the "field research" in typical useage. Isn't it strange to say that to do a certain thing in a foreign country is international social work and to do the same thing in his/her own country is not international social work but domestic ('local' in Chapter 1; 'national' in Chapter 3) social work? Just imagine two cases in which a Japanese researcher analysed of poverty of London in London and then did the same in Tokyo.

Students and professors from China and Korea do research on the problems of Japanese elderly people and give presentations in Japanese academic societies' annual conferences—it is international social work, and is it domestic social work if Japanese practitioners and researchers do the same?

Nothing would be different if you draw some lessons for your own country in 1. a) and b) and in other activities in the following items. It is domestic social work if you draw a lesson for your own country, isn't it?

Replacing the "field research" (1. b)) with "practice", are whatever "practices social workers do in other countries" (2.) international social work? If a United States Christian NGO's work in a Calcutta [Kolkata] slum should be called an international social work practice, why not an Indian nun's work in

68

a Chicago slum soup kitchen? (Physician Task Force, 1985) Do United States professional social workers accept this as an international social work? The engagement in practice in "developing countries" is international social work, isn't it? (e.g., Brown & Pizer, 1987) More seriously—if Japanese social workers' practice in Asian countries could be called international social work, should Japanese researchers' work in the South Manchuria Railway Company Research Department before World War Two and the practitioners' work to transfer Japanese social work to "Manchuria" and the Korean Peninsula be so called? (cf. e.g., Shen, 1995) Is it called international social work if a social worker from the United Kingdom comes to an Asian country and designs a social welfare program, trains social workers for the operation or repeats casework in communities to administer the colonized country smoothly? Suzerain states in the northern hemisphere did much in such countries. Can what they did be termed international social work?

In more basic terms, this approach argues that a Japanese person doing something in Japan corresponds to domestic social work practice, but a Kenyan or an Australian doing the same in Japan constitutes international social work practice (and vice versa). This does not seem very rational.

"International comparative research" (3.) and analysis are just some of the most primitive research methods that are nothing special to social work but are common to all disciplines, fields, and themes. This has always been the case.

"Practice/research on cross-cultural contact" (6.) is not equal to international social work. Cross-cultural and multi-cultural social work is important even in international social work but has nothing to do with only the relations between countries. It is important also within a country. We could not call it international social work.[34*]

---

[34*] In a forum in Tokyo in January 2018 where the Presidents of the IASSW and APASWE (Asian and Pacific Association for Social Work Education) as well as Prof. Lynne Hearly (cf. Chapter 1) attended, the presenters and participants all agreed on this understanding (Matsuo, Akimoto & Hattori, 2019: 76). The forum was organized by the Asian Research Institute for International Social Work (ARIISW), Shukutoku University, cosponsored by IASSW, APASWE, and the Japanese Association for Social Work Education. It was supported by the Japanese Society for the Study of Social Welfare, the Japanese Society for the Study of Social Work, and the Japanese Society for the Study of Social Welface Education.

"Practice/research on internationalization at home" (7.), in the social worker's own countries, may or may not be international social work. It is not easy to call activities international social work when the activities discourage the intake of refugees or encourage migrant workers to be assimilated into Japanese culture and society.

Accepting visitors from other countries, exchanging MOUs (Memorandum of Understandings) with universities of other countries, and being engaged in exchange programs with students, teachers, and researchers (cf. 9. b)), and devoting efforts to the international relations committee of national associations of social work (cf. 10. a)) would not necessarily be called international social work, although they contribute to communication, the promotion of colleagueship, and friendship. Shouldn't these activities be called diplomacy or "foreign affairs" (8.) which are commonly practiced day by day by almost all organizations in today's society including private corporations?

Is it international social work to attend and make a research presentation at a conference (9. c)) which an international social work organization organises, or to be invited by another country and make a keynote speech at an international conference?

Is it an international social work practice to work for a United Nations agency, an NGO, or such a hard-core international social work organizations (10. a)) as the IASSW, IFSW, or ICSW?

Executing joint research projects with researchers from other countries (10. b)) would not necessarily be international social work (Akimoto, 1995a). In a Japan-United States joint research project, is it international social work for a Japanese researcher but just social work for a US researcher to do research on poverty in a big United States city? Suppose a joint research team on problems of Japanese elderly people was formed, is it international social work for Chinese or Korean team members and also for Japanese members, or is it domestic social work for the Japanese members?

The discussion on South-North relationships (11.) would not necessarily be international social work. Are the practice and research of aid activities carried out to expand the market of his/her own country and promote the national interest of his/her own country international social work? Aren't they domestic social work? It is not easy to affirm that the engagement in

ODA (Official Development Assistance) projects is international social work.

## 3. What is International Social Work?
### —Not fields (categories) of activities but norms
### (a way of viewing matters)—

Practice and research under each item in the above list may or may not be called international social work. So, what is international social work? International social work is not a category of activities but rather 'a way of viewing matters' (norms; approach), (Akimoto, 1995a; International social work may be called a branch in this meaning).

This leads to the question of what is 'the way of viewing matters'? The same literature review as that in the section 1 above identified two streams: (1) NASW's *Encyclopaedia of Social Work*[35]—W. A. Friedlander[36]—Y. Kojima and (2) G. Myrdal and R. Pinker—Y. Ashikaga and T. Okada.

### (1) Viewed from the outside

Y. Kojima (1992) writes the following paragraphs:

Even if the legislation and the administration and voluntary welfare services are not yet well prepared in a country...the position of international social work is to examine its imperfection, to develop welfare services for the socially disadvantaged and their families, and to clear frontiers of new practice (p.288).

At the United Nations level, without defining social welfare narrowly, they discuss the guarantee of human rights of women, children, the disabled, the aged, refugees, minorities, migrant workers and others, and criticize and attack mercilessly other countries when their rights are disturbed in other countries or by their own establishment so that the social justice is

---

35    Each edition of Social Work Year Book and Encyclopedia of Social Work, esp. 13th ed. (1957) of the latter.

36    Friedlander, 1961 and 1975.

advanced. Through the process...representatives of United Nations membership countries join their hands to draft resolutions and declarations, to contribute to the advancement of policies on human rights of each country, spending many years, and to make efforts to be concluded into effective conventions and protocols, if an agreement that it is necessary to do so is reached among countries (p.288).

Fundamental human rights have been guaranteed by a state's constitution and laws. What it means is that people can insist on their rights and seek relief based on laws within the extent and limit they provide for, when those rights are encroached. However, if the extent of laws is made limited and changed for the worse, they lose the base of the complaint, and cannot help give in to their fate. Because the guarantee of human rights is under its state's authority, other countries cannot only criticize a country's infringement of foreigners' human rights, which are out of the protection of laws, but are rather criticized as "domestic interference" by the country concerned. Meanwhile, traditionally domestic laws have been stipulated with the idea that "individuals belong to a state," but if the state ratifies the International Convention on Human Rights, and its treaty powers which guarantee individuals' rights, do not rely on the state any more... International legislation makes "people who obey the state" able to live in "a state which exists for individuals" (pp.289-290).

[English translation by TA]

The significance of Kojima is her understanding of social work from outside the state. On the other hand, she discusses only the level of positive law, placing too high a value on the United Nations, and relies too much on the Universal Declaration of Human Rights and the International Convention on Human Rights.

## (2) Beyond the Welfare State to a Welfare World

Y. Ashikaga (1985) and T. Okada (1985) cite G. Myrdal and R. Pinker respectively to write the following paragraphs respectively:

"The fact is that the setting in which the modern Welfare State has been developing in the Western world has been one of progressive international disintegration. It is equally undeniable that the larger part of the complex system of public policies in the interest of national progress, and of the growth of equality and security for the individual, which today make up the Welfare State, have on balance tended to disturb the international equilibrium. They were nowhere conceived and brought into effect as internationally concerted actions. Effects abroad were not taken into consideration." (Myrdal, 1960: 160-161)* In that sense, the modern welfare state is nationalistic. "[T]he strengthening of the ties within the individual nations and the increasing scope of national economic planning have tended to push towards international disintegration" (Myrdal, 1960: 285)*. Thus, the conclusion of the ultimate solution is "...there is no alternative to international disintegration except to begin, by international cooperation and mutual accommodation, to build the Welfare World" (Myrdal, 1960: 176)* (Ashikaga: 187).

[*Myrdal's citation was added by the current author.]

The idea of the "welfare world," which can be obtained by extending the concept of the "welfare state" guarantees the human minimum, rather than national minimum, as a right that derives simply from being a member of human society, and requires world society to fulfil this duty...It is the internationalism of the social welfare that the "welfare state" ought to be extended to a "welfare world," putting the conceptual base of social welfare on the human rights and unlimited altruism. In reality, however, it has been blocked by a thick wall of nationalism. For, as R. Pinker (1979) points out...in his *The Idea of Welfare*, social welfare has an aspect to maintain boundaries and has been confined within an institution of a state because of its national egoism. A state is not only a container but also a wall. Nationalism is necessary but must be open-ended. Internationalism and nationalism are thus two moments that exist within (Okada: 185).

[English translation by TA]

The significance of the above quotes is their concern for the underlying thought. They question the historical meaning and limitation of the welfare state, insert it as a "parameter", and envisage a welfare world beyond it. They let us extract a national boundary, a wall of social welfare, as a central element of international social work.

## Digression for the intellectually curious

### Box 2-2. Why did meanings in the Western world and in Japan became different?

While Chapters 1 and 2 reviewed literature discussing the same subject, "What is international social work?" based on Western-rooted professional social work, why did only Chapter 2 review literature with an interest in the background thought and theories, such as the welfare world, which were still Western-rooted?

The reason may be the language issue. Both use different languages. One is English, the other is Japanese. The English term "social work" has been often translated into "shakaifukushi" in Japanese, which may cover not only social work in the Western sense but also social welfare, social policy, social development, and social wellbeing as well. Naturally a conceptual discrepancy is born in the coverage and meaning. Due to this "misunderstanding" (judging from the original English social work world's point of view), the unexpected conceptual development of social work could be possible insofar as we consider social work on a world scale.

# 4. Not to See and Think from the Perspective of One's Own Country
## —A tentative definition and 'the way of viewing matters' of international social work—

The following is a tentative definition at the most abstract level of international social work with learning from these two streams above and with consideration of the present developmental stage of the world, which will be discussed in the following subsections 5.(1) and (2) on pp.77-80:

> International social work is to think about the welfare of international society (all people in the world) and to make efforts to realize it. The key concept is "judgement from the outside." 'The way of viewing matters' with which we think and make efforts is what exists outside their own country and is commonly usable in the international society.[37]

The prime theme in international social work would be 1) What is 'the way of viewing matters'? 2) Is it possible to form and materialize this international 'way of viewing matters' in today's reality of nation states as the mainstream, and if possible, how? and 3) How are people who think and work with such a 'way of viewing matters' born? Here we touch on 1) and 2). In Chapter 4 we consider 3).

1) What is 'the way of viewing matters'? It is something on the opposite pole of nationalism and national interest. It is the claim from thinking of a welfare world, a citizen of the world, and "as a human being."[38] (Akimoto, 1995a) 'The way of viewing matters' is not only those of the International Declaration of Human Rights and the International Convention on Human Rights. "Positive laws" agreed by each state in the United Nations are easiest to accept as 'the way of viewing matters,' but there would be others. Contrarily, some activities of the United Nations may not be usable

---

37    'The way of viewing matters' may be incorporated into their own country's 'way of viewing matters.'

38    Many NGOs and social work-related people have a liking for these terms to use.

as 'the way of viewing matters' of international social work.[39] NGOs are sometimes different from and conflict with them in opinion. 'The way of viewing matters' here is that social norm in international society. The key is to find what the norms are and formulate them.

2) Is such 'a way of viewing matters' possible? In the reality of the nation-state world, is it possible to force the concession to nationalism and national interest for the welfare world, a citizen of the world, a cosmopolitan, and "as a human being"? Is a welfare world realistic, as well as these other concepts, which are seemingly super-historical and are frequently found in both the mass media and NGO and academic literature recently, theoretically and practically?

Theoretically, we have learned the limitations of welfare states. Philosophically, we have had the ideas of the Western Enlightenment finding their way to the International Declaration of Human Rights. Some articles of a nation-state's Constitution and some laws such as the Labour Standards Act (e.g. Japan), do not distinguish between its own nationals and non-nationals. Some religions have for a long time preached the equality and brotherhood of people before God. There could be other forms of progress.

---

39  The United Nations is meaningful and crucially important, but more sociological analyses are necessary. It should not be forgotten that it is the stage of conflicts of each country's national interests.

# 5. Where Are We Now?[40]

One difficulty is in measuring how far an actual society has already prepared for such 'a way of viewing matters' or norms.

## (1) In an actual society: Solid nation states and national boundaries

Today in reality, national boundaries have also been lowered.[41] For example, a woman who was born in France, moved immediately to Nigeria, received a higher education in the United States, married a Mexican, and is now working in Singapore. She loves all those countries and has difficulty describing her nationality. Needless to say, the numbers of migrants, foreign workers, and refugees are increasing. There exist numerous associations in the sociological sense, both multi-national corporations (Okada, 1985; 185) and non-profit international organizations, which span national boundaries.

There is not only the United Nations but also the EU (European Union), ASEAN (Association of South-East Asian Nations), NAFTA (North American Free Trade Agreement) [ineffective in 2020], etc. The NAALC (North American Agreement on Labor Cooperation), the labour side of NAFTA, stipulates that cases of violation or unsatisfactory implementation of labour laws in a party country go to a review board (National Administration Office) in other party countries. Most discussions and agreements at G7 meetings would have been shouted down as "domestic interference" a few decades ago.

Mutual dependency or the effect of a country's economy on other countries has been dramatically increasing. The world has reached the point where economic superpowers cannot even protect their national interests if they think only of their own interest (Kagami, 1995; Akimoto, 1992: 243). Information encircles the globe in an instant as if there were no national boundaries. The existence of nuclear weapons and the problem of the Earth's ecosystem make national boundaries meaningless (Ashikaga, 1985: 188).

---

40     Subsections (1) and (2) of this Section 5 are from Akimoto, 1997: 28-29 and 29-30 respectively.

41     We have entered not an era of exploring ideas but an era of empirically measuring where we are now heading toward the welfare world, and how much society has prepared for it.

Contrarily, nation states certainly exist and their reality is conflicting national interests. Just remember the simple fact that we still cannot cross national borders without passports which say, for instance, "The Minister for Foreign Affairs of [Country A] requests all those whom it may concern to allow the bearer, a [Country A's] national, to pass freely and without hindrance and in case of need, to afford him or her every possible aid and protection" even though the bearer may not have asked for the patronage of the state.[42*] Even the United Nations is an aggregation of nation states. The agreements and operations of the above organizations abbreviated are also compromised by competing national interests.

Can NGOs with some social cause such as environment protection or "being a woman" surpass national borders? These are the kinds of questions we hear about of late. Even being a class does not surpass national borders. The international solidarity of the labour movement across national boundaries has not yet been successfully achieved. More fundamentally speaking, social welfare today has been designed or is even often defined as the rights of the people from a state or obligations/services of a state to the people. Is it possible to see a human being before his or her nationality?

## (2) In theory: Not a welfare world but internationalized states

While national boundaries have been disappearing much on one side, nation states have firmly continued to exist. In such a setting we need to examine the following questions. What is a welfare world? How will it be achieved? Where are we now on our way to a welfare world?[43*] Here we discuss only the third question.[44]

Today is said to be an age when we are required to be good citizens of a

---

42*   Many European people spontaneously refer to EU and Shengen Agreement areas and insist on the change of the meaning of national boundaries, but we will not get in this subject here. Seeing from the whole world, these areas (countries) share just small parts, and the change pertains to the relation only among those countries and the "national boundaries" between those member countries and non-member countries have firmly existed.

43*   The concept of 'welfare world' today may be different from what was imagined and thought of in the time of Pinker and Myrdal.

44    Strictly speaking, to discuss the latter without discussing the former two is irrational.

nation, good international citizens, and good world citizens all at the same time. A state and its social welfare could be thought of in this analogy. We are requested to be a good nation state providing good domestic social welfare, to be a good internationalized state with good internationalized social welfare, and to have a perspective on a welfare world[45] and world welfare, at the same time.

The importance here is the second term, that is, an internationalized state and its internationalized social welfare. Because of internationalization or even globalization,[46] a state and its social welfare must be internationalized.

Internationalization implies triple points of discussion. Firstly, the basic nature is still national although the period for the judgment on the national interest might be longer than in the first term, that is, a state and its domestic social welfare. In this sense, a welfare world and world welfare will not necessarily arise as an extension of the internationalization of each state and its social welfare.

Secondly, internationalization requires the erasure of national boundaries to some extent. It does not deny a state as a policy subject but refuses to attach a special meaning or importance to a specific state. For example, we do not think that Japan is a special state. We start from the point that Japan is a state which is just the same as other states. It does not start from the perspective of the Japanese, but from one of all peoples. Furthermore, it often leads us to start not as a Japanese but as a human being or an individual. In a way, it requires us to be cosmopolitan before being international (Akimoto, 1992: 243). In other words, international social work contains within it a path to a welfare world. Is the development from within (or the denial of self) possible? If possible, how?

Thirdly, "internationalization" can be used to describe various activities in the process of a state's more abrupt economic, social, and cultural expansion. Sometimes the word is a euphemism for imperialistic invasion. The internationalization of the economy is the independent variable and the internationalization of social work is the dependent variable. The timing

---

45    The relation between a welfare world and the world state has not been fully discussed yet.

46    The difference and relation between internationalization and globalization are not referred to here.

coincides perfectly with the appropriate time lag. Even a developmental project can be for poverty alleviation or for a "developed" country's economic expansion. More difficult is that a project carries both aspects at the same time.

**(3) The location of your country**

[The following is the case of Japan. Each reader is expected to rewrite the content of this subsection replacing "Japan" with his/her own country.] (The insertion for this book publication.)

We need to exercise caution with Japanese discussion on international social work. (1) Almost all Japanese respondents and writers in our surveys, interviews, and literature reviews created the preceding list of items perceived only from a Japanese viewpoint, and only in relation to Japan and the internationalization of Japanese social work. Most of them were busy asking about the role of Japan and Japanese contribution, or the doctrine of atonement. They never leave behind their nationality. (2) The period when discussion on international social work in Japan grew is suggestive. It was from the latter half of the 80s, which coincided with the expansion of the Japanese economy into other countries, especially Asia.

The essence of international social work is 'the way of viewing matters' of the international society, that is, not from national interests.[47]

# 6. Summary

People have conducted various activities and given them the name of international social work as practice and research on and in other countries;

---

47    Some people may argue that today in a shorter term in human history, the surging mass unemployment and nationalism in "developed" countries is a more central subject for international social work.

on issues and problems which arise in the bi-lateral or multi-lateral relationships or on a global scale; on the North-South relations; on cross-cultural contact; about "internationalization at home" as well as international comparative research; "foreign affairs"; international exchange; and international cooperation/collaboration.

However, to do these activities is not necessarily international social work. All that concerns other countries do not come under the concept of international social work. They may or may not be. International social work should be defined not as a category of activities but rather as 'a way of viewing matters,' or efforts towards the welfare world envisaged beyond welfare states.

Today is a time when to be a nation state, to be internationalized, and to have a perspective for a welfare world are required at the same time. With this recognition, we won't miss key elements of international social work today, that is, national boundaries, national interests, and nationalism, as well as a dream for the welfare world. Practice/research and chattering with the lack of recognition of where we are now are not only useless but are also hazardous. International social work is a challenging topic but at the same time a risky one.

International social work is redefined as efforts of the international society whose 'way of viewing matters,' or norms, are ones not from your own countries as to fit today's developmental stage of the society. International social work implies an orientation against national interests and nationalism.

# References

Akimoto, T. (1992). Kokusaika to rōdō sōsharu wāku: Genjitsu no kokusaika, shiten no kokusaika, gainen no kokusaika [Internationalization and Labor Social Work: Internationalization of Realities, Internationalization of 'the way of viewing natters,' and Internationalization of the Concept]. In S. Sato, (Ed.). *Kokusaika Jidai no Fukushi Kadai to Tenbō* [Welfare Issues and Perspectives in Days of Internationalization] (pp.233-249). Tokyo: Ichiryūsha.

Akimoto, T. (1995a). Shakaifukushi ni okeru kokusaika: Kokusaika to nashonarizumu [Internationalization of Social Welfare: Internationalization and Nationalism]. In Ichibangase, Y. (Ed.). *Nijū-isseiki Shakaifukushi-gaku* [The 21 Century Social Welfare] (pp.156-169). Tokyo: Yūhikaku.

Akimoto, T. (1995b). Kokusai-shakaifukushi wo tsukuru: Kokusai-shakaifukushi no jissen/kenkyū to kijun [To Create 'the International Social Work': Practice/research and 'the way of viewing matters' of International Social Work],' *Jurist*, Special Issue, November 1995 Yū hikaku (in Japanese), which was based on a presentation at the Japanese Society for Social Welfare Studies' annual conference held at Doshisha University on October 8, 1994.

Akimoto, T. (1997). Requestioning international social work/welfare: Where are we now? —Welfare: world and national interest. *The Journal of the Japanese Society of Social Welfare Studies*, 1, 23-34. The English translation of Akimoto, 1995b with some revisions and the revised title.

Ashikaga, Y. (Autumn, 1985). Kokusai-shakaifukushi josetsu [Introduction to International Social Welfare]. *Social Work Research [Sōsharu Wāku Kenkyu]*, Vol.11, No.3.

Brown, J. L. & Pizer, H. F. (1987). *Living Hungry in America*. Macmillan. Translation: Aoki. K. (1990). *Gendai Amerika no Kiga* [Hunger in the Present United States ]. (Nan'un-dō).

*Encyclopedia of Social Work*. (NASW). Each edition.

Fasteam, I. J. (1957). International Social Welfare. *Encyclopedia of Social Work. 13th ed*. NASW.

Freidlander, W. A. (1961). *Introduction to Social Welfare*, 2nd ed. Englewood Cliffs, NJ: Prantice Hall.

Furukawa, K. (1994). Kokusaika-jidai no shakaifukushi to sono kadai: Hikaku shakaifukushi no kisoteki shomonndai wo chushin ni [Social Welfare in the Days of Internationalization and its Challenges: Focusing on Basic Issues of Comparative Social Welfare] *Social Welfare* [Shakaifukushi-gaku] (Japanese Society for Social Welfare Studies) Vol.35 No.1 (the 50th volume of the set).

Hagiwara, Y. (1995). Ajia no shakaifukushi [Social Welfare in Asia] Chuō Hō ki Shuppan.

*International Social Work*. Sage Publications.

Japanese Society for Social Welfare Studies (1994). *Shakaifukushi ni okeru Kokusai-kyōryoku no Arikata ni kansuru Kenkyū* [Research on International Collaboration in Social Welfare] (basic research). Japanese Society for Social Welfare Studies.

Kagami, M. (1995). *Hitobito no Ajia Nakamura Shōji-cho (Shohyū)* [Asia of People by Shōji Nakamura (book review)] *Asahi Shimbun*. Jan. 15 Morning edition.

Kendall, K. A. (1993). Sōgo ni izon shiau sekai no naka no shakaifukushi [Interdependent Social Work in the World], *Shakaifukushi Kyōiku Nenpō* [Social Work Education Annual Report] (Japanese Association of Schools of Social Work) Vol.14.

Kojima, Y. (1992). Kokusai-shakaifukushi Kakuritsu no Kiban [The Foundation of the Establishment of International Social Work"]. In Sato S. (Ed.). *Kokusaikajidai no Fukushi-kadai to Tenbo* [Welfare Issues and Perspectives in the Era of Internationalization] (pp. 278-303). Tokyo: Ichiryūsha.

Kojima, Y. & Okada, T. (Eds.). (1994). *Sekai no Shakaifukushi* [Social Work in the World]. Gakuensha.

Kojima, Y. & Healy, L. (1993). A Comparative Research on International Social Work Research in Japan and the United States. *Shakaifukushi Kyōiku Nenpō* [Social Welfare Education Annual Report]. Vol.14.

Matsuo, K., Akimoto, T. & Hattori, M. (2019). *What Should Curriculums for International Social Work Education Be?* (The 3rd Shukutoku University International Forum; 20 January 2019). Asian Research Institute for International Social Work (ARIISW), Shukutoku University, Japanese Association for Social Work Education (JASWE), and Japanese Society for the Study of Social Work (JSSSW).

Miki, K. & Akimoto, T. (1998). Bunken wo tōshite mita nihon no 'Kokusai-shakaifukushi' Kenkyu [Literature Review: 'International Social Work' in Japan]. *Social Welfare* (Social Welfare Department of Japan Women's University). 31-42.

Mohan, B. (1987). International Social Welfare: Comparative Systems. *Encyclopedia of Social Work*. NASW, Silver Spring, MD. 18th ed. 957-969.

Myrdal, G. (1960). *Beyond the Welfare State*. New Haven and London: Yale University Press. Supervising translation: Kitagawa, K. (1963) *Fukushikokka wo koete* [Beyond the Welfare State] Diamond Sha.

Nemoto, Y. (1989). Kokusai shakaifukushi no enkaku [A History of International Social Welfare] In Nakamura, Y. et al. (Eds.) *Shakaifukushi Kyōshitsu* [Social Welfare Class] (enlarged, revised edition) Yūhikaku.

Okada, T. (Totaro) (Autumn 1985). Kantōgen [Foreword]. *Sosharu waku Kenkyu* [Social Work Research], 11(3), 185.

Okada, T. (Toru) (1993). *Shakaifukushi Kyōiku Nenpō* [Social Work Education Annual Report] (Japanese Association of Schools of Social Work) Vol.14.

Physician Task Force on Hunger in America. (1985). *Hunger in America: The Growing Epidemic*. Middletown: CN, Wesleyan University Press.

Pinker, R. (1979). *The Idea of Welfare*. London: Heinemann Educational. Translation: Hoshino, M. & Ushikubo, N. (2003) *Shakaifukushi: Mittsu no Moderu* [Social Welfare: Three Models ] Reimei-shobo.

Romanyshyn, J. M. (1971). *Social Welfare; Charity to Justice*. Random House.

Sanders, D. S. & Pedersen, P. (Ed.). (1983). *Education for International Social Welfare* (Hawaii: CSWE/University Hawaii School of Social Work).

Shen, J. (1995). *Manshūkoku ni okeru Shakaijigyō no Tenkai* [Evolution of Social Work in "Manchukuo"] (Dissertation).

Sitaram, K. S. (1976). *Foundation of Intercultural Communication*. (Carbondale, IL: Southern Illinois University). Translation: Midooka, K. (1985) *Ibunka Komyunikeshon—Ōbei-chūshin-shugi kara-no Dakkyaku—* [Cross-cultural Communication] Tokyo: Sōgensha.

*Social Work Year Book*. (New York: Russell Sage Foundation). Each edition.

Tani, K. (1993). Kokusai fukushi kyoiku no kadai [Tasks of International Welfare Education] *Shakaifukushi Kyōiku Nenpō* [Social Welfare Education Annual Report] Vol.14.

Warren, G. L. (1937). International Social Work. Russell H. Kurtz (Ed.). *Social Work Year Book. 4th Issue.* New York: Russell Sage Foundation.

# Chapter Three

## A New Construction of International Social Work

Chapter 3 approaches a new understanding of the term 'international social work' and sets out a proposal for a new construction of international social work itself, being based on the results in Chapters 1 and 2, and taking lessons from them.

This chapter begins by taking two of the models of the conceptual development of international social work from Chapters 1 and 2 respectively. They are models, so do not necessarily coincide with chronological historical actualities in content. Between the two models, there are five major differences.

These differences are as follows: 1. The inductive construction from the review of actual history vs. the deductive construction from 'the theory of the State'; 2. dealing with the phase when there were practices which were same as or similar to those under international social work in its later phases but having no names or terms as such, as 'pre-history' or as a part of the history of international social work; 3. the focus on 'value' vs. on 'the way of viewing matters'; 4. the understanding of social work (or the distinction between social workers and social work, and between "social workers" who do social work as a gainful occupation and people who do social work; and 5. the dissemination of the existing mainstream social work through globalization vs. the new construction of international social work from zero or based on and comprehending various 'indigenous' 'social work' among all people, localities, countries and all kinds of social work, which may not have the name and concept of 'social work.' While learning from the models, a brief tentative response to the questions raised at the end of Chapter 1 will be provided.

After these 'warming-up exercises,' this chapter will proceed to the new construction of international social work. The following steps will be taken: The examination of the meaning of "international," nations and national borders, the specification of the purpose and the target population for whom international social work works, and the identification of 'the way of viewing

86

matters' (cf. 'value' in Chapter 1; 'norm' as used in Chapter 2) to be incorporated, and international social work's relationship with globalized 'national' ('local' in the words of Chapter 1; hereinafter to be referred as 'national' in this chapter) social work and with the development of social work itself to the next stage. The summary and conclusion will be shown in the form of a new definition, which connotes the elements above. Lastly, for new visitors to this subject, an overview of the newly constructed International Social Work will be made, being unafraid of duplication.

# 1. Two Models of Conceptual Development of International Social Work and Questions on the Achievement of International Social Work of Western-rooted (Professional) Social Work (Follow-up of Chapters 1 and 2)

## 1.1 Simplified Models of the Conceptual Development of International Social Work

Figure 3-1 represents the simplified models of the conceptual development of international social work, one developed from the summary table (Table 1-1) of the mainstream (Western-rooted professional) social work in Chapter 1 with some help from the findings of Chapter 2, and the other developed from the interpretation and lessons of Chapter 2.

The development of the concept of international social work is divided into four phases in the first column. The phases are as follows:

◆ Phase I: The birth of international social work
   This is the phase in which there are "No words, no concepts," but there is virtual (identical) international social work following the nomenclature in the later phases.
◆ Phase II: The birth of the term "'international social work'" and its growth
   This is the phase of "International" social work. All social work related to 'international' is named international social work.

Figure 3-1. Simplified models of the development of the concept of Inter-

| Phase | | 'A Theory of the State' |
|---|---|---|
| I | **The Birth of ISW**<br>No words, no concepts | The birth of nation states and national borders<br><br>**'Mainstream' Model**<br>(Prehistory)　(Chapter 1-origin) |
| II | **The Birth of the Term and its Growth**<br>"International" social work<br>(Social work related to "international") | (Period I) → (Period II)<br><Social work related to other countries and beyond, crossing and concerning national borders> (by social workers)<br> |
| III | **The Maturity of the Concept**<br>"International social work"<br>(An independent concept)<br><br><br>Exploration of the concept-"What is ISW?"<br>⇩<br>Definitions<br>(The final product) | (Period II) → (Period III)<br><Certain categories of social work activities/functions><br>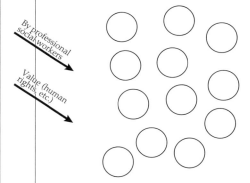<br><Certain categories of social work activities/functions with certain values> (human rights, social justice, democracy, the promotion of the profession, etc.), performed by professional social workers. |
| IV | **Re-examination under Internationalization/ Globalization and the future of ISW**<br><br>For the population of the whole world | (Period III)<br>The globalization of problems, standards & practices<br><br>ISW will disappear or expand.<br><br>Globalization (dissemination) of existing Western-rooted professional sosial work with or without indigenization<br><br>A global profession |

< >: definitional understandings in respective Phase/Period

national Social Work (ISW) from Chapters 1 and 2

## Model (Chapter 2-origin)

<Social work related to other countries and beyond, crossing and concerning national borders>
Virtual ISW activities following the nomenclature in the later phases

→ are not necessarily ISW.

The second birth of ISW, being outside of the state sovereignty

<Social work activities with the certain 'way of viewing matters'>
Viewed by eyes from the outside;
Compound Eyes;
Eyes beyond/from the outside of nation states; from the world

· Reemphasis of the constituency of all people on the earth;
· 'The way of viewing matters' which puts no special significance on any specific countries and regions including one's own.)

<Social work with a certain way of viewing matters>
Performed by anyone, to promote the wellbeing of all people on the earth. No special significance of any specific countries and regions including one's own.

ISW continues as long as nation states and national borders continue to exist.

Construction of ISW based on and subsuming various social works (from zero to an ISW to be applicable for all people, countries and social works)

Development of social work to the next stage

### <SW & Nations>

Social work

National borders

(ISW)    SW

Development of social work

SW transferred to and embraced by a state

The limit of nation states= welfare states

Spinning out of the sovereignty of states

ISW    NSW

Beings or organizations out of nation states e.g. UN, INGOs

(The world federation of nations)

(Welfare world)

**SW:** Social work
**NSW:** 'National' social work
**ISW:** International Social Work

◆ Phase III: Maturity of the concept

"International" social work in Phase II turns into the term 'international social work,' and the exploration of the concept, "What is international social work?" is pursued to its final definitions.

◆ Phase IV: Reexamination under internationalization/globalization and the future

This is the phase of self-conflict and reexamination to make international social work that of the population of the whole world, partly related to globalization.

## (1) Mainstream model, Chapter 1-origin

The second column of Figure 3-1 shows the mainstream model converted from Chapter 1, Table 1-1, with some help from the fruits of Chapter 2. It begins with the first use of the term 'international social work,' and the whole development is divided into three phases (Periods) instead of the four of the first column above. Phase I of "No name, no concept" is missing and treated as "Prehistory."

Period I of the model (Phase II in the first column of Figure 3-1) represents years of "international" social work. All social work 'activities' that are related to other countries or beyond, crossing and concerning national borders are regarded as international social work. In the actual history of mainstream international social work, Jebb's presentation at the 1928 international social work conference was the first example of its use. It referred to the activities of international organizations such as the Red Cross and Save the Children and the need for joint research work, under the name of international social work. Warren was the first to write an article dealing with this, titled, "International Social Work" in the 1937 *Social Work Yearbook*.

Period II of the model (Phase III in the first column) is the period when the concept of 'international social work' —what international social work is—is explored. Certain categories of 'activities' (acts or 'functions' as it is referred to in some parts of Chapter 1) are named as such among all social work activities that are related to other countries or beyond, crossing and concerning national borders. In mainstream history, even Warren in the previous period identified activities exceeding national borders to serve for

90

domestic case work (e.g., immigrants), practices in countries outside of the social workers' home countries, aid and assistance to war and disaster victims and depressed people in other countries, and working in international organizations. In addition, through this phase, exchange (of information, knowledge, opinions, ideas, experiences, and colleagueship through conferences, mutual visits, and joint research), comparative research, cross cultural practices as well as other international-related activities were also counted as international social work. In the process, two key elements—"by professional social workers" and "value" (e.g., human rights, social justice, the promotion of professional social work, and democracy)—were added as necessary elements, and the various combinations of these activities were discussed as definitions. The final product (definition) of this model becomes as follows (cf. Figure 3-2):

> "Certain categories of social work activities related to other countries performed by professional social workers, based on certain values (e.g., human rights, social justice, democracy, the promotion of the profession)."

Period III (Phase IV in the first column) is the time when the future of international social work is questioned under globalization. The entire social work, including 'national' social work, is internationalized/globalized (cf. 2.6 pp. 116-121) and put in an international/global context. Problems, standards and practices of social work are internationalized/globalized. The element of "international"/"global" penetrates every corner of social work and 'national' social work. All people are required to have "international"/"global" eyes (lenses) and be involved in social work.

Thus, international social work ceases to exist, being absorbed into 'national' social work. At the same

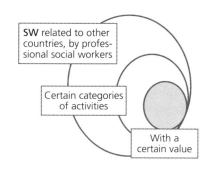

Figure 3-2.
The mainstream model definition

SW: Social work

time, international social work endlessly increases its importance and expands and globalizes the existing mainstream Western-rooted social work to the whole world, with or without indigenization. Social work has become a global profession.

## (2) 'A theory of the state' model, Chapter 2-origin

This model is backed up by 'a theory of the state' while owing a debt to the above mainstream model. 'A theory of the state' here is a nickname given to the model which gives its attention to a nation and has its birth and development from a nation state, a sovereign nation, to the welfare state, its limitation, and further to the welfare world, and their relationship with social work. Myrdal's and Pinker's theories were referred in Chapter 2.[48] 'A theory of the state' here does not mean the reference to such grand theories as those of Platōn, Bodin, Spinoza, Rousseau, and Marx.

In the beginning, there is Phase I. International social work is born with the birth of the nation state with national borders. Some areas of social work which had been carried out without being conscious of national borders, naturally could not avoid being outside these borders as they were when national borders were first drawn. At the time, there was not yet any such term as 'international social work,' but there were almost identical international social work activities following the nomenclature in the later phases.

Phase II is the stage when the name 'international social work' is given to those activities. It is the same as "Period 1" of the mainstream model above. The only difference is that activities here do not necessarily need to be ones carried out by social workers.

In Phase III, the "international" social work in Phase II leaps to become "international social work." Nevertheless, "international social work" is not deemed to be certain categories of activities and their combination of categories as in the mainstream model, but is rather deemed to be a certain

---

48    The later development of their (Myrdal's and Pinker's) theories and other alternative theo-
      ries for the welfare of all people in the world after 'welfare state' is not referred to in this
      book.

'way of viewing matters' (cf. 'value' in the 'mainstream' model). Those categories of activities that do not have such 'a way of viewing matters' are not international social work although they are certainly representative 'candidates' for being considered so.

The content of 'the way of viewing matters' is "eyes (views) from the outside of or beyond nation states," or "eyes (views) from the world," or "compound eyes (multiple views)." Behind this 'way of viewing' there is a 'secret story' on the second birth of international social work, that is, social work's relation to states (cf. the right column of Figure 3-1, Figure 3-5, and Figure 3-8).

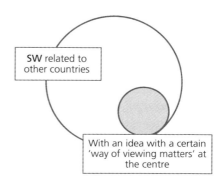

**Figure 3-3.**
**State theory model definition**

SW: Social work

Social work, in its development, gradually transfers its activities and functions to a state, which eventually embraces social work. The Welfare State is its ultimate form. Facing the limits of the nation state, international social work breaks through these walls to become an independent entity leaving 'national' social work behind. International social work is now out of the sovereignty of nation states. The tentative final definition of international social work under this model is as follows (cf. Figure 3-3):

> "Social work that is related to other countries, performed by anyone, with a certain 'way of viewing matters', to promote the wellbeing of all people on the earth equally. (No specific importance is put on any specific countries or regions including one's own.)"

Phase IV is the stage when international social work reexamines its own concept and faces self-contradiction in the progress of internationalization and globalization.

International social work will continue to exist as long as nation states and national borders continue. They will not disappear in the near, or even medium future. Internationalization/globalization does not mean the end of nation states.

International social work could be the promoter of the globalization of existing mainstream social work itself, to disseminate itself to the world but also be 'the person standing watch' over its globalization. While mainstream international social work starts with its own social work and makes efforts to disseminate it to the whole world, the international social work of this model starts with social work in an unfixed form and tries to make for a consolidating social work connoting all types of indigenous social work—Buddhist social work, Islamic social work, non-professional NGO social work, social work by country, and the social work of "being indigenous" as defined by the United Nations, as well as mainstream social work.[49] International social work must be linguistically and logically applicable to all people in all countries and regions on the Earth and all kinds of social work. International social work contributes not only to the development of 'national' social work, but also that of the whole of social work to its next stage.

---

49  "[T]he definition of the United Nations and mainstream Western Social Work" is "'native people,' who 'live within geographically distinct ancestral territories' (IFSW; Commentary note of IASSW/IFSW Global Definition) such as Maori, Inuit, and Ainu in (in case of Japan). We treat Buddhist people in Asia as indigenous people...Indigenous people in our usage here are not necessarily associated with Western colonization and hegemony and not necessarily confined as the minority in their current countries (cf. above commentary note) but must have originated in the community, society, area, region or nation in old days although 'how old' they must go back has not rigidly been defined. Included in indigenous social work are Buddhist social work, Islamic social work, Hindu social work, some non-religious social works, Bhutanese social work, Vietnamese social work, Thai social work, etc. as well as social work by indigenous people in the meaning of UN and IFSW's definition above" (Akimoto, et al., 2020: 66-67).

## 1.2 Brief Discussion on the Achievements of the International Social Work of Western-rooted (Professional) Social Work— Questions Raised at the End of Chapter 1

Six questions from (a) to (f) were raised at the end of Chapter 1 (2 (3)) on 'the final products' (definitions) of mainstream international social work and on 'international social work under globalization.' Elucidatory discussion on the two models in the subsection immediately above (1.1, pp.87-94) has provided us with brief tentative answers to some of the questions and elaborated on some other questions for further discussion in the following Section 2 of this chapter. This is another preparation for the construction of a new international social work. Answers should be integrated into any newly constructed definition of international social work.

### (1) Three questions on 'the final products' (definitions) of mainstream international social work

(a) "Is it appropriate for those activities/'functions' which were raised in functional definitions to be called those of international social work?"
The answer to this question was given in the 1995 article published outside the Western, non-English-speaking world (Chapter 2). It listed all activities done under the name of international social work and concluded that they were "not necessarily" international social work. Without certain 'norms' or 'the way of viewing matters,' they are not international social work. The mainstream Western-rooted social work world had replaced 'norms' or 'the way of viewing matters' with 'value' as written in Chapter 1.

(b) "Is it appropriate to include the 'value' elements such as human rights which were mentioned in "value-focused definitions" and "combined definitions" under international social work?"
It may be acceptable to include the 'value' in the definitional factors at its abstract conceptual level if so desired, but the content of the 'value' to be filled in, for example, human rights and social justice, is not appropriate and acceptable in a double meaning. First, they are 'values' of social work as a whole and not specific to international social work, and second, they are the

most typical core 'values' of Western-rooted professional social work. One may or may not accept the common-sense equation Social Work = Western-rooted Professional Social Work. The matter pertains to the understanding/definition of social work itself, not to international social work which we are now discussing. We are not able to discuss this point here. We shall put it aside for another time (2.1. (1), p.99).

(c) "Must those activities/functions of international social work in "functional definitions" and "combined definitions" be carried out by professional social workers?"

This question also pertains to what social work is, and not what international social work is. See the last few lines in subsection (b) immediately above. International social work does not necessarily have to be carried out by professional social workers unless you believe in the equation above. Social work may be understood more broadly, considering social works in the world—if you distinguish between social work and social workers and also between those people who do social work and social workers who work as a profession, an occupation, or a job. Suppose international social work could be performed only by professional social workers from a Western-rooted social work world, then the great majority of the people on the Earth would be excluded from international social work service, and serve only as an object for international social workers to work on or only if opportunities should be given.

The above functional definition and combined definition have "by professional social workers" as a necessary condition, and the value-focused definition has "any social work in the world" as a necessary condition, but those conditions could be mutually interchangeable between the two types of definitions.

## (2) Three questions on "international social work under globalization"

Some of the essence of the answers has already been presented in the last part relating to Phase IV of the section 1.1.(1) and (2) above (pp.90-94). However, some elaboration of the questions will be made, even though there may be some redundancy.

(d) "If the 'local' practice is put in the global context, is the globalized ('local') practice still 'local' social work, or is it international social work? Will international social work continue to exist? If so, what are the roles and functions of international social work which is coexistent with such globalized 'local' social work? What will it look like?"

Everything in society is globalized. Social work is also globalized, and 'local' ('national') social work is globalized, too. Social work and 'local' ('national') social work are put in a globalized context, and global elements penetrate every corner of social work and 'local' ('national') social work. Is, then, the 'local' ('national') practice in a global context or the globalized 'local' ('national') practice still 'local' social work, or is it international social work? Will 'local' ('national') social work absorb and swallow up international social work, and will international social work disappear? If not, what will its roles and functions be, and what will it look like in the future? What will the relationship between international social work with globalized 'local' ('national') social work and the globalized social work be? What we are discussing is "What must international social work under the globalization be?" not "What is 'local' social work under globalization?"

(e) "How does international social work deal with the globalization of social work itself?"

Should 'the final products' (the definitions) that contain the problems questioned in the above subsections (a) to (c) be disseminated to the world as to do so is one of the conventional roles, functions, and responsibilities of international social work? Social work to be globalized is that of Western-rooted professional social work. It is the globalization of social work itself in the sense of the transfer of matters and standards from the centre to the peripherals. Western-rooted professional social work tends to be critical of globalization because of its negative effects. However, Western-rooted professional social work is indifferent to or even unconscious of the globalization of social work itself in this sense—its values, knowledge, skills, education, and profession—all over the world including the non-Western world. How will international social work deal with this globalization of social work itself? Should international social work reject other forms of social work other than Western-rooted professional social work and disseminate Western-rooted professional social work to the world while it insists on being "international" and of and for the whole world, carrying with it the name of international social work? It would imply a self-contradiction, wouldn't it? How should international social work understand the globalization of Western-rooted professional social work itself?

(f) "What is the contribution of international social work to the development of social work itself to its third stage?"

On the other hand, what contribution will international social work make to the development of 'local' ('national') social work, and social work as a whole? Can social work and 'local' ('national') social work develop to the next stage without international social work and its contribution? Due to the limitation of 'local' ('national') social work, international social work was born from within 'local' ('national') social work. Once it was born, international social work brings in its 'way of viewing matters' and other features and elements to the 'local' ('national') social work and regulates it one way or another. 'Local' ('national') social work, in turn, may shout back to international social work blaming it for its "globalization" but as far as it accepts any, it changes itself and develops, and through the process, social work itself changes and develops. Without the contribution of international social work, not only 'local' ('national') social work but also social work itself, which originated in Europe (Stage I) and matured in North America (Stage II), could not develop into the next stage (Stage III), the stage in which it serves people all over the world.

## 2. A New Construction of 'International Social Work'

Now it is the time to construct the concept of 'international social work.' We will owe the above two models, the 'mainstream' model and the 'theory of the state' model, particularly heavily the latter, but our construction is not one of the 'theory of the state' model itself. We will mainly try deductively to construct an 'international social work' that would satisfy the lessons we have learned from the above Chapters 1 and 2 and Chapter 3.1, although in social work, the importance of an inductive approach is often emphasized.

## 2.1 Groundwork

### (1) International + social work: putting 'social work' in a black box

When people say that there are a variety of understandings of what international social work is, for the most part, this variety comes from variations in the understanding of the latter half of the term 'international social work,' that is, 'social work.' Almost all people in the social work community in the world today are believers in Western-rooted professional social work. They take the equation 'social work = professional social work' for granted. Both the definition of Healy and that of Cox and Pawar, for example, understand 'international social work' as functions by professional social workers or the aim to promote the profession of social work (Ch.1, pp. 33-37).

There could, however, be other understandings of international social work in the world. Even if we accept the above equation, professional social work in a postindustrial society and that in a pre-industrial society or in a society that is beginning to industrialize could not be the same. Or must social work be defined as the product of industrialization? Social work could vary in content even among "developed" countries and even among "developing" countries, depending on the tradition, culture, and political, economic, and social systems of each country. Even the IASSW/IFSW's global definition, a typical expression of Western-rooted professional social work, pays attention to the diversity among regions. For example, refer to a series of works by Akimoto and his team on Buddhist social work since the early 2010s for further discussion on this topic (e.g., Sakamoto, 2013-15; Sasaki, 2013; Akimoto, 2015, 2017; Akimoto, et al., 2020; Gohori, 2017-2022).

Here, we cannot start by asking the question "What is 'social work'?" The answers would be too varied. Refraining from asking this question, let's continue our discussion assuming that there is more than one kind of social work in the world, particularly as we are now going to discuss 'international social work' that refers to the whole world. We will only leave the understanding and interpretation of this part ('social work') to respective readers—although most of them would understand it to be Western-rooted professional social work—for the time being until we reach the last part of this chapter to make the story simpler. What we should question here is the first part of the term, 'international social work,' that is, the understanding of 'international.'

## (2) Inter + national: "nation" as the core and "between"

The word "international" is comprised of two parts, "inter" and "national" ("nation").

### (i) Nation

In this chapter, 'nation' is used in the sense of "a country, considered especially about its people and its social or economic structure," and not of "a large group of people of the same race and language." It is used above in the sense of a nation state defined as "a nation that is a politically independent country," (*Longman Dictionary of Contemporary English*, 6th Edition), and not limited to "a sovereign state of which most of the citizens or subjects are united also by factors which define a nation, such as a language or common descent[50]" (*Oxford Dictionary of English*, Second Edition Revised).

The original meaning of the word 'nation' and the history of the birth of modern nation states in Europe would support the second usage in the meaning of races or ethnic groups, and even today, many people in Western societies, especially in its birthplace Europe, may first imagine 'nations' in this sense when they hear the words 'nation,' 'national,' and 'international.' One of the representative definitions of international social work given in Chapter 1 has retained the understanding—that international social work is "social work activities and interest which exceed the borders of state and culture" (Sanders & Pederson, 1984: xiv; underlined by the current author)[51]. The meaning of the above has, however, shifted toward the usage of politically independent states, through the history of sovereign nation states

---

50    Each type of sovereign nation state has its own features to be discussed separately but it is a matter within international social work.

51    Huegler, Lyon and Pawar (2012) uses the term of new "nation states" (p.11).

100

in Africa and other regions (See Box 3-1).

### (ii) Inter-, international, and international social work

The first part of 'international' is 'inter.' The prefix 'inter' means between or among. 'International' literally means "existing, occurring, or carried on between nations" (*Oxford Dictionary of English*, Second Edition Revised) or at the interface between nations.

'International social work' is the social work relating to more than a nation in the broadest sense (Ch1 1.2(2); 1.3(2)). More than a nation could mean from two neighbouring countries to a few or several countries, to all countries in a region (e.g., South Asia, the Balkan States, Latin America, ASEAN, North Africa, Western Europe) and ultimately up to all 200 countries throughout the world.[52]

### (iii) National borders

"National" ("Nation") is the core word, and without "nation," neither "international" nor international social work could linguistically and conceptually be possible. The 'nation' will be sometimes replaced with "national borders" below in this chapter to imply "between nations" and the conceptual and physical limits, to avoid being drawn into a discussion on 'the theory of the state' itself too deeply, and to make the operationalized discussion easier. Sanders and Pederson (1984) cited in the above subsection (i) straightforwardly defined international social work as "social work activities and concerns that transcend national...boundaries."

---

52  Healy says that international social work in this sense covers a broader range than the expression, 'global social work.' (The 3rd International Academic Forum of the Asian Research Institute for International Social Work (ARIISW), Shukutoku University, held in Tokyo on January 20, 2018.

## Box 3-1. Dictionary definitions of international, nation, and nation state

**A. International** (between a) countries and b) nations)
◆ a) connected with or involving two or more countries (*Oxford Advanced Learner's Dictionary, 8th edition*)
◆ b) existing, occurring, or carried on between nations (*Oxford Dictionary of English, Second Edition Revised*)
◆ b) relating to or involving more than one nation (*Longman Dictionary of Contemporary English, 6th Edition*)

**B. Nation** a) folk or ethnic group (putting countries aside), b) country or state (being conscious of folk), c). country or state or peoples (without being conscious of folk)
◆ a) a large body of people united by common descent, history, culture, or language, inhabiting a particular state or territory (*Oxford Dictionary of English, Second Edition Revised*)
◆ b) a country, considered especially in relation to its people and its social or economic structure; a large group of people in the same race and language (*Longman Dictionary of Contemporary English, 6th Edition*)
◆ b) a country considered as a group of people with the same language, culture, and history, who live in a particular area under one government; c) all the people in a country (*Oxford Advanced Learner's Dictionary, 8th edition*)

**C. *Nation(-)state*** transition from a) a state based on folks to b) & c) a state based on sovereignty
◆ a) a group of people with the same culture, language, etc. who have formed an independent country (*Oxford Advanced Learner's Dictionary, 8th edition*)
◆ b) a sovereign state in which most of the citizens or subjects are united also by factors that define a nation, such as language or common descent (*Oxford Dictionary of English, Second Edition Revised*)

- c) a nation that is a politically independent country (*Longman Dictionary of Contemporary English, 6th Edition*)
- Modern nations that are formed on the basis of (racial/ethnic) communities...These modern nation states were first formed under monarchy sovereignty, but bourgeois revolution rejected them and instead established the principle of popular sovereignty. In Europe, in the 17th to 19th centuries, these nationalistic movements arose and nation states were formed one after another. This nationalism spread to Asian and African regions around WWI, and the independent movement of anticolonialism arose in various places in the period after World War II. But these countries were at an immature stage of becoming a modern nation in the European sense...Political units which first appeared in the form of racial/ethnic states were not ones whose subjects were single race/ethnic in the strict meaning, and many of them featured mixed racial/ethnic composition. The sovereign nations which have been their basic constituents since the formation of modern international society showed the features of popular states rather than racial/ethical states. . . (*Buritanika kokusai daihyakka jiten* [Britannica International Encyclopedia], *Britannica Japan, 2014*) [English translation by TA.]
- ...there are no nations which fit the definition as it stands. Firstly, nations which do not embrace the problem of racial/ethnic minorities seldom exist...and, although the formation of nation states are phenomena of modern and present times, there could still be some which could be classified into types which differ in their closeness to the definition...In some countries in the third world which obtained the right to self-determination after World War II, by the liberation from colonial rule, the regional borders have been decided arbitrarily regarding language and culture, and national integration is very weak(*Shin shakaigaku jiten* [New Encyclopedia of Sociology], Yūhikaku, *1993*). [English translation by TA.]

## 2.2 Framework

### (1) Two types of international social work

International social work is social work related to more than a 'nation' (hereinafter to be sometimes referred to as nation, state, and country interchangeably, although the meaning of these terms is, academically speaking, of course, different and some objections may be raised). In the past, it was enough for social work to take a look within a 'nation.' However, it became necessary to exceed the sovereign nation or national borders due to the internationalization of society. Internationalization presented limits on nation states and thus 'national' social work ('national' social work here means social work at each nation's level or 'of' or 'in' each nation, not social work administered by a government. In Part I of this book, we will use the term 'national' social work although such other expressions might be possible as state social work, local social work, domestic social work, social work country by country, and one's own country's social work).

There could be two different ways of exceeding national borders, which have given birth to two types of 'international social work.' The difference comes from the disputant's position or from where they start thinking and arguing: one way could be from inside a specific 'nation,' most typically one's own 'nation,' using it as a base for further expansion to provide better service to their cases and policies, and the other from outside individual sovereign nations, keeping equal distance from them and as an independent entity.

In the former, ('national') social work simply extends its activities beyond national borders to provide services, or better services, to people 'in' or 'of' its own nation and to promote the wellbeing of those people. These social work activities that relate to other countries are named here as "international social work (A)." For example, to work for international migrants in the social workers' own country, they will have to work with other countries; and to gain new knowledge and skills, they will have to attend international conferences and exchange research results (Chapter 1).

In the latter, facing the limit of a state, a new entity named here as 'international social work (B)' which separates itself from 'nations' and 'national' social work, is born to provide better services to people not of their own one specific 'nation' but of more than one 'nation,' up to all the 200 'nations' and regions of the world to promote their wellbeing. For example, they will work for the resolution of conflicts between two or more countries, disease prevention, and better working conditions, and may work for the ILO, the Red Cross, or Save the Children, and will put their own country to one side for the time being (cf. the right bottom circle in Figure 3-4).

Both types are beyond the nation state and its limits but while the former aims to promote the well-being of the people of a nation state, the latter aims to promote the wellbeing of peoples of more than a state or all states in the world, which are outside of its own state. The former concerns itself with other states and 'national' social work following its own needs while the latter first sets itself up as a separate entity from each nation state and 'national' social work, and concerns itself with each nation state and 'national' social work. The latter sees things by viewing and considering them all as a whole.

The former, 'international social work (A),' is of, by, and for its own 'nation' and its people, and thus is fundamentally part of a 'national' social work however closely it works with other countries. We hereinafter call the latter, i.e., 'international social work (B),' as International Social Work (with capitalized initials).

## (2) Nations and International Social Work: structural elements of social work and their locational relationship

Figure 3-5 shows the structural elements of social work (International Social Work, 'national' social work, and social work as a whole) and the locational relationship among them. Social work is composed of 'national' social work (small white circles with dark gray ovals within) and International Social Work (a gray oval), which is an independent entity segregated from 'national' social work. In other words, the two parts, 'national' social work and International Social Work, have come together to make up social work. The lower right figure is this observation from the point of view of 'national' social work.

Figure 3-4. Two ways national borders could be exceeded

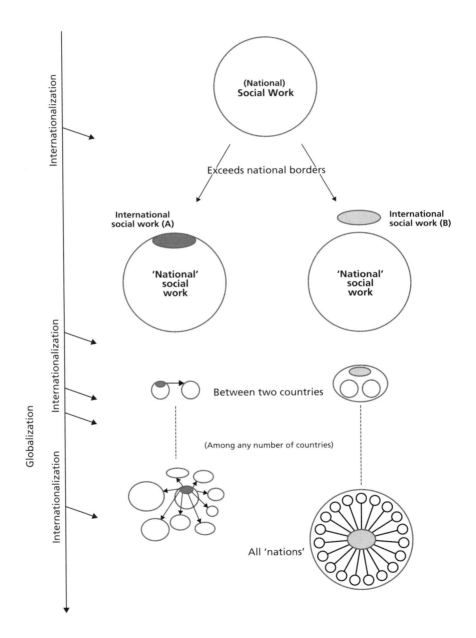

Figure 3-5. Locational relationships among international social work, 'national' social work and social work

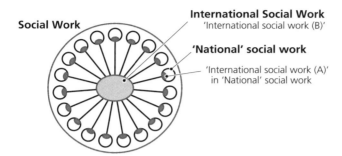

## 2.3 Core elements of International Social Work

We proceed with the inquiry and the construction of International Social Work in the meaning of 'international social work (B).'

Core elements of International Social Work are (a) to (d) below. International Social Work is not special. It is part of social work as a whole just as 'national' social work is. Purposes, principles, values, and other elements of International Social Work are basically the same as those of 'national' social work. Suppose 'social work' = 'Western-rooted professional social work'—although we put social work in a black box at the beginning of this section (2.1(1) p.99)—the purpose would be to alleviate and solve the difficulties and problems in people's lives and promote their wellbeing (see IASSW/IFSW Global Definition). The fundamental principles or values of both International Social Work and 'national' social work are social justice and human rights. The field of actual practice of International Social Work would be both inside and outside of the practitioner's own country. It is also the same as in 'national' social work, which is practiced by social workers both inside and outside of their home country.

Consistency with the core elements involved in 'national' social work is first required. But stepping into a new field of "international" or introducing the new ingredient of national borders, some revisions and additions may become necessary. This is nothing unique to the topic of "international." It is also the case with other new fields[53] and when new ingredients are introduced. The major revisions and additions to International Social Work are as follows ((a) to (d)). Possible items that may be still hidden or items with a potential of which we have been unaware will become evident sometime in the future.

(a) The key term
The key term in 'International Social Work' is 'between nations' or 'national borders.'[54] The modern sovereign nation forms the core of our inquiry on

---

53    In Chapter 2, it was written that international social work was not certain fields, but the meaning is different here.

54    Sanders and Pederson (1984), "social work activities and concerns that transcend national and cultural boundaries (1.2 (2) p. 96)."

'international social work.' The antonym[55] of International Social Work is 'national' social work with national borders.

**(b) The task**
The task of International Social Work is social work beyond or related to national borders in problems, standards or practices[56] (See Ch.1 and Ch.3.1).

**(c) Constituency**
Constituents, or the target population, of International Social Work, are all people (eight billion; UN *World Population Prospects 2022*) in all countries and regions (about 200 as of 2022) of the world, not simply the people in one's own nation.

**(b) + (c) Purpose**
The purpose of International Social Work is to alleviate and solve the difficulties and problems in people's lives and to promote the well-being of people all over the world, not only those of the people in one's own country.

**(d) 'The way of viewing matters'**
International Social Work's greatest feature is its certain 'way of viewing matters.' 'The way of viewing matters' in the literal sense could connote value, which the mainstream Western-rooted professional social work referred to in Chapter 1 as such, the purpose and the aim, the principle, the philosophy, the ideology, and perception. 'The way of viewing matters' could be interpreted as a 'yardstick' (ruler, measure, or standard) in an operationalized form.

But the content of 'the way of viewing matters' specifically here is 'the way of looking at things' with eyes from the outside or more than one pair of eyes. International Social Work views matters by leaving behind and not sticking to a specific nation, most typically one's own country. It does not see things through putting one's own country or people at the centre.

International Social Work does not look at things with a single yardstick

---

55    To extract the essence of "international social work," we should provide an antonym.

56    Also in concepts and theories (Akimoto, 1992).

but does so by applying two yardsticks or more, which could hopefully be developed into a common yardstick for the use of all parties. Looking at the thinking in Western-rooted professional social work, conventions of the United Nations and its affiliated and related organizations as well as human rights, social justice, and other concepts could be examples of those common yardsticks, (cf. Friedlander, 1975) although they are not necessarily the common yardsticks we mean here. Ours exceeds these levels, eliminating value factors as much as possible. The following two considerations should be made.

(i) Social work without 'the way of viewing matters'
Firstly, unless it passes this test of having 'the way of viewing matters' or yardsticks, we cannot refer to or define any social work activities as International Social Work even if these activities are related to other countries. They are 'national' social work, which aims at the promotion of the well-being of one's own nation and people.

The items that were listed in Chapter 2 as "these are not necessarily international social work" are not necessarily "these are not International Social Work" (in capitals). If they pass the test of 'the way of viewing matters', they are International Social Work. The point is that we do not call anything International Social Work unless it has been screened by 'the way of viewing matters' above.

(ii) Erasing national borders
In other words, the core meaning of 'the way of viewing matters' of "International Social Work" is to regard all nations and peoples or all people and their groups at an equal distance regardless of their nationalities. International Social Work does not give specific values to any specific nations or peoples. We regard them as being the same even while they are different.[57] It does not attach a label of either superiority or inferiority to any specific states or peoples. Just think of the clamor for the superiority of the so-called

---

57    If they are the same and single, the cooperation, collaboration, and joint work could not become a topic to discuss. Both journeys to seek not for differences but for sameness and not for sameness but for differences would start.

Germanic race, the Anglo-Saxon race, the Han race, the Yamato race, etc., even when replacing 'race' with 'nation' and 'people.'

Ultimately, if one views matters by erasing national borders, a very different world may come to the fore. We would see the world using class, race, gender, religion, language, functional communities as well as other indices before national borders or nationality[58]. People may insist on using such terms as "world citizens[59]," "Earthians," and "being human beings," although they are not theoretically, historically, or legally plausible at present or in the near future.

In reality, national borders firmly exist—however far internationalization and globalization proceed, and people, things, money, information, etc., break down national borders here and there (Akimoto, 2004). Even main players in "international social work," e.g., the United Nations, nation states, international NGOs, religious organizations, multi-corporations, independent firms, and individuals and their groups, are not free from national interest and nationality.

(a) + (b) + (c) + (d) The idea (*idee*)[60]

'The idea (*idee*)' will be used below in this chapter as the roundup concept of (a) to (d) above. It could include a historical perspective for the future and dreams[61]. The meaning of the idea (*idee*) here is close to one in philosophy[62] rather than one in daily life—a "thought or suggestion as to a possible course of action" (*Oxford Dictionary of English*, 2nd Ed. Revised, Oxford University Press, 2005).

---

58    During periods of war today, these factors are subdued under nationality.

59    The concept of citizenship requires a government that responds to their rights. A world government has not yet come into being.

60    *Rinen.* "The fundamental thought of how the matter is to be the idea which transcends experiences." (*Japanese Language Dictionary*, Shōgakukan, 2006). "It is used as the purpose for decision and interpretation without the ontological implication" (*Kōjien*, ver.6, Iwanami Shoten, 2008, 2014: English translation by TA).

61    Cf. Footnote 49.

62    *Philosophy* (in Platonic thought) is an externally existing pattern of which individual things in any class are imperfect copies: (in Kantian thought) a concept of pure reason, not empirically based in experience (*Oxford Dictionary of English*, 2nd Ed. Revised, Oxford University Press, 2005).

## 2.4 Birth of International Social Work and the Historical Development of its Relation with 'National' Social Work and Social Work as a Whole

Here we throw in the time factor.

(i) The first birth

Without nation states, no international social work would have been plausible, not only linguistically but also historically. The birth of international social work owes much to the birth and the existence of modern sovereign nation states, which are defined by 'people,' 'sovereignty,' and 'territory.' National borders embody the conceptual and physical limits of nation states. Logically speaking, 'international social work' was born when national borders were born. Some of the social work activities until that moment might remain (a) outside the newly-drawn national borders as they had been, or (b) as some contacts and activities beyond national borders from the need to provide services to their domestic clients inside the newly-drawn national borders (cf. 'international social work (A)'). This was the first birth of international social work. Social work before this moment had nothing to do with or no consciousness of national borders.

(ii) The second birth—spin-off and boomerang

International Social Work, 'international social work (B),' was born from another limit of ('national') social work[63] as a spin-off ( 1) in Figure 3-6). This is the second birth of 'international social work.' Once it was born, the newly-born international social work boomeranged to intrude into 'national' social work. It started and continued conveying its core elements (cf. the above section 2.3 pp.108-111) including 'the way of viewing matters' as well as various other thoughts and practices with 'the way of viewing matters' implied to 'national' social work ( 2) in Figure 3-6). 'National' social work may accept, resist, or reject them together with the messages and demands International Social Work sends in ( 3) in Figure 3-6). As far as it accepts any

---

63    Strictly speaking, "'national' social work" could be said to have been born as a result of the birth of "International Social Work." Until then, it was "social work."

Figure 3-6. The birth and boomerang effect of International Social Work

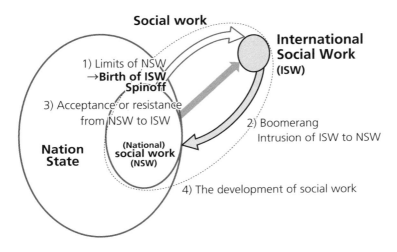

of them, however, those accepted become part of its 'national' social work and the social work itself, and contribute to the change and the development of 'national' social work, and eventually the change and the development of social work itself to the next stage ( 4 ) in Figure 3-6). In the case of Western-rooted professional social work, the next stage means its third stage in which it will serve the whole world after the first stage (birth in Europe) and the second stage (growth in North America).

(iii) The existence outside of sovereignty

However, the biggest treasure which this circular movement has left us was the birth of International Social Work which is located outside the sovereignty of any nation and 'national' social work, but within social work. Now as social work is composed of 'national' social work and International Social Work, it essentially includes the part that is outside the sovereignty of any nation states.

## 2.5 The *Idealtypus*[64] and the 'Actual Being': International Social Work and International Social Work´(dash)

Hereinbefore, the discussion was mainly held at the *Idealtypus* (ideal type; philosophy) level. We had dropped the factor of 'actual being' as much as possible up to this point.

Now, we throw in this factor. International Social Work in an actual society cannot be free from individual nation states and 'national' social work in actual societies. International Social Work in actual society has been distorted from the ideal type of International Social Work under construction above. We call this distorted International Social Work as International Social Work´(dash) (hereinafter to be referred to as International Social Work´(dash)) in this chapter.

Firstly, International Social Work is structurally composed of 'national' social works of all states, which are different in size and power. All nation states are looking out for their own national interest, and each 'national' social work works for the benefit of its own people whom it serves. Secondly, not only structurally but also in the process of daily operation, International Social Work in an actual society is always under those nations and 'national' social work with the differences in power and does not function neutrally. International Social Work´(dash) has skewed towards 'national' social work of nations with power in their administration and operation (Figure 3-7).

The actual existing International Social Work is not that of the pure ideal international social work presented in the above subsection 2.3, but a distortion of that, even if it may pretend to be equal in distance from all nations. However, International Social Work exists holding the above-mentioned idea (above 2.3, p.111) as an impregnable tower and directs the actual existing distorted International Social Work´(dash) towards an ideal International Social Work.

'National' social work on the opposite pole makes an effort to bring

---

64    A methodological concept in social sciences by Max Weber. "Types or models made of essential factors which were selected from among many phenomena to measure, compare or evaluate real cultural phenomena which are very fluid and scattered" (Japanese Dictionary (Nihon Kokugo Daijiten), Shōgakukan, 2006) (English translation by TA).

Figure 3-7. International Social Work´(dash): International Social Work in the actual society

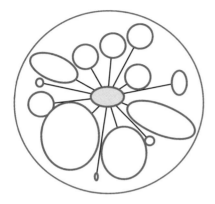

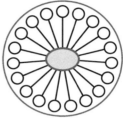

International Social Work closer to itself for its own interest, but it cannot help but consider, and has considered, the idea of International Social Work. International Social Work´(dash) is in a tug of war between International Social Work and 'national' social work, which have different starting points and goals.

Metaphorically, think of the United Nations. The United Nations exists outside individual sovereign states as an independent organization. Nevertheless, the United Nations is structurally composed of individual sovereign states which have different sizes and powers and operates under its organizational conditions. While those individual sovereign states have sought and fought for their national interests and benefits, they have also worked together and cooperated and collaborated through compromise. The Universal Declaration of Human Rights and many conventions are, for example, regarded as the highest-level common yardsticks that were agreed to by all or the majority of sovereign states, but, in reality, they were adopted and have been administered by those member states with a greater voice and power and in specific historical, political and social conditions. Nevertheless, the existence of the United Nations is generally regarded as being fair, valuable, and indispensable by the majority of states.

## 2.6 Environmental Factors: Internationalization and Globalization

Both factors of time and actual existence are thrown in.

### (1) The internationalization of society and social work

Behind the story from the second birth of International Social Work to the boomerang in the section 2.4 (pp.112-113), the current of internationalization flowed, although to be more exact, it had been running ever since the first birth of 'international social work,' that is, the formation of nation states and national borders.

Internationalization "[o]riginally" means "to show the relative relation between countries," but the definition varies. A few examples of common usage of the word are: (a) "To transform a nation from a self-sufficient, closed system to an interdependent, coexistent system"; (b) "To assume its own due share of obligation and responsibility to stand abreast with other nations"; and (c) "Widely to open the door to the world for the inflow of people, things, culture, information, etc. from other nations" (*Britannica International Encyclopedia (Buritanika Kokusai, Dai-hyakkajiten)*, Britannica Japan, 2014). [English translation by TA.]

Society has been internationalized, politically, economically, and socially. Social work, which is part of it, is no exception. The internationalization of society internationalized social work in two ways. Firstly, it facilitated the birth and growth of International Social Work. Secondly, it put 'national' social work in an internationalized context and infused it with an "international" element in all its aspects.

### (2) The internationalization of 'national' social work

(i) The three drives of the internationalization of 'national' social work
The internationalization of 'national' social work has come about in three ways: 1. extending itself outwards to satisfy with immediate needs of its own

Figure 3-8. Internationalization by society in general and International Social Work

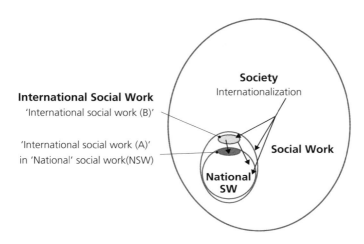

clients and with interests of its own and its own state for more knowledge and better services; 2. becoming a "good international" state to be accepted with respect by other states;[65] and 3. being required and forced to change by outside forces.

Regarding 1., we may remember the description of the birth of 'international social work (A)' (2.2 (1) p.104 and 2.4 pp.112- above). Regarding 1. and 2., refer to (a) and (b) (p.116) of the definition of internationalization in the immediate above subsection 2.6 (1) and also to the first two terms of the qualification to be "a good person of today" which was mentioned in Chapter 2 (5.(2))—being a good citizen (national), a good international[ly-minded]

---

65  "We believe that no nation is responsible to itself alone, but that laws of political morality are universal; and that obedience to such laws is incumbent upon all nations who would sustain their own sovereignty and justify their sovereign relationship with other nations" (The preamble of the Constitution of Japan).

citizen, and a good world citizen at a time. The requirement and the force in 3. come both from the society directly and through International Social Work which was born through the internationalization of society (Figure 3-8).

These 1. to 3. are not necessarily in a time series. International Social Work facilitates and reinforces each of these three steps of the internationalization of 'national' social work above, together with society in general (Figure 3-6).

(ii) The whole 'national' social work is fully internationalized

Problems that social work works for are internationalized, standards (yardsticks) that social work uses are internationalized, and actual practices that social work is engaged in are internationalized (Ch.1 1.3(3-1))[66]. All subfields of social work, e.g., child welfare, disabilities, the elderly, poverty, and mental health, are internationalized. Even the basic classes on child welfare and disabilities, for example, could not be completed without referring to the UN's Conventions on the Rights of the Child and the Rights of Persons with Disabilities respectively, and the situation of other countries both at the policy and program level and the reality level[67]. 'National' social work must be considered and practiced in the social context of internationalization. Otherwise, nothing in social work could be understood and achieved effectively.

(iii) The substance of internationalization and globalization: one-directional

'National' social work may be willing, reluctant or forced to accept those messages and demands and to be internationalized. The term 'internationalization' was originally a neutral concept used to describe a phenomenon (2.6 (1) pp.116-118 above), but the substance of internationalization tends to be one-directional—from social work "developed countries," that is, the North or the West, to social work "developing countries," that is, the South or non-the West[68]. The latter copies the former with longing and admiration or obeys the former with humiliation. The sense of imperialism and colonialism may be

---

66   Concepts are, too.

67   For example, the Americans with Disabilities Act (ADA), advanced policies and practices for the elderly people in Sweden, and mass poverty in the world.

68   See the usage of the term 'international social work' in Bhutan, Vietnam, and Thailand in Chapter 1, and in Japan also in Chapter 1.

implied (cf. ACWelS (Asian Center for Welfare Society)'s Internationalization-Indigenization research project (Matsuo 2014) supported the findings).

This "one directional" quality in internationalization has been taken over by the discussion on globalization. Since around the 1990s, the word globalization began being used, overlapping with the word internationalization, and sometimes replacing it interchangeably or overriding unconsciously in the mainstream international social work community even though the meaning and concept of both words are, of course, different.

There are various definitions of globalization, but a definition by Ohno fits our discussion here:

Globalization does not simply mean the situation whereby each country intensifies contact and competition through trade, investment, finance, information, and personal exchange. Each period of the world's economy has its own geographical and industrial centre. Globalization is a process, with a clear direction and hierarchical structure, in which values and systems of the country at the centre diffuse to other regions by following and coercion. It is "self-evident" in the central country's eyes that their civilization is superior. Globalization implies both the sense of superiority and the sense of mission to extend the benefits to regions that have not yet enjoyed them. Furthermore, it is undeniable that globalization has a side whereby the central country forces other countries to participate in fields where it has an advantage under the rules it has laid down, and reproduces its superiority on a progressive scale. [Translated by the current author.]

Ohno, K. 2000. *Globalization of Developing Countries—Is the self-sustainable development possible?* Tōyō Keizai Shinpōsha.

That which was written on internationalization in the first paragraph in (iii) on the previous page (p.118) could be simply repeated if the word 'internationalization' were to be replaced with the word 'globalization.' The only notable difference from internationalization is the emphasis on the more explicit and conscious one-directional relationship with the centre (sender) and peripherals (receiver), overriding the euphemism of internationalization.

Once, even unipolar theory was in fashion (cf. Akimoto, 2007: 686-690). In the case of social work, what is at the center is the social work of "developed" countries or Western-rooted professional social work.

## (3) International Social Work under internationalization and globalization

The discussion in subsections (1) and (2) avobe was mostly about 'national' social work under internationalization and globalization. Here we shall be discussing the relation of internationalization/globalization to International Social Work, not that of internationalization/globalization to 'national' social work.

International Social Work was facilitated by the environmental condition of the internationalization of a society in its birth and growth, but 'international social work,' in turn, facilitated the internationalization/ globalization of 'national' social work (and even the internationalization/ globalization of the society).

International Social Work brings in 'national' social work not only 1) its 'way of viewing matters' and various thoughts and practices under it but also 2) what is one-directional under internationalization and at the centre under globalization, namely, Western-rooted professional social work. 'Value' tends to be the subject most frequently referred to but knowledge and skills could also be so.

'National' social work retorts in the voice of "Globalization!," "Westernization!," "Social work imperialism!," and "Professional colonialism!," beyond "Domestic interference!" some years ago, in response to what has been brought in, and also against International Social Work (and the society) which had been the agency of this importation. More accurately speaking, International Social Work is a promoter of internationalization 1) in the paragraph immediately above and a preventer of 2). 'International Social Work' may be a mover for both internationalization 1) and 2). Some people involved in international social work in the Western-rooted professional social work community even promote it as a "global profession" without hesitation under the name of International Social Work.

What we have been exploring is what International Social Work is, and not what specifically the international social work of Western-rooted professional social work is. What we have been interested in with International Social Work is that it can be commonly applicable to or intimate with all social work and all parts of the world. We cannot discuss International Social Work without considering the international social work of other types of social work including Buddhist social work, Islamic social work, various NGO's social work, and as well as other indigenous social work.[69] We sealed the inquiry of what social work is in a black box at the beginning of this section. International Social Work aims to deliver social work to all eight billion people of all countries and regions around the world.

## 2.7 The Future: Unsolved Questions

### (1) Will International Social Work cease to exist?

'National' social work was put in the internationalized context and had the "international" element in every corner of itself (2.6 (1) p.116). 'National' social work is supposed to be fully internationalized. Then, will international social work become unnecessary and cease to exist? This was one of the questions raised at the end of Chapter 1, and discussed briefly in 1.2 (2) (d) in this chapter. As far as the International Social Work we are constructing is concerned, the answer is simply "No" although the name of the 'international social work (A)' (2.2 (1) p.104) may,[70] conceptually, losing its distinction from other parts of 'national' social work.

International Social Work will not cease to exist unless sovereign states cease to exist. Neither International Social Work nor International Social Work´(dash) will disappear shortly while national borderlines have been changing from solid lines to broken lines, and the spaces between the broken lines have been becoming wider. Some may argue that the original question "Will 'international' social work cease to exist?" should have rather been "Will 'national' social work cease to exist?" But the answer and reasoning to this new question would not change.

As long as a nation state continues to exist—it will—and as long as a

---

69    See footnote 49.

70    Or may not, or maybe even strengthened.

world state is not born—it will not—International Social Work will be necessary. The role and function of International Social Work will be the same as today: 1. carrying the torch of the original idea of International Social Work, and 2. managing International Social Work (actual International Social Work) as a field of cooperation, collaboration, competition, and compromise, whereas 'national' social work tries to work in its own interests while partly understanding the idea of International Social Work.

Imagine the governing boards of the United Nations and IASSW (International Association of Schools of Social Work). The United Nations is composed of individual sovereign nation states, which compete and compromise national interests in reality and pursue UN ideas. Think of the board members of the IASSW—executive officers and board members elected by the general member body and board members sent in as national representatives. From which side do you see matters, the UN or IASSW side or the individual member country's side? In reality, some executive members may work as if they were national representatives for their own countries, with various degrees. However much their original ideas are distorted, they have their own significance of existence. However much actual International Social Work (dash) is distorted, it exists as International Social Work.

## (2) Are there any common yardsticks that could avoid this criticism of globalization?

Internationalization/globalization forces us to see what is at the centre or the strongest, as common yardsticks crossing national borders or even as global standards. The makeup of globalization in our case is Western-rooted professional social work or its values, knowledge, and skills. 'International Social Work' possibly functions as its promoter while 'national' social work raises the objection of "Globalization!"

Are there any yardsticks common worldwide that could dodge the criticism of globalization? If there are, how can we find them? Indigenization cannot be the answer. What was indigenized is still Western-rooted professional social work. Some minor modifications would have to be made in quality or quantity to make the substantive whole body accepted (seeing from the sender's side), or to accept it (seeing from the receiver's side). (See

122

the ABC Model in Buddhist social work and its extension in Akimoto, 2017: 22-23 and 2020: 65-68).

Should we think not from the self or the center but from others or the peripheral, that is, indigenous social work in our case? Some common yardsticks may be found if we observe such social work to identify and isolate their yardsticks and consolidate them inductively and all-inclusively.

Or shall we return to the society before national borders were born while we are looking for common yardsticks usable in the society after the national borders were solidly drawn, overcoming, and erasing them?

See Figure 3-9. At one time, in each locality "social work" existed although the term social work was not used. It was 'indigenous' social work. No national borders existed physically and/or within consciousness (I in the Figure). Nation states and national borders were born. Social work was divided into two parts, outside and inside the borders. Most were located inside, within a nation (II in the Figure).

Social work became nationalized although the understanding of social work same as in II could be maintained as far as the way of seeing 'social work before a nation.' Social work gradually transferred some part of its activities to the nation (III in the Figure). "National social work" in the meaning of social work by governments (hereinafter to be referred as "state social work"), not in the meaning of social work geographically bound to a territory, was born and grew. It was gradually institutionalized and eventually embraced, subsumed, and confined by the nation.[71] The welfare state and professionalization and national licensing/certificate programs may be the symbolic culmination. Social work becomes subordinate and even a tool of states (III→IV in the Figure).[72]

During this process, international social work spun off from 'national social work' with the limit of national borders, to be created as an independent entity, which is not under the sovereignty of nation states.

---

71  The speed and the degree of embracement, subsumption, and confinement vary in each nation's social work. Some parts of social work could remain outside 'state social work' while remaining inside 'national social work' as far as the individual identity as social work is preserved.

72  In a more historically accurate picture, the attachment on the right shoulder of IV (cf. Figure 3-6) could be attached to III.

We may find some primitive fundamental common yardsticks applicable to all levels of societies including indigenous societies (I). No killing, no stealing,[73] goodwill, love and compassion, charity, voluntary work without expecting returns,[74] humanism, philanthropy, and social care, for example, might be candidates for those yardsticks although they are certainly too primitive. "They are not social work," would be a spontaneous response from people involved in mainstream Western-rooted professional social work. Social work must be only theirs. "Social work" has not been patented for monopolization by Western-rooted professional social work, which is not serving and cannot serve all people, in all parts of the world.

We are discussing distinguishing social work and those who serve in the field of social work. Among them, there could be social workers who are engaged in social work as a job, and among them, there could be professional social workers (1.2 (1) (c) p.96).

Again, "what social work is" is not the topic of this book. We put this issue in a black box at the very beginning of this section (cf. The 4th International Academic Forum on Buddhist Social Work, December 20-21, Tokyo, Japan; Gohori, J. (Ed.) (2020; 2021)). We are not discussing the International Social Work of Western-rooted professional social work. Our International Social Work must be applicable to all social work. This way of viewing matters, erasing national borders and nationalities, may have been rooted in social work as if it were a DNA molecule. We will see and think of a totally different world to find highly common yardsticks.

---

73    Cf. the Ten Christian Commandments, and the Five Buddhist Commandments.

74    From this point of view, professional social workers, who work for money or as a job, are not those who are doing social work, and professional social work is not social work.

Figure 3-9. Social work and nations and international social work

II

Nation
→(the birth of ISW)
and NSW

IV

NSW
SSW

Limits of NSW
→Birth of ISW
spinoff

International
Social Work

Nation
State

Resistance
Acceptance

Boomerang
Intrusion of ISW
into NSW

e.g.
Welfare state

Institutionalization of SW
inclusion in the Nation

SW before a nation

I

SW
in a locality

(Indigenous SW)

NSW

Transfer of services
to the Nation

III

SW subordinates
to the nation
(SW=the nation's)

e.g. licensing
professionalization

The development
of NSW and SW
(to the third stage)

V

SW: Social work
SSW: State social work
NSW: 'National' social work
ISW: International Social Work

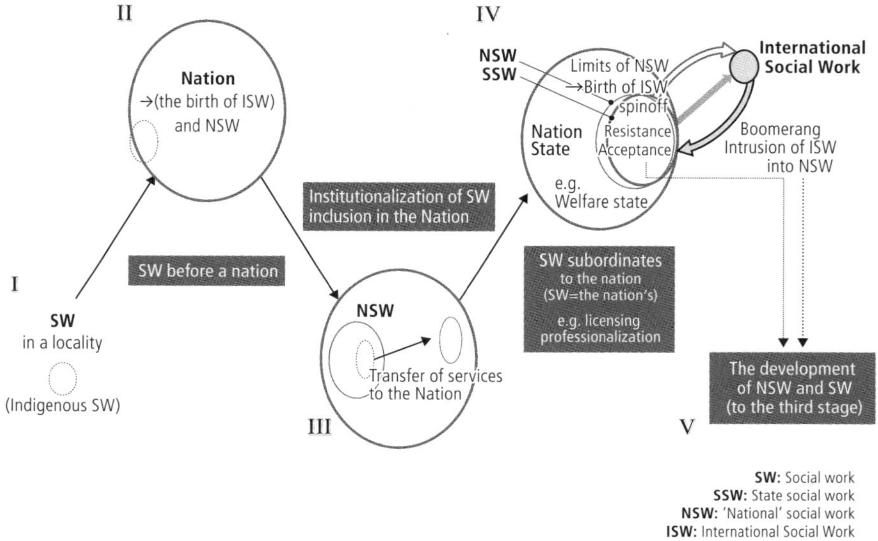

# 3. A Newly Constructed Definition and Conclusive Summary

## (1) A Definition of International Social Work

Though still tentative, the construction work has been completed, giving us the following definition of International Social Work:[75]

International Social Work[1] is social work[2] beyond, crossing, or relating to national[3] borders, and is backed up by certain ideas.[4] Its constituency comprises all people of all countries worldwide,[5] and its aim is to promote

---

75     As far as a definition is concerned, minimizing factors and components could make it more inclusive in content while paraphrasing them would be also necessary to guide readers to a better understanding.

their wellbeing. 'The way of viewing matters[6] is to see with eyes from the outside of nation states including one's own country, with 'compound[7] eyes, or with one or more common yardsticks. International Social Work does not give any special importance, superiority, or inferiority, to any specific countries, peoples or nationalities[8]. The antonym of International Social Work is 'national' social work[9]. International Social Work is to be commonly compatible with all indigenous[10] social work[11].

1) 'International social work (B)' (2.2 (1) p.104)
2) The social work that each reader assumed and put in a black box at the beginning of the previous Section 2.1 (1) p.99). Not necessarily limited to Western-rooted professional social work.
3) Includes "regional" in the equivalent sense to "national"
4) Includes philosophy, principle, value, purpose, aim, the way of viewing matters, yardstick, measure, norm, etc. Being paraphrased as in the following three sentences.
5) Not people of one's own country and region. 'Nation' was mainly used in the body of this book, but 'country' is used here for easier understanding.
6) The way of looking at things, purpose and aim, value, yardstick, measure, standard, perspective, approach, etc.
7) 'multifaceted'
8) Other elements within and outside of the idea are not different from those of social work as a whole as International Social Work is part of it, together with 'national' social work.
9) 'National' social work here means social work in each country, not by a government.
10) The usage is different from UNESCO/IFSW definitions (cf. the footnote 49).
11) Not only for Western-rooted professional social work. It is to have an affinity for social works as a locomotive is connected to a variety of different cars. Cf. compatibility in grafting.

The keyword of International Social Work is "national borders," and the task is social work crossing or concerning national borders. The constituency comprises eight billion[76] people of some 200 countries and regions, not a specific country or its people, particularly one's own. The purpose is to promote the well-being of the whole world. 'The way of viewing matters,' the core of the idea, is to see with eyes from the outside of sovereign states including one's own country, or with multifaceted eyes, and to use multiple or common yardsticks. Besides this, nothing (values, principles, fields of practice, etc.) is different in International Social Work from 'national' (local;

---

76    As of the end of 2022.

domestic; state) social work—at this moment although something different might be identified in the future—as both are part of the same social work.

The antonym of International Social Work is 'national' social work, i.e., social work in each country. International Social Work does not give any special importance, superiority, or inferiority to any specific countries or peoples. Representative actors of International Social Work are trans- or inter-governmental organizations, and international nongovernmental organizations including social work organizations but that could also be any groups and any individuals as far as they hold the above-mentioned idea. The idea here has been used as an inclusive term of the constituency, 'the way of viewing matters,' philosophy, its future direction as well as values, principles, purposes, aims, standards, norms, yardsticks, measures, and other elements.

International Social Work has a common affinity with all social works throughout the world and must be compatible with them. 'Social work' here is not limited to Western-rooted social work but could be any other type of social work. Professionalism and human rights, for example, which the Western-rooted social work cherishes as their purpose and value, are applicable as international social work of Western-rooted professional social work, but may or may not be in such other international social works as the international social work of Buddhist social work, Islamic social work, NGO social work, and other indigenous social work. The meaning of "indigenous" here is different from the UNESCO/IFSW definitions (cf. the footnote 49).

### (2) An opening tour of the new edifice (Summary: Some features of the new International Social Work)

Lastly, let's take our International Social Work visitors on an opening tour to show them some features of the new edifice.

1) All social work related to other countries is not necessarily International Social Work.

All social work related to other countries is not necessarily International Social Work. The meaning is two-fold.

1)-1 Only certain activities with a certain idea

Only certain activities with a certain idea (See the next item 2).) among activities related to other countries are called International Social Work. International social work once leapt from "international" social work to "international social work." In the former, "international" was an adjective to modify 'social work' and meant all 'related to other countries' while in the latter, 'international' is a constituent of an independent three-word term or concept, "international social work." Exploring the concept led to this conclusion above (cf. In mainstream social work, a category or a combination of categories of social work activities (acts; functions) with a certain value, by professional social workers, were and are called international social work).

1)-2 There are two kinds of 'international social work,' but one is essentially 'national' social work

There are two ways for social work to exceed national borders: (A) 'National' social work spreads its wings to cross national borders to serve clients of their own countries better and more efficiently. We refer to it as 'international social work (A).' Think of the cases of migrants and international adoption. (B) An independent entity outside 'national' social works is set up to overview all 'national' social works or all people in the world. We refer to this as 'international social work (B).' Think of conventions and activities by the ILO and WHO, and activities by some international NGOs and individuals. We regard 'international social work (A)' as part of 'national' social work in the sense that it focuses on the benefits of people of one's own country. We regard 'international social work (B)' as International Social Work, which sees it with eyes from the outside of nation states including one's own countries.

2) The Idea: For all people of all countries and seeing with eyes from the outside of one's own country

The "idea" in above 1)-1 is a term inclusive of various elements, but in International Social Work, the following two are core elements:

- The constituency: all people in all countries and regions of the world; and

- with eyes from the outside of nation states including one's own country, multifaceted eyes, or multiple or common yardsticks.

In short, it is seeing all peoples and countries as equal, and exceeding national borders, which coincides with the conclusion in above 1)-2.

The background theory[77] is a theory of the state—the understanding of the birth and limits of modern nation states, the distance of the welfare state to the welfare world, and the erasure of national borders. The terms 'world citizen,' 'cosmopolitan,' 'Earthian,' and 'being a human being' toward which International Social Work has its orientation, help us with the construction of this concept although the criticism that they are super-historical and unscientific concepts cannot be avoided.

3) International Social Work of the ideal type and actual existence

International Social Work in an actual society has been distorted from the International Social Work of the ideal type. International Social Work has been structured, administered, and operated on a set of 'national' social works actually existing in the world with different sizes of power. We call this International Social Work International Social Work´ with a dash.

International Social Work´(dash) in actual society is located somewhere between two poles: International Social Work of the ideal type, and crude 'national' social work working for the benefit of domestic cases in their own countries. A tug of war has been played out between both poles.

While International Social Work´(dash) has grown up along with a trend toward internationalization, it has, in turn, contributed to the internationalization of social work[78] and furthermore to the globalization of social work, that is, the dissemination of Western-rooted professional social work from the center to the peripherals. It is, in a sense, the contribution of International Social Work´(dash) to the distortion of International Social Work itself. The counterattacks from 'national' social work come under the voices of "Globalization!" and "Westernization!" against the force of mainstream Western-rooted professional social work.

Refer to the analogy of the United Nations, which is composed of

---

77    It is based on the discussion of Western philosophy.

78    It was originally neutral.

individual nation states with their different sizes and powers. It contains the idea of peace and prosperity for the whole world but the reality has been distorted by the differences of size and power of each country in structure, administration, and operation.

4) International Social Work is for all social work, not only of Western-rooted social work

International Social Work is of all people of all countries of the world and all forms of social work which may exist already and/or latently in the world. It is not only of Western-rooted social work. For example, human rights and professionalization could be acceptable as a value and a purpose, as part of the idea, as far as we discuss international social work at the level of International Social Work of Western International Social Work, but they may or may not be acceptable once we begin discussing International Social Work at the world level, which covers and considers the whole world.

International Social Work and its idea must have a universal connection to various other types of social work throughout the world as if it were a locomotive that could be connected to a variety of different railway cars. International Social Work must have an affinity with all social work. The expression of the International Social Work of Western-rooted social work, the International Social Work of Islamic, Buddhist, or NGOs' social work...is linguistically and conceptually self-contradictory.[79]

5) The future

5)-1 Will International Social Work cease to exist?

Will International Social Work vanish if internationalization/globalization proceeds?

If society is internationalized/globalized, 'national' social work will be put in an internationalized/globalized context, the element of "international"/ "global" will penetrate every corner of 'national' social work, and 'national' social work will be internationalized/globalized. The concept of 'National'

---

79    We are not able to go into the subject of 'what social work is' here, besides confessing that we are not believers in the equation, "social work = Western-rooted professional social work"  (cf. 1.2 (1) (b) p.95).

130

social work may diminish itself, in the sense of the loss of its uniqueness, by accepting and embodying the idea of International Social Work. But this is a matter of 'national' social work under internationalization/globalization.

What we must discuss here is the destiny of International Social Work under internationalization/globalization. International Social Work ('international social work (B)' p.104) will continue to exist as long as nation states continue to do so[80] although 'international social work (A)' may disappear in the sense that the distinction between it and other parts of 'national' social work will blur and disappear. The role and function of International Social Work will continue being to fill the gap between International Social Work and International Social Work´(dash) and orient International Social Work´(dash) towards International Social Work of an ideal type, carrying the torch of the ideal type of International Social Work.


5)-2 Out of sovereign nations and the contribution to the development of social work

The significance of International Social Work is to have located itself outside nation states, or 'national' social work, and to have remained within social work. Social work is now composed of 'national' social work and International Social Work. Having a part that is not under the sovereignty of nation states in itself, social work has developed an existence beyond nation states not only physically but also conceptually and ideally. It has liberated itself from nation states at least partially. Such terminology as International Social Work of Country A, International Social Work of Country B…is self-contradictory. This form of social work seems to be a newly emerged one but also to be a kind of reversion if one traces back to the origin of social work. The element (being outside of the nation state) seems to have been rooted in social work as if it were its DNA. 'Social work' was born in indigenous[81] localities—although such a term was not used at this time when nations and national borders did not exist or were not in peoples' consciousnesses. Social work emerged under such conditions. Nations were born and national

---

80    Even if the solid line denoting national borders on maps is broken into a dotted line and
      the distance between the dots becomes wider.

81    See footnote 49.

borders were drawn, and eventually embraced social work (See 2.7 (2) and Figure 3-9).

International Social Work brings with it its ideas, thoughts, and practices under it in 'national' social work. 'National' social work would become enriched, from the International Social Work point of view, and further social work itself would and will develop onto the next stage,[82] the stage 'of all people' throughout the world.

This new construction is not Chapter 2's 'A Theory of the State' Model (Ch.3 1.1 (2)) itself but was constructed based on the Mainstream Model in Chapter 2 (Ch.3 1.1(1)), which was mostly based on the understanding and achievements of the international social work of Western-rooted social work, and Chapter 2's State Theory Model which was based on the Mainstream Model and the understanding and achievements of Western-rooted state theories. In this sense, this new structure is also a Western-rooted product and not something that exceeds the understanding and achievements of the Western world, except that the author is from a non-Western, non-English-speaking world, and has a slightly greater respect for the non-Western world.

---

82    The third stage follows the first stage (the birth in Europe) and the second stage (the mutu-ality in North America) as far as Western-rooted professional social work is concerned.

# References

Ahmadi, N. (2003). Globalization and consciousness and new challenges for international social work. *International Journal of Social Welfare*, 12(1), 14-23.

Akimoto, T. (1992). Kokusaika to rōdō sha fukushi—Genjitsu no kokusaika, shiten no kokusaika, gainen no kokusaika [Internationalization and labor social work—Internationalization of realities, Internationalization of 'the way of viewing natters,' and Internationalization of the Concept]]. In S. Sato, (Ed.). Kokusaika Jidai no Fukushi Kadai to Tenbō [Welfare Issues and Perspectives in Days of Internationalization (pp. 233-249). Tokyo: Ichiryūsha.

Akimoto, T. (1995). Towards the establishment of an international social work/welfare concept. Unpublished paper. Japan Women's University, Kanagawa, Japan.

Akimoto, T. (1997). A voice from Japan: Requestioning international social work/welfare: Where are we now? Welfare world and national interest. *Japanese Journal of Social Services*, 1, 23-34.

Akimoto, T. (2001). Kokusai Shakai Fukushi [International Social Work]. In *Encyclopedia of Social Work* (pp. 1-4). Yūhikaku.

Akimoto, T. (2004). The essence of international social work and nine world maps—How to induct students into the secrets of ISW—. In *Social Welfare* (Journal of Social Welfare Department of Japan Women's University), 45, 1-15.

Akimoto, T. (2007). The Unipolar World and Inequality in Social Work: A response to James Midgley, 'Global inequality, power and the unipolar world: Implications for social work', *International Social Work*, 5, 686-690. [Central Conference, The 33rd World Congress of Schools of Social Work, International Association of Schools of Social Work (IASSW), August 28-31, 2006, Santiago, Chile.]

Akimoto, T. (2007). Social justice and social welfare policies beyond national boundaries—What Should We Question? (Proceedings) presented at The 50th Anniversary Celebration of Establishment of Korean Academy of Social Welfare International Conference, "Human Rights and Social Justice: Rethinking Social Welfare's Mission." Seoul University, Seoul,

Korea. April 20, 2007. <Reprint> *Shakai Fukushi* [Social Welfare] No. 48. March 2008. <Partial reprint> "Social justice in an era of globalization: must and can it be the focus of social welfare policies?—Japan as a case study." Reich, M. (Ed.). (2016). *Routledge International Handbook of Social Justice*. Routledge.

Akimoto, T. (2017). Seiyō senmonshoku sōsharu wāku no gurōbarizeshon to bukkyō sōsharu waku no tankyū [The globalization of Western-rooted professional social work and the exploration of Buddhist social work] In Gohori, J. et al. (Eds.). *Seiyō-umare Senmonshoku Sōsharu Wāku kara Bukkyō Sōsharu Wāku e* [From Western-rooted Professional Social Work to Buddhist Social Work] (pp. 1-44). ARIISW- Gakubunsha. (Japanese version: pp.1-53).

Akimoto, T., Fujimori, Y., Gohori, J., & Matsuo, K. (2020). To make social work something truly of the world: Indigenization is not the answer. In Gohori, J. (Ed.). *The Journey of Buddhist Social Work—Exploring the Potential of Buddhism in Asian Social Work* (pp. 62-69). ARIISW-Shukutoku University.

Cox, D. & Pawar, M. (2006/2013). *International Social Work: Issues, Strategies, and Programs*. Sage Publications, Inc.

Friedlander, W.A. (1975). *International Social Welfare*. Prentice-Hall.

Gohori, J. (Ed.) (2020/2021). *The Journey of Buddhist Social Work—Exploring the Potential of Buddhism in Asian Social Work;* and *Social Work Academics Resisting the globalization of Western-rooted Social Work—Decolonization, Indigenization, Spirituality, and Buddhist Social Work*. ARIISW-Shukutoku University.

Healy, L. M. (1990). [International content in social work education programs worldwide]. Unpublished raw data.

Healy, L. M. (2001). *International Social Work*. Oxford University Press.

Healy, L. M. & Link, R. J. (Eds.). (2012). *Handbook of International Social Work: Human Rights, Development and the Global Profession*. Oxford University Press.

Hokenstad, T. et al., (1992). *Profiles in International social Work*. NASW Press.

Huegler, N., Lyons, K. & Pawar, M. (2012). 1 Setting the Scene. In Lyons, K. et al. (Eds.). *Handbook of International Social Work*. Sage Publications.

Hugman, R. (2010). *Understanding International Social Work: A Critical*

*Analysis*. Basingstoke, Palgrave-Macmillan.

Jebb, E. (1929). International social service. *International Conference of Social Work [Proceedings]* (Vo. I, pp.637-655) First Conference, Paris, July 8-13, 1928.

Johnson, H. W. (1996). International activity in undergraduate social work education in the United States. *International Social Work*, 39(2), 189-199.

Kojima, Y. (1992). Kokusai Shakaifukushi no Kiban [Foundation of International Social Welfare]. ( In Sato, S. (Ed.). *Kokusaika-jidai no Fukushi Kadai to Tenbō* [Welfare Issues and Future in Days of Internationalization (pp. 278-303). Ichiryūsha.

Lyons, K. (1999). *International Social Work: Themes and Perspectives*. Ashgate Publishing Limited.

Lyons, K. et al. (2006). Globalization and social work: International and local implications. *British Journal of Social Work*, 36(3), 365-80.

Lyons, K. et al. (2012). *The SAGE Handbook of International Social Work*. Sage Publications.

Matsuo, K. (Ed.). (2014). *Internationalization and Indigenization*. ACWelS (Asian Center for Welfare in Societies-Japan College of Social Work).

Matsuo, K., Akimoto, T. & Hattori, M. (Ed.). (2019). Kokusai Sōsharu-wāku Kyōiku no Karikyuramu wa Ikani Arubeki-ka? [What Should Curricula for International Social Work Education Be?] (The Third Shukutoku University International Academic Forum, Jan. 20, 2018). Asian Research Institute for International Social Work (ARIISW), Shukutoku University.

Nakamura, Y. (1986). Zadankai: Mokuzen ni Sematta Kokusai Shakaifukushi Kaigi [A Round-table Talk: Soon Coming International Social Work Conference]. *Gekkan Fukushi* [Monthly Welfare] (1986.4.28), 12-38.

Ohno, K. (2000). Tojōkoku no Gurōbarizeishon—Jiritsu-teki Hatten wa Kanō ka? [Globalization of Developing Countries—Is Self-sustained Development Possible?]. Tōyō Keizai Shinpōsha.

Payne, M. & Askeland, G. A. (2008). Globalization and International Social Work: Post Modern Change and Challenge. Ashgate Publishing.

Stein, H. (1957, January). An international perspective in the social work curriculum. Paper presented at annual meeting of CSWE, Los Angeles, CA.

Warren, G. (1937). International social work. In Russell H. Kurtz. (Ed.). *Social*

*Work Year Book.* 4th Issue. New York: Russell Sage Foundation.

Xu, Q. (2006). Defining international social work: a social service agency perspective. *International Social Work*, 49(6), 679-92.

# Chapter Four

## The Essence of International Social Work and Nine World Maps[83*] —How to Induct Students Into the Secrets of International Social Work—

What is the essence of International Social Work? How can we pass on this essential knowledge to students? This chapter[84*] is a tentative summation of the author's ten-year teaching experience[85*] at Japanese schools of social work.

## 1. What Is International Social Work?

### (1) What International Social Work is not

To practice or conduct research on or in other countries is not equal to international social work. This would be the same if you did this jointly with social work practitioners or professors from other countries. To make an international comparison is not international social work, regardless of drawing lessons for your own country. Comparative analysis is just one of the most basic research methods. To be engaged in practice or research on assistance to the Two-Thirds World is not international social work. This would not change if you refer to "North-South relations."

"Cross-Cultural Social Work" is, of course, not international social work. To devote your energy and talents to international social work organizations such as the IASSW (International Association of Schools of Social Work), the IFSW (International Federation of Social Workers), and the ICSW

---

\*    marks next to footnote numbers indicate the new insertion on the publication of this book.

83*   This chapter is a reprint of the article (2005) published in Social Welfare (Journal of Social Welfare Department of Japan Women's University) No.45, 2004, with minor corrections and changes. It was originally orally presented at the IASSW (International Association of Schools of Social Work) Board Seminar at Addis Ababa University, Ethiopia, on 20 January 2005.

84*   [In the original] "paper."

85*   Mostly the 1990s.

(International Council on Social Welfare) is not international social work, either. Working with other organizations outside of one's own country is "foreign affairs" activities, which are requisite to almost all kinds of organizations at present. These are all valuable and important but not necessarily international social work (Akimoto, 1997: 26-27) (Ch.2 1 & 2).

## (2) What International Social Work is

What is International Social Work? (a)International Social Work is social work that is concerned with national boundaries.[86*] It is "international" social work. It deals with problems related to or across national boundaries or efforts beyond national boundaries, to solve those problems. (b)International Social Work thinks of and acts for the well-being of all people on this Earth—around eight billion people[87*] in 200 countries and regions—not the well-being of one country or one people. International Social Work is not "national" social work. It is social work beyond the welfare state. (c) International Social Work does not attach any special meaning or importance in value to any specific country or people. It requires not egocentrism and ethnocentrism but "compound eyes". (d)Ignorance and innocence, including those of history, will jeopardize International Social Work both in its practice and research (Ch.3 2.3).

The definition or the understanding of international social work has of course changed over time. Period[88*] I occurred around the 1930s, before World War II. There were four ways of breaking national boundaries: serving international social case work (e.g., regarding immigrant and international adoption); internationally assisting disaster and war sufferers and distressed minority groups; holding and attending international conferences; and working for international cooperation in transnational organizations (e.g., the League of Nations, ILO (International Labour Organization) and the International Committee of the Red Cross). They were termed international

---

86*   In Chapter 3, the term "national borders" was mainly used. "National borders" and "national boundaries" have been used interchangeably in Part I of this book.

87*   As of 2022. [In the original] 6.4 billion people.

88*   [In the original] "Phase". It has been changed to "Period" to conform with the message in Chapter 1. Hereinafter same.

social work (cf. Warren, 1937: 224 and 1939: 192; Ch.1 1.1)[89*].

After World War II, aid and assistance to the South by the North became a major form of international social work. This Period II lasted until the 1970s to 80s. The practice and the research on and in other countries or with people of other countries were also considered as international social work. These were other ways to transcend national boundaries. Being engaged in the promotion of international exchange and "foreign affairs" was also termed international social work by some people (Ch.2 1). We are now in Period III, the next state (Akimoto, 1997: 33).

## 2. How to Convey the Essence of International Social Work

How can we convey the essence of today's international social work mentioned in the two paragraphs above to students in a session or two? [Data on which this section is based are all from classes in Japanese universities. All readers are expected to read the following sections replacing words "Japan" and "Japanese" and Japan-related examples and explanatory descriptions with those of your country, people, and equivalent examples and explanatory descriptions. In Subsection (0) below, Pacific-centred [MAP a] and [MAP b] should be replaced with world maps which are the most commonly used ones in each reader's country. In Subsections (1) to (3), students' perceptions and responses would vary depending on the country or region and/or students' backgrounds. Try the same experimental tests with your students and rewrite paragraphs. The comparative study would be interesting and fruitful.][90*]

**(0) Two blank world maps**

The first lecture on International Social Work starts with a blank world map [MAP a]. The map is handed to students and instruction is given. "Look at

---

89*   Some insertions and changes.

90*   [ ]: New insertion.

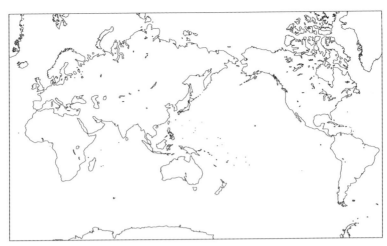

**MAP a**

Source: https://www.freemap.jp/itemDownload/world/world1/1.png (retrieved 8 Nov. 2022) (replaced the map originally used in classes).

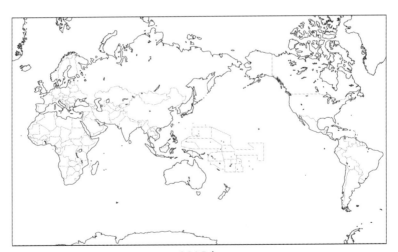

**MAP b**

Source: https://www.freemap.jp/itemDownload/world/world1/3.png (retrieved 8 Nov. 2022) (replaced the map originally used in classes).

*The dotted lines may not necessarily reflect the actual national border lines. (See 2 (1)). Some countries may not be appropriately represented.

*The height and width ratio of the original maps have been changed by the current author for the page design.

the attached map and write down your feelings and thoughts (20 minutes)." Immediately after they are turned in, another blank world map [MAP b] is handed to the students and the same instruction, "Look at the attached map and write down your feelings and thoughts (20 minutes)" is given. The map is the same as the previous map [MAP a] except for the dotted lines drawn on it. From these two maps and their comparison, almost all ingredients, or the essence, of International Social Work can be extracted.

There are four points:

## (1) The keyword: National boundaries

The key word, or the core concept, of International Social Work, is a "national boundary." The sole difference between the two maps is the dotted lines. Because of these lines, various problems happen. International Social Work deals with problems caused between and across, and efforts beyond national boundaries to solve those problems.

Generally, for the first map, bright and positive comments tend to be made, as far as Japanese undergraduate students are concerned. For example, "Roomy," "Peaceful," "Unity," "Wholeness," "Conflicts and wars between countries seem to be absurd," "My worries seem to be trivial," and "This Earth is not only for human beings but for all animals and plants." Many refer to seas and continents—their portions, shapes, and historical shifts. For the second map, dark and negative comments tend to be made. For example, "Jumble," "Conflicts and wars," "Strife and feuds," and "Competition and hatred." There are of course some opposite ideas and comments. Attached at the end of the chapter is the list of words, phrases, and sentences given by students. [Appendix, pp.151-160.]

International Social Work is, however, not the social work of the first map. Many practitioners and scholars seem to define international social work as such. They praise words, concepts, and expressions such as an Earthian, a citizen[91] of the world, and a crew member of the spaceship *Planet Earth*. Such understanding, however, encounters criticism as being "superhistorical," unscientific, and irresponsible; ignoring and erasing national boundaries when seeing, thinking, and acting.

We are still in the midst of nation states today, although national boundaries have certainly been broken down in various ways—by goods and services, capital (or multinational corporations), people, information, etc. See the first page of your passport. Japanese passport, for example, reads:

> The Minister for Foreign Affairs of Japan requests all those whom it may concern to allow the bearer, a Japanese national, to pass freely and without hindrance and, in case of need, to afford him or her every possible aid and protection.

The state acts as if it were your "guarantor" or "patron" while you have not asked it to do so. We cannot go anywhere outside our country without a passport.[92*]

Although it may be appropriate to have the concept of a world "citizen" as a long-term goal to which we are directed, we are only somewhere on the way toward this. Seeing the past and the future, we have to know where we are now and think of what we should do. We must always carry the two maps in our pockets, in our minds, in International Social Work. "This is the time when being a good (national) citizen, a good international man/woman, and a good world 'citizen' is called for all simultaneously."

What are national boundaries? When and how were they born? They were man-made and relatively recent in the history of human beings. They are a product of modern nation states. Even today some boundaries have been

---

91    The present concept of "citizens" was constructed in relation to a state in modern Western theories. Citizens have rights to be free from, to demand, and to be entitled to receive services from a state. From whom and to whom are those rights of "citizens of the world"?

92*   Except for "within countries under the Schengen Convention," etc.

142

newly drawn and re-drawn.[93] Some boundaries may be possibly erased or eliminated tomorrow or someday in the future.

## (2) The subject: All people on the Earth

International Social Work cares for the wellbeing of all people in this world—eight billion[94*] people in 200 countries and regions—not the well-being of one country or one people. It sees both the Two-Thirds World and One-Third World and their relations. International Social Work is in that sense social work beyond the welfare state, for the welfare state is not only a container of social welfare but also a wall of social welfare (cf. Pinker, 1979). International Social Work can be constructed only on the limitation of the nation-state.

The second map visualizes people's lives in concrete terms. Within the space surrounded by the dotted lines, various people live their lives with and under various political, economic, social, cultural institutions and situations, as well as various natural conditions.

The second map tends to emphasize these variations and differences. International Social Work begins its journey seeking differences. The first map makes us feel the similarities and the commonalities that are not partitioned as in the second map. International Social Work begins a journey seeking commonalities. International Social Work begins journeys in two opposite directions.

More interestingly, viewing the first map again after seeing the second map hints, suggests, and gives the possibility of seeing things not by a national boundary but by other criteria—such as class, social strata, gender, religion, tribes, and indigenous people/invaders—for analysis and practice, freeing us from the constraints of national boundaries. Not to see the world by country does not mean to see things flatly. To go beyond national boundaries does not mean to make a comparison between and among countries but rather to acquire a way of viewing matters that is not influenced

---

93    MAP b, which was a map made in the early days of the 2020s, may not reflect the newest national borders when readers read this book. Some border lines may be new and some others may vanish, which may serve as a good lesson for the understanding of the features and meanings of national borders (rewritten in this publication).

94*   As of 2022. [In the original] 6.4 billion people.

by national boundaries.

## (3) 'The way of viewing matters': Not egocentric and ethnocentric but with "compound eyes"—from outside nation states

International Social Work does not give any special position, meaning, or importance in value to any specific country or a specific people. It requires "compound eyes." All International Social Work practitioners and researchers are expected to view things not only with the eyes of their own country but also with the eyes of other countries and the eyes of the whole—not only from the inside but also from the outside.

Almost all students used the word "Japan" or "Japanese" at least once in their answer sheets. They think only from the stance of their own country. A personal sense of belonging is natural and healthy up to a certain level. Few comments were however given from the angle of other countries or peoples.

One assignment I gave in a class in May 2004 was the following: "Three Japanese nationals [a freelance photographer, a freelance writer, and a volunteer child welfare activist who were critical of the Japanese government's dispatch of the Self-Defense Forces of Japan to support the United States Iraq war and were in Iraq for humanitarian assistance, ignoring

MAP c
Source: Waido Sekai Zenzu [Wide World Map]. To–bunsha, Tokyo.

## MAP d
Source: LE MONDE. Projection Van der Grinten mondifiée MICHELEN.
\* The original map had national flags around it but they were trimmed away by the author.

## MAP e
Source: Classic Map of the World (HAMMOND Incorporated. Mamplewood. NJ).

\*The height and width ratio of the original maps (MAPs c, d, and e) have been changed by the current author for the page design.

the Japanese government's 'advisory recommending evacuation',] have been kidnapped [by an Iraqi armed group]. Map the feelings, the understanding, the thoughts, and responses of the various players or stakeholders." The three hostages, their families, their friends, the organizations they belonged to, the Japanese government, the United States government, the Iraqi government and various other governments, NGOs, the general public in various countries, their sub-populations, various segments of Iraqi people, and many others...The question itself had a fundamental flaw. Why wasn't it phrased as "We kidnapped three Japanese," or in the active voice?

On the other hand, many students pointed out that the two maps were Japanese world maps because Japan was located in the centre. There are typically three kinds of world maps today—the "East Asian countries/the Pacific Ocean-centred world map [MAP c]," the authentic "European world map [MAP d]," and the "American world map [MAP e]." How "arrogant" they are! (Not only that of Eastern Asian countries but also of the other countries.) They put their own countries in the middle. Particularly, the "American world map" bravely cuts the Eurasian Continent in half, putting its eastern half on the west side and its western half on the east side.

In addition to egocentrism, the emphasis on the theory of the elite and the superiority of one's own, e.g., Sino centrism, Zionism, the elite and the superiority of the Germanic people, the Japanese, and the Anglo-Saxons,[96] seems to be a common character of all countries. These are on pole opposite to International Social Work.

A map is a dangerous thing. It can control your way of thinking about and seeing the world. Not only among countries but also in North-South relations, a severe bias has been infused. The equator was not located at the centre of the three maps above. The North has been unproportionally magnified. Peters' Projection [MAP f] is a challenge to this bias although the part at the very top is still drawn disproportionately wide.[97] Both at the national level and also at the individual level, discriminatory, superior, or

---

95*   A new insertion.

96   People may define each of these terms or concepts differently, sometimes positively and sometimes negatively.

97   This is unavoidable when we use a plane to represent the surface of a sphere.

**MAP f**
Source: World View, Peters Projection Map (WorldView Publications: Oxford, UK).
*The height and width ratio of the original map have been changed by the current author for the page design.

disdainful views are baneful.

### (4) The preparation: Overcoming ignorance and innocence

Ignorance and innocence as well as popular beliefs are fatally detrimental to International Social Work in its practice and research. Some examples:

(a) Looking at the two blank world maps, many Japanese students start their comments with "Japan is a small island country" in their answer sheets. The notion has been a persistently prevailing common knowledge in Japan. Is Japan small? Yes, but how small is it among all countries in the world? Japan is the 60th biggest among some 194 countries and regions, according to a data book (Ninomiya Shoten, 2001: 18-24)—a third from the top. There are only three countries in Europe that are bigger than Japan: France, Spain, and

Sweden. Japan is the 11th[98*] largest in population, and 6th or 8th biggest, depending on the source, in terms of area (with its Exclusive Economic Zone considered). Can we discuss International Social Work with this misperception? Japan is an island country. Yes, but so what? So it has an island country mentality, that is, an insular spirit. It is narrow-minded. There are many island countries in the world—Iceland, the United Kingdom, Cyprus, Madagascar, Qatar, Cuba, Jamaica, New Zealand, Papua New Guinea, Sri Lanka, Tuvalu, Philippines, Indonesia...Do they share the same insularity?

(b) [MAP g] is a 1507 map obtained at the Vatican. Where can we find Japan? "Nowhere," responded a sales staff member wearing a robe, who was attending the display desk.[99*] What does this mean? There are two serious implications. One, in the brains and minds of the people who made and used this map, Japan—where millions of human beings were living—did not exist. Their world was different from the reality. Two, how do people feel about being ignored? Maybe not comfortable. To put it bluntly, it is a form of conceptual genocide. How terrible this is! Users as well as cartographers crossed out millions of people's existence.

The next assignment to students was "Simply write as many country names as possible (15 minutes)." To be shameful, the Japanese college students in my classes were able to write only around 60 country names on average (the maximum was 137), a third of all existing countries. What does this mean? Can you practice and study International Social Work with so little knowledge?

(c) [MAP h] is hard for the author to display in front of people, especially Asian colleagues. Taiwan, the Korean Peninsula, and some Pacific islands are painted red as in Japan, and the northeastern part of China is orange. This is a map taken from an atlas published in 1939 and is proof of Japanese imperialism, colonialism, and aggression. Few students had seen this map. Although many said they knew the historical facts, they could not imagine

---

98*  UNFPA State of World Population 2022 [In the original text, Japan was 9th] .

99  I am not sure if the answer was correct or not. A small island at the east end may be intended to be Japan without identification.

### MAP g
Source: Waldseemüller's World Map, 1507 (Wychwood Editions).
*The height and width ratio of the original map have been changed by the current author for the page design.

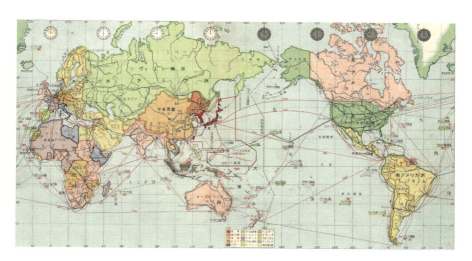

### MAP h
Source: *Shinsen Dai-chizu, Nippon-hen* [New Atlas: Japan] Michio Moriya, (Teikoku Shoin. Tokyo, 1939) pp. 2-3.
*The original map had colours and weather signal flags around it but they were trimmed away by the author.
*The height and width ratio of the original map have been changed by the current author for the page design.

what had really happened because it was all in the distant past, from their perspective. To these young people, it didn't personally involve them and wasn't a part of their life.

On the other hand, many students do seem to have innocently no discriminatory feelings against the people of those countries that Japan once invaded, at least at the conscious level. They become friends with young people[100*] of those countries without hesitation while older generations[101*] have some conflicting feelings regardless of their political or ideological position— reactionaries, conservatives, liberalists, or radicals. "We had not even been born during that period of aggression," say young students, implying that they are not responsible for history. Is this excuse acceptable for those whose countries were once invaded?[102] Can you practice or research International Social Work with this innocence? "It is not only Japan that invaded, killed, and exploited" other countries, say some people. But it is a fact Japan did. It is not easy for a Japanese to work in Asia.[103*]

(d) Asian countries are our neighbours. Is this commonly accepted view correct? There is a field named Telegeography. At one time, a map drawn by the volume of telephone and facsimile. communication (1990-91)[104*] was presented in an article in a journal (Staple, 1994: 29)[105*] ["MAP i Japan Communication Continent" (omitted)]. The proportion of the space of Japan covered by Country A (e.g. 23% in the case of the US) shows the volume of the information sent to the country among all the information sent out to all countries from Japan, and the proportion of Japan in the space of Country A (e.g. 4% in case of the US) shows the volume of the information sent to Japan

---

100* Remember that the original article of this chapter was written at the beginning of the 2000s.

101* Remember that the original article of this chapter was written at the beginning of the 2000s.

102 "You are enjoying an affluent life as a historical inheritance. We must inherit our history as a whole."

103* Akimoto, T. (2003). One-page policy statement was distributed when the current author ran for Board Member-at-large in the 2003 IASSW election.

104* Today Internet communication, which was not so common at the beginning of the 90s, would be even more important and the map might be significantly different.

105* The proceeding two sentences have been slightly changed.

150

among all the information Country A sent out to all countries. Neighbouring countries for Japan seem to be North American countries and European Community countries, but not Asian countries.[106*] Most Asian countries are distantly located. Are we ready for International Social Work?

There is no need to summarize this short story to this point. Please make an equivalent story, replacing "Japan" and "Japanese" with your own country and your own people, and think and practice.

---

106* The proportion has significantly changed in these few decades.

# References

Akimoto, T. (1995). A Voice from Japan: Requestioning International Social Work/Welfare: Where Are We Now? *Japanese Journal of Social Services*, 1, 23-34.

Ninomiya Shoten (2001). *Data Book of the World*, Vol.13.

*Pinker, R. (1979). *The Idea of Welfare*. London: Heinemann.

*Staple. C.G. (1994). Terejiogurafi kara mita sekai [The world seen from Telegiography]. *The TeleGiograpy*. 25-32. Cf. *TeleGiograpy*, (yearbook). International Institute of Communications and TeleGeography, Inc.

*Warren, G. (1937 and 1939). International social work. In R. Kurtz, (Ed.). *Social Work Yearbook*. Vol. 4 and 5 (pp.224-227 and pp.192-196 respectively). New York: Russell Sage Foundation.

* New insertions for this chapter. They were not included in the original article reprinted for this chapter.

## [Appendix] Two blank world maps

The following comments, grouped by topic (e.g., "A small island country"), were given by 38 undergraduate students, mainly sophomores and juniors, in the first session of the 2004 International Social Work class of Japan Women's University, Tokyo, Japan.

Two blank maps were handed to students and the following instructions were given. "Look at the attached maps and write down your feelings and thoughts about them within 20 minutes." (See pp.139-141).

Students have not learned about international social work yet. These comments are similar to those given by students in other classes at Japan Women's University and other universities in the Tokyo area in the past ten years. See Section 2. (0) and (1) (particularly, its first and second paragraphs, pp.148-150) of Chapter 4. Also see the first paragraph of Section 2, Chapter 4, p.139.

## Comments about both maps [MAP a & MAP b]

### "A small island country"
1. Japan is a small island country.
   Japan is really small.
   How small Japan is!
2. Island countries are few.
   I feel insecure about the lack of links with other countries.
3. It's a great matter that Japan is a world economic power while it is really small.

### "Japanese world map"
4. This is a Japan-centered world map.
   Probably Japanese made it.
   It's natural to put your own country in the middle, but I sense some egocentrism—Japanese supremacy.
   What do world maps in other countries look like?
5. It's rather unnatural to put France or the United States in the middle while we are Japanese.
   It's important to love your own country.

## Comments about the first map [MAP a]

### "Broad and spacious and peaceful"
1. Broad, spacious, open.
   I feel refreshed.
2. Peaceful.
   What trivial matters we fight over!
   Wars and strife between states seem absurd.

153

**"Unity and a whole"**

3. The world looks to be one.

   I feel intimacy with all of it.

   I feel I could go anywhere just now.

   I don't feel the distance between countries.

   All countries look alike although they have been partitioned and have their own cultures and policies.

   Some places are now at war and others at peace and some places are poor and others are wealthy, aren't they?

4. Without national boundaries, not an end but continuity is seen between Europe and the Middle East.

**"Continents"**

5. Not countries but continents come to our eyes.

6. The shapes of the continents are interesting.

   All continents fit each other to make a big continent.

   Once upon a time, all continents were connected, people say.

   The phrase:

   "All people are brothers and sisters" comes to mind.

7. The Earth is made of land and sea.

   The oceans look much bigger than the land. .

   The Pacific Ocean is huge.

   Is this how the Arabian Peninsula and the Mediterranean Sea were always shaped?

8. Some parts of today's land may disappear in the future due to global warming, and the area of seas and oceans may become larger.

   Environmental problems should be discussed more as the world is connected into one.

**"Six billion [sic][107*] people and not for human beings alone"**

9. Are people living on small islands in an ocean? If yes, how are they living? In each place, many kinds of people are living different lives. How wonderful it is for those people to live at the same time on the same Earth with their respective norms and standards.

10. The world population has exceeded six billion.[108*]

11. This Earth belongs not only to human beings but also to animals and other life.

12. The world is certainly big, but the universe is much bigger.

**"My existence and my worry"**

13. Here I am living in this universe, just like one little speck of dust, worrying and struggling. The whole idea seems comical in a way.

    "I" could be dotted on this map only with a precision instrument. It's pitiably cute for a human being to strive over such a tiny life. My worry seems to be a very small matter.

---

107* As of the beginning of the 2000s when the original article was written. Now (2023), it should be replaced with "eight billion."

108* Ditto.

154

**"Part of a whole"**

14. All countries are on this one planet and connected by land and sea.
    The world is linked together.
15. Japan is small and part of the large world.
16. This map presents only the essential framework of the world before us.
    Why has what used to be one come apart?

**"Poverty"**

17. How many people are living happy lives with sufficient living standards now?
    The gap between the rich and the poor is huge even though we are on the same Earth: Why?
18. Japan is full of goods but there are also poor countries in the same Asia.
    Every day, thousands of thousands starve to death.
19. Somewhere far from or very near to us, many people on this map have no security, not even the assurance of a daily meal.
    In Japan, too, some people are homeless and don't know where their next meal is coming from.

**"Wars & conflicts"**

20. We have wars and troubles right now somewhere.
    Iraq is at war[109*] and many other places I don't know have poor security.
    Many people have become victims.

**"National boundaries & states"**

21. There might be no wars without national boundaries.
    Nationality changes and laws and institutions all become different once you cross a national border even by one centimetre.
22. There may be no need for us to have the unit of a "state." Because of a "state," nationalism sprouts, and the distance between "our" country and "their" countries is born while all states are on the same continents of the Earth. This has produced wars, discrimination, poverty, etc. In terms of social welfare, we think of that of our own country even though society is composed of all continents on this Earth.
23. We call people from other countries "*Gaijin*" (Foreigners. strangers, aliens, or outsiders). This is a discriminatory term or a carryover from 400 years of national seclusion. It sounds as if we were rejecting them.
24. It is necessary to know about Japan if we want to bring up true "international men and women."
25. The world is one. The Japanese, the Americans, and the people of Africa are really all one race: the human race...race is not important. I would like to say so. But it would be whitewashing. The culture and religion of each district and country, which have been built up through history, have become sources of trouble, produced many victims, making mutual understanding among people difficult. Seeing and hearing recent Iraqi related

---

109*  The original article of this chapter was written in early years of the 2000s.

155

incidents and news. I have been convinced that I, a pacifist, and those who want to "solve" the problem with war and force have no common words and could never reach a mutual understanding. The only commonality among us is the simple fact that we are all human beings who are living on this map. There is nothing else to share. Everything else is quite different

**"Perception"**

26. The Japanese do not seem to be proud of being part of Asia although we are part of Asia. They yearn for the character of Europe of which they have nothing in common (not hair colour, skin colour or temperament). Japanese are attracted even by the sound of the word, "Europe" itself. How about other Asian people? Do they also revere Europe? How do the Europeans perceive Asians? What does Japan, a small country, look like in their eyes?

**"Modesty"**

27. The world I know is just part of the whole.

I only know something about tiny Japan.

There are many places and countries that I don't know.

With this poor knowledge can I study International Social Work?

28. There are people live in totally different environments and have different customs. It's important to know of them.

29. The world is big and each country has various problems which I really know nothing about. I wish I had taken an interest in them.

It's necessary to see various countries and places.

30. Watching the news about Iraqi problems, I am little concerned with them, while they have happened within a distance of only ten centimetres on this small scale of a map.

What percentage of people in this world lack basic necessities--clothes, food, and houses? Even now many people are involved in wars and violent incidents somewhere. But I don't know nor do try to know even where. I am only concerned with something around myself. I feel I am very a small person.

**"Aspiration"**

31. I live in a small city in the small country of Japan and there's a lot that I haven't seen, yet I would like to see and know more.

I want to see as many people as possible.

32. I want to get out of this small Japan into the big world to have various experiences.

**Other comments**

33. Europe seems smaller than I thought. It is unbelievable for me that countries in such a small Europe had the power to divide the world.

34. The closeness between countries does not depend on the distance.

35. All the talk about globalization seems trivial when we look at tiny maps like these.

36. Until when will Japan be ruled and controlled by the United States even while we are located far from each other? I feel uneasy.

37. I wonder if the world will rain ruin on itself someday.

## Comments about the second map [MAP b]

**"Narrow, cramped and closed"**

1. Jumbled.

   How narrow the world is!

   Only with national boundaries added, the world looks smaller. I am choked with being cramped.

   Crowded.

   Closed.

2. The feeling of liberation in the first map has gone somewhere.
3. The map with national boundaries seems unnatural. The map without them seemed better.
4. I am somehow sad with this map, particularly after looking at the first map.
5. Dotted lines are unpleasant.

   They look like a patchwork of dinosaur skeletons.

**"Piecemeal"**

6. The world has been divided into small bits and each of them has been fenced. Seas are also divided into territorial waters. The world is more fragmented.
7. If people live in a smaller divided space, the world they think of also becomes smaller.
8. The world looked to be one in the first map but it's now firmly divided.

   The world looks like not one but an aggregate of various countries.

**"National boundaries"**

9. In this map, there are national boundaries.

   We are accustomed to this map with national boundaries that were artificially drawn.

   Everything would differ if we went a step beyond a national boundary.

   You would feel foreign unreasonably.

10. I feel the distance between countries.
11. What is a national boundary? How was it decided? What was used as a basis for the decision?

    What meaning was there in drawing the line?

    Shapes of countries have been drawn by the hands of men/women, except for island countries like Japan.

12. Why did shapes become so complicated as these?

    Why aren't the lines straight? It would be easier to handle this with straight lines.

13. It is apparent that the straight border lines were drawn artificially by people.
14. The national boundary lines in Africa are frightening, and tell the history of competing European countries' invasions.

    I feel very sad. Borderlines in Africa make me disconsolate.

    I learned in schools that many of the national boundaries in Africa were decided by European and American countries without consideration for tribal or religious relations.

    Thinking about whose colony each country was, I feel the cruelty afresh One nation should never rule another.

15. How different are the people on both sides near a border?

157

16. On one hand, there are many people who aren't convinced by the present map lines, and on the other hand, there are many people who don't care about them.

17. The meaning of national boundaries would be different in Japan, an island country, and in Europe and America where many countries are closely located.

    How do people feel in a country immediately neighbouring other countries?

    How do people feel with people on the other side of the borderline whose language, food, and buildings are different?

**"A state"**

18. National boundaries expel the view of continents.

    The world grasped by a state is presented rather than the world by a continent.

    The relationship between states, being good or bad, comes to the fore.

19. With national boundaries, human beings made distances between themselves by themselves.

    People became unable to come and go freely anymore. Always distinguishing you from others and putting them far from you, people won't walk toward each other.

    The strong insistence of a state drives people not to cross dotted lines and to accept what exists only within the border to reject all others from horror.

20. Without national boundaries, we think of "people living in the same world." With national boundaries, we distinguish people of our country and people of other countries, e.g., Japanese and foreigners.

**"Wars, conflicts, struggles, competition and hatred"**

21. It's strange—being divided by dotted lines, states now start insisting on their rights and territories.

    Many countries competed, hated, and repeatedly fought each other. It's too sad when they are neighbours.

    National boundaries remind me of many wars over land. I heard many tragic stories about national borders.

22. Seeing wars in the past and territory disputes today, human beings seem to be creatures that always want to expand their territories. For me what's important is how more people become happier rather than how more territory is obtained. The size of a country is not the determinant of affluence.

23. Human beings have repeated wars over national boundaries for many centuries. Japan also invaded other countries before and during World War II to expand its territory, but I cannot help wondering why people stick to their national boundaries. territories and interests. People will probably continue fighting for them forever.

24. People have been afflicted by the national boundaries that they made, haven't they?

    Many people have suffered with national boundaries.

25. It does not seem to be important to me which countries are strong and which countries are weak. The world looks flat: I don't feel the difference between rich and poor on this map.

26. In the name of religion, people killed each other. Is belief in a religion justifiable for killing people?

**"The shape and the size of countries"**

27. Big countries, small countries, and countries like particles.

    A country like a dot or a huge country like Russia is equally a country.

    The size of the land does not parallel the affluence of the country.

28. I am tempted to put in colours.

29. There are many countries in Africa.

    There are more countries in the Southern Hemisphere.

    The Southern Hemisphere contains many "developing countries" in it.

30. Racial discrimination is firmly rooted but countries of Blacks, Whites, and Yellows are roughly the same in number and area. It is unreasonable and unfair to discriminate against each other.

**"Visualization"**

31. Each country is now spending time at its own pace, ways, and values.

32. The actual lives of people, e.g. special products, folk costumes, and animals, can be visualized.

    I can imagine the politics, laws, cultures, religions, and languages in each country.

    What do people eat for breakfast in each area surrounded by lines? The difference in characters by region interests me.

33. Since cultures, races, and others differ, the world may be interesting, but in reality, the differences have sadly caused conflicts.

**"Aspiration"**

34. I have been to some countries but haven't been to many.

    I have started thinking that I want to go this country or that island.

    I would like to travel to many places.

**"Erasing national boundaries"**

35. Lines of national boundaries are obstacles.

    I think national boundaries are unnecessary. Their value has been disappearing in this time of internationalization, globalization, and the information society.

36. Various new phenomena beyond national boundaries have been occurring, e.g., the destruction of nature.

    National boundaries have reached a limit today. We have to strive for the solution of the problems on a global scale.

37. I wish all these lines would vanish someday from this world.

38. What if there were no national boundaries? I am curious.

    I am fearful. I have a hunch that the worst thing would happen.

39. Dotted lines cannot be erased so easily. They seem to have existed from the old days.

40. The problem for us is how to overcome the concept of a "state."

**Other comments**

41. Besides national boundaries, many invisible borders have not been shown here in the world. Human beings are creatures that want to create "borders" from ancient times.

42. Many common problems exist within each dotted line such as the gap between the

extremely rich and poor and wars and racial conflicts.

43. It is great that English is the common language of the world. But I wonder if it is good or not for all people to be able to speak English.

# Epilogue

## The reason for this publication

Discussion held in Part I of this book was at the conceptual level. The book was originally compiled and directed towards leading veteran international social work theorists, researchers, educators, and practitioners around the world. This new International Social Work, however, ought not to interest or be accepted among most of them and their followers, who are based on the equation "social work = Western-rooted (professional) social work." That is fine. The author truly respects them and their international social work.

The author's intention in this book is not the redefinition and the reconstruction of their international social work, but the construction of a new international social work. The newly-constructed International Social Work is that of all eight billion people in the world. It concerns them equally, and their wellbeing, difficulties, and problems in life, i.e., "social work needs" in the words of Western-rooted social work. Western-rooted (professional) social work has served and will be able to serve only part of them, in quality and quantity.

## A few clues to understand the new International Social Work

Through test discussions, lectures, and reading in the process of writing, editing, reviewing, and printing, the new International Social Work found newcomers to its field to be interested in it and to easily understand and accept it when the following few clues were given.

1. Its locational relation to Western-rooted professional social work: The new International Social Work is located outside Western-rooted (professional) social work while embracing it as described above (cf. p.165). The new International Social Work is not based on the equation that 'social work' is equal to 'Western-rooted social work,' which was assumed to be born through the industrialization, at the end of 19th century, or after "charity." Otherwise, the overwhelming majority of people would be left outside social work. International Social Work must have affinity with and be coexistent with all kinds of social work, not only Western-rooted (professional) social work. Most of those kinds of social work do not or may not, of course, use the term "social work", particularly in English, for

themselves.

2. Its standing position in relation to sovereign nations: It is also located outside sovereign states while always keeping them in mind. Social work had supposedly existed before national borders, in consciousness or in reality, and gradually shifted its functions to states, eventually to be embraced by them. Part of the social work spun off from them as international social work, to become an entity outside their sovereignty while remaining within social work. International social work views matters from and for the whole, not from and for respective national interests. Social work itself resumed the view before national borders with such International Social Work included in it (Chapter 3 2.7 (2)).

3. The explicit distinction between social work and social workers: What the new International Social Work discussed was not on social workers and their activities/functions, but on social work, which was the subject of our research. Also, the distinction has been consciously made between (professional) social workers and those who do social work regardless of whether it is their occupation or not.

In addition, to understand the new International Social Work, the following basic preparative knowledge (primitive theories beyond the social work discipline and simple statistical facts) is necessary: 1. the birth, growth, and change of nation (sovereign) states and national borders; 2. the relation among nationalism, internationalism, and cosmopolitanism; 3. language issues and policies; 4. the geographic distribution and the diversity of people; 5. the geographic distribution of (professional) social workers on the Earth; 6. the diversity of societies by industrialization and education; 7. Wars and social work; 8. various other knowledge.

## Some dilemmas to be tackled—the expectation to future generations

The discussion of this book has been uncompleted. Some discussion has been expected to the next generations.

1. While International Social Work was defined to free it from bonds to sovereign nations, those who practice it have not been freed from nationalities. How to accommodate this dilemma? To become a no-

nationality person for oneself is usually not allowed, nor is it easy.

2. While the orientation to "welfare world" after "welfare state" was proposed, the theoretical development of its idea and/or its alternative ideas in this half a century has not been reviewed nor considered in this book.

3. While the construction of International Social Work of all people on this earth would be possible only being based on all kinds of indigenous (cf. Ch.3 1.1 (2) footnote 49) social work in the world, those indigenous kinds of social work have not been conscientized, discussed, and constructed as social work yet. The only social work that has been revealed in a systematized tangible form today is Western-rooted (professional) social work.

4. The 'value' (human rights, social justice, democracy, etc.) which the international social work of the Western-rooted (professional) social work takes for granted was replaced with 'the way of viewing matters' in the new International Social Work. This new International Social Work aims to eliminate or minimize the value factor as much as possible for (international) social work to be a scientific discipline and deal with or skirt around both the current dysfunctional United Nations and the conflict-ridden international society. However, if e.g., "the view from the outside (of nation states)" is thrown in to fill the content of 'the way of viewing matters,' it might be still deemed to be a value.

5. This book attempted to construct a new international social work, but the product is far from what the author dreamed of. This book started with the literature review of international social work of Western-rooted professional social work (and only that by English-speaking people), listened to people from the non-Western, non-English world, and made a new proposal applying a kind of 'a theory of the State.' But the 'state theory' was also Western-rooted. In this sense, this new International Social Work is also a Western-rooted product, and not one that exceeds the understandings and achievements of the Western world, except that the author is from a non-Western, non-English-speaking world and that a little heavier respect was given to the non-Western world. No matter how far Sun Wu-K'ung flew, he could not escape from the palm of the Buddha's hand. Someday someone will hopefully construct the real international

---

\*     The title of the book has intentionally adopted "of" neither "for" nor "by".

social work based on and applicable for the whole population, or all societies and countries and regions, on this planet.

At last, the most important inquiry on practice now is how the practices (including policy, etc.) that readers have been currently engaged in under the Western-rooted (professional) social work would alter or not alter if they take this new interpretation of international social work. We expect our future generations to obtain the proof positive and its record. Meanwhile, if we suppose that this International Social Work must spread into the mainstream social work community, one strategically effective route might be how to connect and lead 'international social work (A)' to 'international social work (B)' (Chapter 3 2.2 (1)).

Is the concept of international social work—and thus, social work—effective without an understanding of this book, in the current war-ridden world?

## Deciphering the new International Social Work

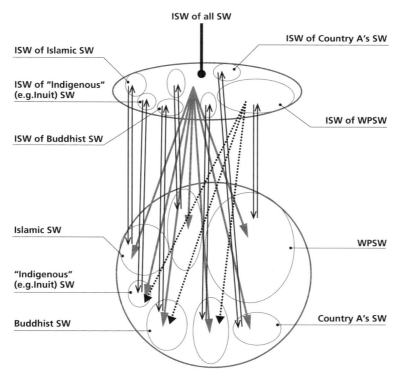

**SW:** Social work
**NSW:** 'National' social work
**ISW:** International Social Work
**WPSW:** Western-rooted professional social work

1. International social work of Western-rooted professional social work can serve only part of the whole.

2. International social work of the social work which was born and grew in a certain culture and society could work effectively in that culture and society, but couldn't in the different culture and society on which it is not based.

3. The new International Social Work has affinity for all social work and compatibility in all cultures and societies.

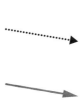

165

**Part II**

# The Foundations Underpinning the Construction

Masateru Higashida
Hiromi Satoh
Taichi Uchio
Ayako Sasaki
Takeshi Sato-Daimon
Josef Gohori

# Chapter Five

## Birth, Growth and Transformation of Borders and Nation-states

### Masateru Higashida, Hiromi Satoh

Look at a globe or a map. You will see that nations are separated by "lines" that appear as if they are indisputable and objective "facts." News programs, documentaries and films[1] sometimes show people confronting the stark realities of borders and experiencing immense difficulties in crossing them. Borders literally denote the boundaries that separate two or more nations and have been politically and socially constructed throughout history by human beings. However, these seemingly simple and self-evident boundaries incorporate complex aspects that indicate why it is crucial to question their underlying themes. Indeed, the interdisciplinary research on borders elucidates diverse dimensions and points of discussion. In this chapter, we will first conceptually define borders before overviewing varied aspects related to them by referencing fundamental knowledge obtained from discrete encyclopedias and introductory books on border studies (e.g. Diener & Hagen, 2012, 2024). We will then briefly trace the history of borders and discuss events and issues related to them. Based on these preliminary queries, we will present the perspectives illuminated by multifarious discourses on borders. This chapter aims to present inquiries conducted on borders and present the conceptual insights attained on the topic rather than to scrutinize or detail particular historical episodes or discourses. Therefore, some parts of the discussion that follows may appear sketchy.

## 1. What is a Border?

Lexically, a border denotes a boundary line defining the territory of a state (Kitamura, 1977, p. 54). It has been defined as "[a] boundary line established

---

1    For instance, the movie 'The Syrian Bride' directed by Eran Riklis is set in the Golan Heights and depicts the difficulties associated with crossing borders.

by a state, or a region, to define its spatial extent" (Mayhew, 2009, p. 56). More specifically, a border may be described as "[a] form of BOUNDARY associated with the rise of the modern NATION-STATE and the establishment of an inter-state GEOPOLITICAL order" (Sparke, 2009, p. 52).

These definitions clarify that borders can only be appropriately described if we understand several related key concepts underpinning them, including state, boundaries or borderlines, frontier and sovereignty (Newman, 2017). A state or sovereign state is defined as "[a] territorial unit with clearly defined and internationally accepted boundaries, an independent existence, and responsibility for its own legal system" (Mayhew, 1997, p. 471). A modern state comprises three elements: a nation or a group of people who have an experience of belonging to the state, a territory that is demarcated by borders and sovereignty or autonomy in self-government.

The state of sovereignty is identified "as the exercise of supreme authority and control over a distinct territory and its corresponding population and resources" (Diener & Hagen, 2024, p. 6). The term boundary may be defined in several ways according to many facets;[2] however, it may be described in direct relation to borders as "[a] line around the edge of an area: a perimeter. …a boundary is a strict line of separation between two (at least theoretically) distinct territories, where a border is an area of interaction and gradual division between two separate political entities" (Mayhew, 2009, p. 57). Conceptually, a borderland indicates a territorial range surrounding the boundary line. Apart from these notions and terms, the word frontier is used to denote indeterminate peripheral zones or cross-border regions.

## 2. Some Aspects of Borders

Borders may seem like undeniable physical boundaries separating nations, but they are studied from various perspectives. This section outlines the findings of contemporary interdisciplinary studies to convey a foundational understanding of borders and to overview their general forms, functions and

---

2      For example, '[a] point or limit that distinguishes one social system or group from another and identifies and regulates who may participate in it' (Mayhew, 2009, p. 57)

types.

Borders or boundaries are generally categorized into natural and artificial in form. Natural borders are based on ecological features such as mountains, rivers, lakes and valleys. Artificial borders include human-made objects such as walls and fences or delineate boundaries defined by latitudes and longitudes. Another example is the famous border along the 22nd parallel North between Egypt and Sudan.

Boundaries, including national borders, principally discharge the functions of creating, occupying and governing territories, including places and spaces, and to distinguish them from other territories. In other words, boundaries separate "the social, political, economic, or cultural meanings of one geographic space from another" (Diener & Hagen, 2012, p. 5). Further, borders function as permeable filters: they allow the transfer of people and goods across them but such movements may be directionally asymmetrical and could vary depending on the prevailing political and social situations (Diener & Hagen, 2012, 2024; Longo, 2018).

Interactions between nations at borders are conceptually categorized into four types (Martinez, 1994). First, "alienated borderlands" are extremely closed and are exemplified by political and military tensions. Second, "coexistent borderlands" indicate that limited agreements are possible but long-term cooperation is unexpected for political or military reasons. Third, "interdependent borderlands" occur in places where open negotiations and trade are conducted to the extent that they do not harm national interests. Finally, "integrated borderlands" may emerge where all barriers to cross-border exchanges are removed and a shared identity that transcends culture may be formed.

Additionally, interdisciplinary academic discussions exist on diverse border-related aspects. In particular, certain interdisciplinary initiatives have been introduced: for instance, Border Studies and Borderland Studies (Diener & Hagen, 2012, 2024; Strassoldo & Bort, 2000). Researchers and institutions with diverse academic backgrounds such as international relations, international politics, geography, sociology, linguistics and anthropology, among others, have used distinctive lenses to research borders. For example, the perspective of social constructivism considers reality to be socially constructed through interactions among individuals. Therefore, discourses describing borders as objective facts are critically analyzed or deconstructed by social constructivist scholars (Lybecker et al., 2018). This chapter does not introduce each viewpoint in detail. However, it does emphasize the need to contemplate borders from multifaceted perspectives. Borders must also be regarded as dynamic processes that entail the engagement of varied actors and not merely as static and objective facts. In other words, it is important to understand the political and social functions of borders and even to apprehend the process of boundary drawing, rather than just to perceive the fixed and physical boundaries that exist at a certain point in time (Diener & Hagen, 2012, 2024). The next section overviews the history of borders as a prerequisite for the comprehension of such issues.

## 3. The History of Borders: Their Birth, Development, Change and Disappearance?

A range of discourses can be observed on the history of borders. The dominant narrative describes that boundary-making began in Europe and spread to many other areas across the world through colonization. However, some researchers (e.g. Iwashita, 2015) have posited the necessity of attending to the history and discourses rooted in the West as well as to the diverse processes involving people and society. This section will examine some border-related genealogies.

Many boundaries across the world were formed gradually and over time. The spectrum of frontiers and boundaries has historically been depicted in every form of administration, including city-states, empires and nation-states, indicating a complex rather than linear process (Longo, 2018). On the one hand, humans or the societies they have constituted, have drawn boundaries and categorized phenomena everywhere since antiquity. Such drawing of lines on land and territory is directly linked to the concept of delineating borders (Strassoldo & Bort, 2000). Meanwhile, when human habitation (ecumene) was limited in prehistoric times, there was no felt need to distinguish boundaries with fixed lines. Frontiers were then expanded substantially even without being named (Takagi, 2013).

The origins of the modern state system[3] are believed to be traced in pre-modern Europe to at least as far back as the 11th century. The initial construction of the state was grounded in the feudal system and the structure differed significantly from modern states. Researchers have indicated that by the late Middle Ages (around the 14th to 15th centuries) "the modern state system began to form... as centralized governments exercised increasing political and economic control over defined territories" (Diener & Hagen, 2024, p. 38). Ambiguous areas such as overlapping boundaries and peripheries remained as frontiers in each state (Diener & Hagen, 2012, 2024).

The Peace of Westphalia, concluded in 1648 in the western section of the Holy Roman Empire, is symbolic in mainstream discourses on the formation of modern borders. This peace treaty followed the Thirty Years' War, which began in Europe in 1618 because of religious conflicts between Catholics and Protestants. Some scholars have explained that the sovereign states that negotiated this treaty had produced long-standing order in the European region because they were promised the right to choose among the myriad Christian sects that existed within their borders and were conferred the right to form alliances (Diener & Hagen, 2012, 2024). However, recent studies in international relations and international sociology suggest that the discourse on the modern international order born out of the Peace of Westphalia is "a story" or a myth constructed through the lens of Anglo-American international relations and international law. Thus, the dominant narrative is "mythologized" (Kawamura, 2016).[4]

Further, scholars have posited that the concept of sovereignty is itself not fixed. Borders have gradually diverged from their primary function "as a buffer-line dividing states from each other, contra inter-state war or invasion" in the early period of the Westphalian systems to their current avatar as "filtration-sites, protecting states from the movement of people" (Longo,

---

3   The concept flourished over long periods as a dominant political construct even in ancient city-states (Diener & Hagen, 2012, 2024).

4   In particular, the publication in 1814 of a history of international law in Europe from the Peace of Westphalia to the Congress of Vienna (*'Histoire des Progres du Droit de Gens en Europe depuis la Paix de Westphalie jusqu'au Congres de Vienne'*) by the American scholar Henry Wheaton, described the treaty as the beginning of modern international law. This account is believed to have contributed to the stated mythologization (Kawamura, 2016, p.173).

2018, p. 5). In addition, scholars have indicated the impermanence of the established boundaries and have noted that attempts were made later to stabilize borders (Strassoldo & Bort, 2000).

Woodrow Wilson, the 28th President of the United States, announced the Fourteen Points, a statement of principles for peace after World War I. While having different contexts with the Peace of Westphalia, they both address sovereignty[5] (Davis, 2016). The Fourteen Points also include principles related to self-determination. Emphasizing ethnic identity and highlighting territorial reorganization might have influenced the formation of nations based on ethnic majority, albeit the complex historical process (Diener & Hagen, 2012, 2024).

In parallel, European states advanced their borders through colonization, which entailed border formations in other regions. In literal terms, these colonizing "states began mapping and reorganizing those lands to conform to the territorial state model that was emerging back in Europe" (Diener & Hagen, 2024, p. 46). The first such attempt dates historically to the Treaty of Tordesillas in 1494, after which colonization was promoted by the European powers. Colonization began in Africa with the opening of the Indian route in the 15th century and the undertaking of religious activities by Christian missionaries. The slave trade was subsequently implemented in the 16th century and the foundations of economic exploitation by chartered companies were laid. Expeditions by explorers for inland development resulted in large-scale governance by European states from the late 18th to the 19th centuries (Diener & Hagen, 2012, 2024; Miyamoto & Matsuda, 2018). The Scramble for Africa, including its invasion and division, commenced explicitly at the Berlin Conference in 1885.

Global transformations were affected when World War II ended in 1945 and independence movements gained traction in Asian and African countries. However, colonial boundary lines remained almost unchanged and were inherited as national borders because numerous nations resisted the redrawing of their borders (Diener & Hagen, 2012, 2024). As time passed, political and academic discussions about frontiers and borders in Europe

---

5    For example, Articles 5, 7 and 12 of the Fourteen Points.

were refocused after the fall of the Berlin Wall in November 1989. After the Cold War, federal republics attained independence because of the dissolution of the Soviet Union; new administrative divisions in the federation became national borders and the functions of other boundaries also changed (Strassoldo & Bort, 2000).

Globalization has caused wide-ranging information, technological innovation and norms to transcend national borders and political affairs related to the control are observed even in outer space (Diener & Hagen, 2012, 2024; Longo, 2018). The state of borderlessness has been discussed at regional levels in conjunction with the organizational process of supranationalism, as seen in the integration of the European Union (Diener & Hagen, 2012, 2024; Moravcsik, 1998; Takagi, 2013). Such developments have significantly changed the positioning of borders; however, they do not imply the dissolution or imminent disappearance of national borders (Longo, 2018). Rather, the birth of a "borderless" space simultaneously creates new borders outside that space: for instance, the exclusion of foreigners from that space, while also highlighting its distinction from other boundaries[6] (Iwashita, 2015).

Historically, borders have been drawn, erased and redrawn frequently during transitions between sovereign states, often due to the hegemonic actions of a powerful sovereign state. However, such actions do not imply a return to a world without borders. The process of creating a border is likely to be irreversible: once a border line is drawn on a map, it cannot be erased. It is almost a fallacy to assume a world without any political divisions in the contemporary context, but we can probe the characteristics of discrete types of borders (Longo, 2018).

A growing interest is currently observed in the concept of border management in the real world[7] (Diener & Hagen, 2012, 2024; Takagi, 2013). In particular, countries in the West have attempted to institute joint border management initiatives using digitalization and technologies, including big

---

6　As an example, while borderlessness has increased within the EU and border permeability has increased, it 'has been accompanied by a hardening of the borders between EU and non-EU states' (Deiner & Hagan, 2012: p. 109).

7　Researchers also state that '[t]hese "transnational social fields" can be organized to facilitate collective action beyond the traditional nation-state system' (Deiner & Hagan, 2012: p. 86).

data, to act against illegal immigrants and refugees (Longo, 2018). Events and issues related to borders must thus be examined in the context of such a changing world.

## 4. Problems and Issues Related to Borders

Diverse dimensions may be noted in the associations between national borders and the various issues emanating from them (Strassoldo & Bort, 2000). This section will address both macro-level issues between nations and the relationships that confront individuals vis-à-vis international social issues. First, at the international level, two or more countries that share borders can dispute the locations of borders and the territories under their purview. Such problems are labeled "border issues" and can lead to wars or armed invasions. Such disputes sometimes become apparent when clear economic or military benefits can accrue to the involved nations from peripheral areas including undetermined boundaries. Clashes can also arise over boundaries formed without ethnic and cultural considerations or over annexed boundaries (Takagi, 2011).

Second, we must focus on people who confront border issues and populations that do not fit within the framework of borders and nations. In other words, the standpoint, positionality and experiences of the concerned people are important. For example, scholars may explore the intersections of the transnational identities, lived experiences and activities of such stateless populations. Typically, this state of deterritorialization is exemplified by experiences related to immigration, refugees and international adoptions, among others, where people must transcend borders. Scholars must also contemplate the reconsideration of the self-determination rights of the (ethnically) marginalized (Diener & Hagen, 2012, 2024). Moreover, research conducted in the vast region of Southeast Asia (Zomia), has confirmed the existence of people who continue to distance themselves from a specific state (Scott, 2009). The existence of such people underscores the significance of the perspectives and experiences of people over the viewpoints or dominant discourses of nations apropos their frontier territories.

In broader terms, many scholars contend the need to address discrete global cross-border social issues such as poverty, human trafficking, child protection and welfare, wars and civil wars, forced migration, public health issues, themes related to women and gender, natural /human-made disasters and climate change (Healy & Thomas, 2021).

## 5. Summary and Implications

This chapter outlined the definitions, types, functions and history of borders and overviewed other associated issues and related concepts. The findings of this inquiry suggest that examining borders and even their transgressions can enable the reconsideration of inter-state relations as well as human existence itself. We must recognize that borders incorporate dimensions that "center on fantasies of exclusion and binary logics of interiority/exteriority, us/them, identity/difference" (Longo, 2018, p. 1). Nevertheless, we can also employ a critical and multifaceted perspective[8] to rethink borders and nations and discuss the world. Such outlooks envision and enable new horizons of discussion that do not necessarily rely only on the knowledge accumulated in the West[9]. Scholars have demonstrated such possibilities by postulating the necessity of disciplines such as "border studies" (Iwashita, 2015).

---

8     Longo (2018) exemplifies a sociological and interpretive perspective of borders, exhibiting a normative viewpoint. The meanings and intentions of such perspectives do not necessarily align with Tatsuru Akimoto's (Part I) suggestions about the ways of viewing matters and compound eyes in international social work.

9     For example, boundary studies have been stated to require the following elements. First, scholars must collect a more wide-ranging set of cases from around the world, for instance, from Asia and Africa. Second, Western discussions should not be dismissed as inapt to the realities of, for example, Eurasia. Instead, scholars should enhance interactions and disseminate their re-examinations of Western theories (Iwashita, 2015, p. 176).

## Acknowledgements

This work was supported by JSPS KAKENHI Grant Number JP23H00900.

## References

Davis, M. P. (2016). The historical and theoretical evolution of collective security (including in the Baltic Sea region) from the 1648 Westphalia Peace to Woodrow Wilson's 1920 League of Nations. *Security and Defence Quarterly, 10*(1), 75–98.

Diener, A. C. & Hagen, J. (2012). *Borders: A Very Short Introduction.* Oxford University Press.

Diener, A. C. & Hagen, J. (2024). *Borders: A Very Short Introduction, 2nd edition.* Oxford University Press.

Healy, L. M. & Thomas, R. L. (2021). *International Social Work: Professional Action in an Interdependent World, 3rd edition.* Oxford University Press.

Iwashita, A. (2015). 解説 世界を変えるボーダースタディーズ (F. Kawakubo, Trans.). In Diener, A. C. & Hagen, J. (Eds.). Borders: A Very Short Introduction（境界から世界を見る―ボーダースタディーズ入門）(pp.173–182). Iwanami Shoten. (in Japanese)

Kawamura, S. (2016). 近代ヨーロッパ秩序の萌芽―ウェストファリア神話以前における国際関係思想の展開. In Yamashita, N., Ataka, H. & Shibasaki, A. (Eds.). ウェストファリア史観を脱構築する―歴史記述としての国際関係論 (pp.172–185). Nakanishiya Shuppan. (in Japanese)

Kitamura, Y. (1977). 人口分布と文化地域. In Ogawa, I. & Ide, S. (Eds.). 地理学要説 - 地理学における地域研究 (pp.17–57). Bunka-shobo Hakubun-sha. (in Japanese)

Longo, M. (2018). *The Politics of Borders: Sovereignty, Security, and the Citizen After 9/11.* Cambridge University Press.

Lybecker, D. L., McBeth, M. K., Brewer, A. M. & De Sy, C. (2018). The social construction of a border: The US–Canada border. *Journal of Borderlands Studies, 33*(4), 529–547.

Martinez, O. J. (1994). The dynamics of border interaction: New approaches to border analysis. In Schofield, C. H. (Ed.). *Global Boundaries* (pp.1–15). Routledge.

Mayhew, S. (1997). State. In Mayhew, S. (Ed.). *A Dictionary of Geography, 2nd Edition.* Oxford University Press.

Mayhew, S. (2009). Boundary. In Mayhew, S. (Ed.). *A Dictionary of Geography, 4th Edition.* Oxford University Press.

Miyamoto, M. & Matsuda, M. (2018). 新書アフリカ史　改訂版. Kodansha. (in Japanese)

Moravcsik, A. (1998). *The Choice for Europe: Social Purpose and State Power from Messina to Maastricht.* Cornell University Press.

Newman, D. (2017). Borders, boundaries, and borderlands. In Richardson, D., Castree, N., Goodchild, M. F., Kobayashi, A., Liu, W. & Marston, R. A. (Eds.). *International Encyclopedia of Geography: People, the Earth, Environment and Technology.* John Wiley & Sons. https://doi.org/10.1002/9781118786352.wbieg1039.

Scott, J. C. (2009). *The Art of Not Being Governed: An Anarchist History of Upland Southeast Asia.* Yale University Press.

Sparke, M. (2009). Border. In Gregory, D., Johnston, R., Pratt, G., Watts, M., Whatmore, S. (Eds.). *The Dictionary of Human Geography, 5th edition* (pp.52–53). Blackwell Publishing.

Strassoldo, R. & Bort, E. (2000). National border relations. In Borgatta, E. F. & Montgomery, R. J. V. (Eds.). *Encyclopedia of Sociology* (pp.1931–1939). Macmillan.

Takagi, A. (2011). 世界の境界線. *Chizu Joho, 30*(4), 12–19. (in Japanese)

Takagi, A. (2013). 境界. In Human Geographical Society of Japan (Ed.). 人文地理学事典 (pp. 108–109). Maruzen Publishing. (in Japanese)

# Chapter Six

## Nationalism, Internationalism and Cosmopolitanism: A Comparative Analysis of the Concepts

### Taichi Uchio

Political organizations have evolved to foster a sense of unity among their members, even in the absence of direct interpersonal connections. This evolution, which has been particularly prominent in the pre-modern era, has been accompanied by a transition from societies composed of small familial bands to larger tribal societies. This period also witnessed the emergence of chiefdoms, which are characterized by the dominance of specific kinship groups. Over time, the nation-state emerged as a socially stratified, centralized political entity that uniquely possesses legal authority over the armed forces. Within the nation-state, individuals' rights and responsibilities are defined by statutory laws rather than kinship ties. Moreover, nation-states are territorially bound, with individual membership typically determined by birth or parental heritage.

The nation-state asserts sovereignty over a distinct territory, fortifying a collective sense of national identity by constructing a unique national culture and historical narrative. This chapter begins with a discussion of the Peace of Westphalia in 1648[10], which created the foundational framework of the modern nation-state. This treaty marked the inception of a system of coexisting sovereign states in Europe, each defined by its territory, populace and system of governance. Over time, this system of states spread across the globe, shaping the contours of contemporary international society.

The ensuing discussion explores the themes of nationalism, internationalism and cosmopolitanism. These concepts reflect the diverse nature of national societies and the trajectory of human civilization.

---

10    The Peace of Westphalia emerged after the Thirty Years' War, spanning 1618 to 1648. This extensive conflict, which involved major European powers, was driven by religious and political motives and resulted in widespread destruction and chaos.

# 1. The Meaning of Each Term

## 1.1 Nationalism

Nationalism, as an ideology or movement, accentuates the distinct identity of a specific ethnic group or people, underscoring their cohesiveness and uniqueness within the framework of the nation-state. Nationalist ideology is intricately woven into the tapestry of the nation-state, and it is nurtured and shaped by the nation's legal system, social welfare policies, educational structures and other institutional frameworks. Moreover, a homogeneous group identity is also central to nationalism. This collective identity, which is commonly referred to using the terms "nation" or "people," is unified by shared identity markets, including lineage, language, culture and history.

Nationalist discourse strongly promotes cultural and political independence, as well as the development of an individual ethnic or national group; this process is often intimately related to power dynamics. This tendency can manifest in various forms, including the principles of national self-determination and non-interference in internal affairs, as well as the independence movements of sovereign nations. Furthermore, nationalism is critical in fostering internal integration within a nation while also differentiating the nation from external entities.

The academic discourse on nationalism is multifaceted and includes many perspectives. One of the pivotal questions in nationalism studies pertains to the origins of nationalism itself. In this context, scholars ask, "Is nationalism an extension of pre-modern societal structures or inherently a product of modernity?" This debate continues to be a subject of extensive scholarly debate and research.

Antony Smith (2010) highlights the historical persistence of peoples, positing that nationalism is deeply ingrained in pre-modern histories and traditions. Smith asserts that ethnic groups coalesce around shared historical experiences, forming the foundation of the nation-state. Conversely, Ernest Gellner (1983) perceives nationalism primarily as a product of industrialization and modernization. Gellner argues that the nation-states formed as a response to economic and societal transformations, with national consciousness emerging as a product of a new shared culture and modern education systems. Smith's theoretical framework, termed "ethnosymbolism," adopts a perennialist perspective that traces the origins of nationalism back to a time before nation-states. In stark contrast, Gellner adheres to the principles of social constructionism, treating nationalism as a social construct that has emerged out of modernity.

In addition, Benedict Anderson (1991) contributed to nationalism studies with his work *Imagined Communities*, which argues that nations are "imagined communities" within which members forge conceptual connections through shared language, history and culture despite never engaging in direct interpersonal contact. This idea contrasts sharply with the in-person interactions of pre-modern tribal societies. In contemporary nation-states, individuals rarely interact directly with their fellow citizens; instead, a collective identity of "we" is cultivated through mass media. Anderson posits that the proliferation of print technology was pivotal in expanding the collective imagination of the nation-state. The widespread dissemination of news media and literature enabled individuals to perceive distant happenings as national events, fostering their sense of belonging to the "imagined community" of the nation. This phenomenon, which became particularly pronounced in the 18th and 19th centuries, played a critical role in the genesis and evolution of national consciousness.

Additionally, in their scholarly work *The Invention of Tradition* (1982), Eric Hobsbawm and Terence Ranger present a compelling argument regarding the genesis of traditions. They challenge the conventional perception of traditions as ancient and enduring practices, instead asserting that many traditions are, in fact, creations that were "invented" in a not-so-distant past. Hobsbawm and Ranger elucidate that these invented traditions have significantly shaped national identities and have been instrumental in symbolically reinforcing the authority of royal and imperial families.

These scholars, whose works align with Ernest Gellner, predominantly support a constructionist paradigm for analyzing nationalism. This perspective holds that nations and national identities are modern constructs that have been shaped by specific socio-political contexts. In contrast, Antony Smith's perspective, which acknowledges people's agency as historical actors, presents a convincing counterpoint to the constructionist framework. Smith's approach underscores the meaningful existence of ethnic groups, whose origins predate the modern nation-state. This enduring lineage of ancestral history is an undeniable reality for many, rendering ethnic groups as indisputable entities.

Thus, the academic discourse on nationalism accommodates seemingly divergent yet possibly reconcilable perspectives. This tension reflects the complex and multifaceted nature of nationalism in the contemporary world.

## 1.2 Internationalism

The prefix "inter-" signifies "between" and denotes interactions or relationships between entities within the same domain. An example of this is the term "international," a familiar adjective in contemporary discourse. "International" is typically used to describe activities or events, such as matches or conferences, involving multiple nation-states.

Internationalism is an ideological framework that advocates for recognizing and prioritizing values and interests that bridge national and ethnic boundaries. This philosophy is rooted in the promotion of international cooperation and the cultivation of multicultural understanding through both bilateral and multilateral engagements. Bilateral cooperation focuses on strengthening ties between two nations, whereas multilateral cooperation involves building broader networks of international actors.

Distinct from nationalism, which is oriented towards national self-interest and sovereignty, internationalism acknowledges the critical role of global cooperation and interdependence. In the contemporary international climate, entities on a larger scale than the nation-state, such as international organizations, play a pivotal role. Following World War II, the United Nations and affiliated organizations fostered a system of multilateral cooperation. A significant milestone in this endeavor was the passage of the Universal Declaration of Human Rights of 1948,[11] which was a watershed moment in the establishment of a shared set of global values.

Nevertheless, critiques of the United Nations often highlight the

---

11     The preamble and articles of the Universal Declaration of Human Rights are available on United Nations Website. https://www.un.org/en/about-us/universal-declaration-of-human-rights

disproportionate influence of major world powers in decision-making processes. The permanent members of the UN Security Council (the United States, Russia, China, the United Kingdom and France), often referred to as the "P5," wield considerable power, including veto rights. This has led to instances where the nationalistic interests of these powerful states impede the practice of genuine internationalism.

Consequently, there are two contrasting perspectives on the international community. Some view it as an arena heavily shaped by power struggles between nation-states, each striving to ensure its security and maintain its authority. Others see it as a platform where cooperation is more productive than conflict. The internationalist perspective aligns with this latter viewpoint, as it advocates for a global order characterized by harmonious relations. A tangible manifestation of this ideology is the concept of human security, which prioritizes the protection and empowerment of individuals on a global scale, expanding traditional notions of national security.

Human security represents a paradigm shift from the traditional concept of national security. That is, whereas traditional national security focuses solely on territorial integrity and the protection of the population, human security prioritizes the safety, welfare and rights of individuals. Originating from the United Nations Development Program's Human Development Report (UNDP, 1994), the concept of human security constitutes a broader and more holistic approach to security. This 1994 report outlined two fundamental aspects of human security: "freedom from fear," which addresses issues such as conflict, and "freedom from want," which targets obstacles such as poverty. It posited that human security objectives could not be attained merely through military force, implying that there was a need to foster peace via developmental initiatives.

A final report issued by the Commission on Human Security (CHS, 2003) that was co-chaired by Amartya Sen and Sadako Ogata further refined and expanded on the concept of internationalism. This report underscored the necessity of both empowering and safeguarding individuals. It broadened the scope of human security to include not just military threats but also economic, health and environmental challenges, recognizing the compound nature of the risks faced by individuals in the contemporary world.

These reports advocated for a comprehensive, multi-actor approach to ensuring human security and rights, emphasizing that responsibility for this task extended beyond the nation-state. Human security, therefore, inherently involves an international commitment to safeguarding individuals to cope with the multiple threats in the modern world.[12]

## 1.3 Cosmopolitanism

The ascendancy of nation-states has been pivotal in the formation of distinct national identities. There has also been a concurrent increase in the emphasis on the necessity for a commitment to solidarity and mutual understanding that transcends national borders. This recognition is particularly pertinent in the context of global challenges that demand a more expansive perspective that transcends the confines of nation-states, prompting a reevaluation of the concept of community on a human scale. This ethos is encapsulated in the concept of "cosmopolitanism."

Derived from the ancient Greek term *"kosmopolitēs,"* cosmopolitanism combines the words *"cosmos"* (world) and *"polites"* (citizen) and literally translates to "world citizenship." Cosmopolitanism is a philosophical and ethical orientation that envisages humanity as a singular, integrated community and cuts across the traditional divisions separating various nations and cultures. When viewed through a cosmopolitan lens, individuals are perceived as part of a global polity that is bound together by universal human values and responsibilities that surpass specific national or cultural affiliations.

The contemporary discourse of cosmopolitanism has been profoundly influenced by the philosophical contributions of Immanuel Kant, who conceptualized human beings as autonomous entities capable of rational thought and moral decision-making. Kant posited that this universal capacity underpins the shared dignity of humanity, a cornerstone of cosmopolitan thought. His notion of the "right of hospitality" (Kant, 1795, Campbell Smith

---

12    In 2022, the JICA Sadako Ogata Peace and Development Institute in Japan published a re-port titled *Human Security Today,* which attempts to update this concept to reflect recent changes in society, including those precipitated by the COVID-19 pandemic. https://www.jica.go.jp/english/jica_ri/publication/booksandreports/20220331_02.html

[Tr.], 1903) epitomized this cosmopolitan ethos, and he argued that given human's shared habitation of the Earth, people should not be treated as enemies upon entering a foreign country. This principle can be interpreted as advocating for a doctrine of universal human rights that transcend national boundaries and identities.

Cosmopolitanism requires an expansive imagination akin to Kant's invocation of common human dignity and a universal legal framework that transcends national boundaries. Nevertheless, cosmopolitanism also acknowledges and engages with the variances inherent in daily human interactions. Writing in the context of the "very modern" era, Kwame Anthony Appiah (2006) further developed this concept, suggesting that cosmopolitanism is a synthesis of universalism and pluralism. While idealistic maxims such as "all humans are brothers" are appealing, they often clash with actual lived reality, where national interests predominate.[13] Appiah contends that it is feasible to respect both human universality and diversity simultaneously in pursuit of a life that is both globally oriented and respectful of regional traditions and cultures.

This interplay between Kant's and Appiah's perspectives forms a philosophical framework that is complementary to modern cosmopolitan thought. Kant emphasizes the cultivation of amicable human relationships within the shared global space of humanity, while Appiah extends this focus to the individual inhabitants of this space and their diverse cultural identities. This dual approach balances the artificial divisions created by national borders with a recognition of the intrinsic dignity and diversity of human beings.

## 2. The History of Each Term

### 2.1 The history of nationalism

The origins of nationalism are directly linked to the evolution of modern

---

13 A prominent recent example of this is the "America First" slogan which has been promoted by the Trump administration.

statehood in the 17th and 18th centuries, which coincided with the decline of feudalism and the rise of more centralized states in Europe. A technological milestone that contributed to this development was the advent of Gutenberg's printing press in the mid-15th century, which revolutionized the production of manuscripts and newspapers. The proliferation of print media was instrumental in standardizing languages and disseminating national news, which, in turn, fostered a shared identity among people and nurtured nationalist sentiments.

Key historical events such as the American Revolutionary War and the French Revolution in the late 18th century were pivotal in propagating nationalism among the broader populace. These revolutions strengthened the principles of national sovereignty and self-determination, embedding them firmly in the political consciousness of the time.

The 19th and 20th centuries, which were marked by imperialism and colonialism, cast a shadow over the narrative of nationalism. Powerful nations in Europe, along with Japan in East Asia, employed nationalism as a tool for asserting their own national identity and expanding their influence overseas. Nationalism, in this context, was often centered around a discourse of national superiority as typified by "civilizing mission,[14]" intended to bring culture and civilization to what were perceived as less-developed parts of the world. Among European powers, this "mission" was referred to as "the white man's burden,[15]" Meanwhile, Japan saw itself as the orchestrator and leader of a "Greater East Asia Co-prosperity Sphere.[16]"

However, nationalism was not solely a vehicle for domination; it also inspired resistance movements among colonized peoples. Oppressed by imperial rule, colonial populations embraced the language of nationalism to preserve their cultural identities and strive for political independence. In the post-colonial era, many nations leveraged nationalism to forge new national

---

14　The civilizing mission was a rationale for military intervention and colonization from the 15th to the 20th centuries, it was aimed at Westernizing indigenous peoples in Africa and, Latin America, etc. and elsewhere.

15　"The White Man's Burden" is the title of a poem written by English novelist and poet Rudyard Kipling in 1899, during the Philippine--American War.

16　The "Greater East Asia Co-prosperity Sphere" is a pan-Asian coalition concept that the then Empire of Japan attempted to establish.

identities, engaging in cultural revitalization, language policy reforms and historical reinterpretation.

Nationalism, as a potent political ideology, has significantly shaped historical trajectories. Its presence is also felt in the quotidian experiences of peacetime. International sporting events such as the Olympics and the World Cup serve as contemporary platforms for the peaceful expression of national pride and friendly rivalry. Through elaborate opening and closing ceremonies, these events celebrate the diverse cultures and traditions of participating nations. The enthusiasm of spectators, which is expressed through national flags and collective chants, exemplifies how nationalism can also manifest in relatively harmonious contexts. This phenomenon represents the uplifting and benign aspects of nationalism, which contrast sharply with its more controversial manifestations throughout history.

## 2.2 The history of internationalism

The evolution of internationalism, which is characterized by cross-border cooperation and solidarity, has undergone significant developments, particularly in the 19th and 20th centuries. Propelled by the socio-economic transformations of the Industrial Revolution, the concepts of international cooperation and solidarity gained momentum in the 19th century. This era witnessed a widening economic gap between wealthy capitalists and the working class, as well as a burgeoning workers' rights movement that transcended national borders and became increasingly international in character. This period also saw the expansion of colonialism and heightened inter-state competition. Amidst rising nationalist sentiment, an international peace movement emerged aimed at avoiding the ravages of war. This century also marked the advent of the women's rights movement, which challenged entrenched patriarchal systems and advocated for economic independence, suffrage and equality for women.

The two world wars of the 20th century, which resulted in a devastating human toll, further elevated the status of internationalism, particularly in the post-war era. The League of Nations, established in 1920 following World War I (1914–1918), embodied a reflection on the atrocities of war. Its core objective was to avert future conflicts through collective security, disarmament and peaceful dispute resolution. The League also tackled various social issues, including labor protections and the rights of minorities. Despite initial successes, the League's influence diminished due to a lack of participation by key nations, such as the United States, and the eventual withdrawal of others, including Japan. The outbreak of World War II (1939–1945) ultimately led to the League's dissolution in 1946. Nevertheless, its existence in the first half of the 20th century was significant for laying the groundwork of international law and the formation of the United Nations.

The United Nations, which was established following World War II, sought to create a more comprehensive and effective framework for international cooperation that could maintain global peace and security. As of today, it comprises 193 member states committed to respecting each country's sovereignty and right to self-determination, which includes non-interference in the internal affairs of other countries. The Universal Declaration of Human Rights (1948) was an early landmark achievement of the UN. This multinational agreement established certain fundamental human rights and freedoms and came to serve as the foundation for much of contemporary international human rights law.

During the Cold War, numerous international organizations embodying the values of internationalism were established despite ideological divisions. Such organizations include UNICEF, UNESCO, the United Nations High Commissioner for Refugees, the UN World Food Program and the United Nations Development Program. These organizations address a broad spectrum of global crises while promoting international cooperation on humanitarian aid, social development and cultural preservation initiatives. This era also witnessed a surge in international peace movements, catalyzed by the threat of nuclear war, which pressured governments to work towards nuclear disarmament and dialogue.

Since the end of the Cold War, conflicts have been increasingly oriented around regional, religious and ethnic disputes. Despite fortified national borders, civil protection is not always guaranteed, and, at times, the state itself may be the oppressor. It is within this historical moment that concepts such as human security, as discussed earlier, gained prominence, reflecting a nuanced understanding of safety and rights in a global context.

## 2.3 The history of cosmopolitanism

The philosophical roots of cosmopolitanism can be traced back to ancient times, notably the Greek philosopher Diogenes of the 4th century BC. When asked about where he was from, Diogenes is said to have declared himself a *"kosmopolitēs,"* (citizen of the world), signifying a nascent form of cosmopolitan thinking. This perspective gained further traction as Greek city-states (*polis*) expanded and people from diverse cultures began to interact with one another, fostering a sense of universal community, particularly among Stoic philosophers.

After the Roman Empire began to expand in the 1st century BC, it encountered an array of cultures, giving rise to a more cosmopolitan milieu. Influenced by Greek philosophy, Roman thinkers like Cicero drew on Stoic principles to begin to articulate notions of a common humanity and ethical duties that extended to all people. Cicero is also credited with provoking early discussions on human dignity.[17]

The Renaissance in medieval Europe, which lasted from the 14th to the 16th centuries, marked a resurgence of humanism and a reengagement with classical thought. This era rekindled an interest in international perspectives, particularly among intellectuals. Subsequently, the Age of Enlightenment in the 17th and 18th centuries saw the further development of cosmopolitan ideals. Philosophers such as Immanuel Kant championed universal principles of morality and envisioned a world where individuals from various nations could coexist peacefully.

However, the emergence of nation-states and the rise of nationalism in the post-modern era, especially during the two world wars, led to a decline in cosmopolitan thinking. Focus shifted towards national identities, overshadowing the values of global citizenship. However, in the aftermath of World War II, the increasing interdependence among nations and the emergence of international organizations signaled a revival of cosmopolitanism.

In the late 20th and early 21st centuries, cosmopolitanism resurfaced as a

---

17    The history of the concept of dignity is detailed in Michael Rosen's book, *Dignity: Its History and Meaning,* published in 2012 by Harvard University Press.

central topic in discussions surrounding global justice, ethics and governance. Contemporary global challenges, such as climate change and the spread of infectious diseases, have prompted a reflection on the centrality of the nation-state. These issues underscore the importance of building cosmopolitan solidarity and advocating for a global perspective that transcends national interests to address the collective challenges facing humanity.

## 3. Comparing Nationalism, Internationalism and Cosmopolitanism in the Context of Contemporary Geopolitics

In the preceding sections, we examined the historical evolution of the concepts of nationalism, internationalism and cosmopolitanism. For our final analysis, we seek to juxtapose these three ideologies and elucidate their differences in the context of the global contemporary landscape.

Since the 1990s, globalization – which is characterized by the accelerated and unimpeded flow of people, goods, money, technology and information across national borders – has become an increasingly pronounced trend. These past decades have been marked by the ascendancy of multinational corporations, which, propelled by the neoliberal agenda of the post-Cold War era, have weakened the traditional role of nation-states as the primary actors in the global economy. Simultaneously, in the realm of geopolitics, a reconstituted international community has gradually supplanted the ideological dichotomy between East and West. This community is defined by a framework of interdependence and cooperation, signaling a significant shift away from the bipolar geopolitical landscape of the Cold War. In this context, the roles of international organizations and non-governmental organizations have expanded considerably, reflecting a diversification of actors in international relations.

This transformation represents a profound challenge to the modern Westphalian system, which is predicated on the sovereignty and territorial integrity of nation-states. The advance of globalization has been accompanied by an anticipation that national borders will continue to diminish in importance. However, the contemporary geopolitical landscape, in fact, contradicts these predictions. That is, rather than eroding nationalistic sentiments, the advancement of globalization has paradoxically contributed to their resurgence. This phenomenon can be attributed to several factors.

The increase in economic immigration, while beneficial for host countries in terms of labor force supplementation, has simultaneously sparked concerns among citizens. These concerns encompass apprehension about job competition, cultural friction within communities and perceived threats to public safety. Among the majority population, such anxieties often manifest as a feeling of being threatened by an influx of immigrants, leading to societal instability.

Seizing on this sentiment, nationalist parties and movements have gained traction by advocating for strengthening national identity and imposing stricter immigration controls. This blend of nationalism with populism has resulted in policy formulations that resonate deeply with national sentiment and traditions. The power of social media in this dynamic cannot be understated; it serves as a potent catalyst for spreading patriotism and chauvinism, sometimes propelled by fake news. This propagation of nationalism and false narratives demonstrates the complexities of the post-truth era.

This resurgence of nationalism in the age of globalization can be interpreted as a counter-reaction – that is, as a backlash against the perceived invasions facilitated by global interconnectedness. This resurgence underscores the tension between global integration and the enduring allure of national identity. This dynamic reflects the nuanced and often contradictory interplay between globalizing forces and the persistent power of nationalism in shaping the contemporary socio-political landscape.

In the contemporary era, which is marked by the multifaceted challenges of globalization, internationalism emerges as a pivotal ideology advocating for enhanced international cooperation and mutual understanding. This perspective is particularly relevant in addressing the complexities engendered by increased economic migration and the resurgence of nationalism, as well as the resulting social divides.

Internationalism is a cooperative worldview that seeks to align the diverse interests of nations towards the pursuit of shared objectives. Today, an outstanding example of this approach is embodied in the United Nations Sustainable Development Goals. These 17 goals encompass a broad range of global aspirations, including poverty reduction, educational expansion, the reconciliation of environmental protection with economic growth and the fortification of international partnerships and governance structures. Achieving these objectives necessitates concerted multilateral efforts, underscoring the importance of internationalism in navigating the global landscape.

Beyond diplomacy and international policy, internationalism also plays a crucial role in mitigating the forces of nationalism within the fabric of everyday life. In societies increasingly characterized by diversity, internationalism mediates the tension between ethnocentrism and multiculturalism. It emphasizes the significance of cross-cultural understanding and education while advocating for public engagement with and appreciation for diverse cultures and values. Instruments such as multicultural education, cultural exchange programs and international symposiums serve as vital conduits for fostering dialogue and enhancing mutual comprehension among people from varied cultural backgrounds.

Furthermore, the relationship between nationalism and internationalism is not inherently antagonistic. In developed countries grappling with demographic challenges like declining birth-rates and ageing populations, nationalist concerns regarding future international competitiveness and influence have prompted a reconfiguration of national identity. In such contexts, the pursuit of multicultural coexistence and the construction of an inclusive national identity that embraces migrant children may emerge not only from liberal ideals and humanitarian considerations but also from pragmatic concerns regarding national survival and prosperity.

In the current global context, cosmopolitanism can be conceptualized as a form of transnationalism. This ideology contrasts with both nationalism and internationalism in terms of its unique approach to global interconnectedness. Nationalism is deeply entrenched in the sovereignty and distinctiveness of nation-states, and it focuses on enhancing internal cohesion and identity. Internationalism, in contrast, promotes inter-nation collaboration, with the nation-state serving as the foundational unit of global interaction.

Cosmopolitanism, however, transcends these paradigms by challenging the very notion of dividing the world into discrete nation-states. It adopts a transboundary perspective that advocates for a relative understanding of national divisions. Unlike nationalism, which concentrates on specific nations or ethnic groups, cosmopolitanism envisions a broader, more inclusive human community that transcends such demarcations. In contrast to internationalism, which is concerned with cooperation among nations and maintaining international order, cosmopolitanism places increased emphasis on individual dignity and universal human rights, surpassing the confines of national boundaries.

Although Kant's ideal of a unified government of world citizens has not become a political reality, the global economy's interconnectedness is undeniable. Political instability in one region can have far-reaching effects, disrupting international trade networks and impacting global markets. Furthermore, advancements in digital technology have enabled real-time information sharing across the globe. Participatory media platforms, including social networking services, online communities and virtual spaces, are facilitating cross-border interactions and fostering empathy, underscoring the growing significance of transnational connectivity.

Significantly, the challenges faced in the current era are increasingly global in nature. The escalating threats posed by environmental degradation, climate change and large-scale natural disasters defy unilateral solutions. These problems cannot be effectively addressed by any single country, nor can they be left solely to the discretion of government leaders, diplomats or international organizations. Rather, they demand a collective response that transcends national policies and strategies. These global challenges implicate our collective lifestyle on this planet, necessitating a cosmopolitan approach that integrates concern for the collective well-being of humanity with a recognition of our shared responsibility to preserve the world for future generations.

# 4. Conclusion

This chapter engaged in an in-depth exploration of nationalism, internationalism and cosmopolitanism, illustrating their distinct yet interconnected discourses. This comparative analysis demonstrated that these concepts fundamentally revolve around human perceptions and imaginations regarding others. These ideologies navigate the complex network of human relationships, with various respective ideologies viewing others as members of an extended family, adversaries or competitors, collaborators belonging to different groups or fellow travelers aboard the same "spaceship Earth."

These philosophical threads have been intricately woven into the fabric of human history, sometimes creating friction and, at other times, fostering progress and transformation. The interaction and evolution of these ideologies have been instrumental in shaping the course of human civilization. As humanity stands at the cusp of a new era of change, it is imperative to recognize that our collective imagination and the perspectives we adopt will significantly influence the trajectory of our world. The choices we make in conceptualizing "others" not only reflect our current ideologies but also shape the contours of our global society. The path we choose – whether it leans towards inclusivity, cooperation and shared humanity or towards division, competition and isolation – will profoundly impact the future landscape of human interactions and global coexistence.

# References

Anderson, B. (1991). *Imagined Communities: Reflections on the Origin and Spread of Nationalism* (Revised and Expanded ed.). Verso.

Appiah, K. A. (2006). *Cosmopolitanism: Ethics in a World of Strangers.* W. W. Norton & Company Inc.

Commission on Human Security. (2003). *Human Security Now.* https://digitallibrary.un.org/record/503749/files/Humansecuritynow.pdf

Gellner, E. (1983). *Nations and Nationalism.* Oxford: Blackwell Publishing.

Hobsbawm, E. & Ranger, T. (Eds.). (1983). *The Invention of Tradition.* The Press of the University of Cambridge.

Kant, I. (1795). *Zum ewigen Frieden. Ein philosophischer Entwurf.* F. Nicolovius. (Kant, I., Campbell Smith, M. (Tr.) (1903). *Perpetual peace: A philosophical essay.* Swan Sonnenschein. https://archive.org/details/perpetualpeaceap00kantuoft/page/n5/mode/2up)

Smith, A. D. (2010). *Nationalism* (2nd ed.). Polity.

UNDP. (1994). *Human Development Report 1994.* Oxford University Press. https://hdr.undp.org/system/files/documents/hdr1994encompletenostatspdf.pdf

# Chapter Seven

## A World Behind and Beyond "Nationality"

Ayako Sasaki

Imagine attending an international conference in Nepal. How would you introduce yourself? Where would you begin? What aspects of yourself would you describe? The way one introduces oneself differs depending on whether it occurs before a lecture or at a reception, to whom one introduces oneself, and in what language one performs the introduction. Would you prefer to use English to introduce yourself and describe where you are from? For example, if you are born and raised as a citizen of country A,[18] where English is not an official language, have an "appearance" that is representative of the people from country A, speak the official language of country A as your first language, and introduce yourself in English with an accent typical of people from country A, your introduction will be accepted at "natural." However, how should you introduce yourself if you are a citizen of country A yet your first language is English, were born in country B, raised in country C, have an "appearance" that represents country D, and now live in country E? The people around you might be confused about who you are and even ask, "Where are you 'originally' from?" They may also comment, "You speak English very well."[19] This is one example of the many microaggressions that people of mixed ethnic heritage and people with culturally and linguistically diverse backgrounds often experience (Ventura, 2018). This is especially true in countries where it is assumed that there is a high level of cultural and linguistic homogeneity among the population. Even in today's globalized

---

18   In this paper, I discuss "country" and "nationality" in terms of the unit in which the pass-port is issued.

19   The second edition of *Microaggressions in Everyday Life* by Derald Wing Sue and Lisa Span-ierman (2020, p. 7) states that the term "microaggression" was first defined by Chester Middlebrook Pierce as "subtle, stunning, often automatic, and nonverbal exchanges which are 'put-downs'." The term has also been defined as "subtle insults (verbal, nonverbal, and/ or visual) directed toward people of color, often automatically or unconsciously." Sue and Spanierman also explains that "while early theorizing focused solely on racial microag-gressions, microaggressions can be expressed toward any marginalized group in our soci-ety" (Sue & Spanierman, 2020, p. 7).

society, in nations across the world, it is still commonly believed that there is a certain "authentic" appearance and name for people born in each country. That is, people expect to see an appearance and name that matches the country's image and that the individual will speak the official, mainstream language as their first language.

As of 2020, there are 281 million people living as migrants across the globe, comprising 3.6% of the world's total population (IOM, 2022, p.2). According to the International Organization of Migration (IOM), the estimated number of international migrants in 2020 was approximately 2 million lower than initially estimated (IOM, 2022, P. 2). In the United Arab Emirates, migrants accounted for 88% of the total national population as of 2022 (United Nations, Department of Economic and Social Affairs Population Division, 2022). Meanwhile, there are over 50.6 million migrants living in the United States (IOM, 2022). Even in countries where the populations are believed to be homogeneous, the percentages of foreign nationals are likely to continue to increase.[20] These data provide an opportunity to critically reflect on the practice of attempting to identify "typical characteristics" that define people from a certain country, as well as the act of linking a person's "nationality" to their cultural and linguistic background, appearance, or name.

In this chapter, I focus on the concept of "nationality" and provide an overview of the discussion of current trends and changes in the context of "nationality." I also explore how "nationality" affects people's lives and its implications for social work practice.

Chapter Seven

---

20 For example, even in Japan, which is often believed to be a homogeneous country, 3.22 million "foreigners" were living in the country as of 2023 (Immigration Service Agency, 2023). Moreover, 7,000 to 9,000 people acquire Japanese citizenship through "naturaliza-tion" every year (Ministry of Justice, 2023), and over 10,000 children with Japanese citizen-ship require Japanese language instruction (Ministry of Education, Culture, Sports, Science and Technology Japan, 2022).

# 1.The Three Meanings of Nationality

What is nationality? For many people who live in the country where they hold citizenship, this question has little significance for their everyday lives. However, in today's globalized society, which is characterized by the active movement of people across the globe, nationality greatly impacts the lives of many people in a variety of everyday situations and spaces. Moreover, it is crucial that social workers in modern society consider how nationality affects people's daily lives and what function nationality serves in society.

Nationality has been discussed in several academic disciplines, such as political science, sociology, international relations and migration and refugee studies. Discussions on nationality have focused primarily on political aspects as well as questions about how people identify in a given country. For example, debates have discussed how patriotism and nationalism are created and maintained in relation to nationality, to what extent people are considered "nationals" in a given country, and how to nurture a collective national identity. In the following sections, I explore how nationality affects individuals by examining the three meanings of nationality: nationality as a basic human right, nationality as proof of identity, and nationality as a tool for realizing a better life.

## 1.1 Nationality as a fundamental human right

The Universal Declaration of Human Rights, which was originally published in 1948, describes nationality in Article 15, which states, "Everyone has the right to a nationality. No one shall be arbitrarily deprived of his nationality nor denied the right to change his nationality" (Universal Declaration of Human Rights, 1948). In addition, Article 7 of the Convention on the Rights of the Child, which was adopted in 1989, states, "The child shall be registered immediately after birth and shall have the right from birth to a name, the right to acquire a nationality and, as far as possible, the right to know and be cared for by his or her parents. States Parties shall ensure the implementation of these rights in accordance with their national law and their obligations under the relevant international instruments in this field, in particular where the child would otherwise be stateless" (Convention on the Rights of the

Child, 1989).

As these excerpts from the international conventions demonstrate, nationality is a fundamental human right because there are many rights and entitlements that require citizenship as a precondition. However, according to the United Nations High Commissioners for Refugees (UNHCR 2023, p.43), an estimated 4.4 million people are either stateless or of undetermined nationality.

One institutional factor that has contributed to this situation is the differences between countries regarding the principle of birthright citizenship. There are two main principles that inform citizenship policies. According to the principle of *jus sanguinis,* a child's nationality is determined by the nationality of their parents, regardless of where the child is born.[21] Countries that adhere to this principle include Japan, Indonesia and China. According to the principle of *jus soli,* children are granted citizenship by the country in which they are born, regardless of their parents' nationality. Countries adhering to this principle include Australia, Canada and Brazil. Many countries have adopted a combination of these two policies, with some allowing for dual or multiple citizenship. However, if a child is born to undocumented parents who are living as foreign nationals in a country adhering to the *jus sanguinis* principle, the parents may forge registering a birth for fear of deportation. This will result in the child becoming stateless. In some cases, undocumented women who give birth alone are detained by immigration authorities. In some cases, only the mother is deported, with the child being left in foster care run by the child protection services of that country or region.

For example, in Taiwan, migrant women employed in elderly care and domestic work often leave their workplaces in search of better working conditions to escape discrimination and exploitation. These women become undocumented migrants, and there is an increasing prevalence of cases where these women give birth outside hospitals and midwifery facilities. These children often end up unregistered and stateless or in the care of

---

21    This explanation is cited from the *Oxford Dictionary,*
https://www.oxfordreference.com/display/10.1093/oi/authority.20110803100027515
(Accessed September 29, 2023).

orphanage services in Taiwan (Wang & Lin, 2023). According to Wang and Lin (2023), as of January 2022, there were 664,733 documented and 50,000 undocumented migrant workers in Taiwan. Moreover, there were approximately 800 undocumented children born to women in these situations. Considering that women sometimes give birth outside hospitals and midwifery facilities, it is estimated that 700 stateless or unregistered children are born each year, indicating that over 20,000 children without birth certificates or citizenship are living in Taiwan at present (Wang & Lin, 2023).

The UNHCR is the main international organization that assists stateless people and "refugees" who have fled their home countries due to a legitimate fear of being persecuted due to their race, religion, nationality, membership in a particular social group, or political opinions and are unable to receive protection in their home country (UNHCR, 1951). According to the UNHCR (2023, p. 45), the largest group of stateless people is the Rohingya. Although there are obstacles to accurately counting and reporting the global population of stateless people, the largest estimated populations of stateless people are located in Bangladesh (952,300), Côte d'Ivoire (931,100), Myanmar (630,000) and Thailand (574,200).

Considering the vulnerable position in which these stateless people find themselves, the UNHCR established the Global Action Plan to End Statelessness (2014–2024) as a guiding framework[22]. This action plan encourages states to take one or more of the following ten actions to end of statelessness: "(1) Resolve existing major situations of statelessness. (2) Ensure that no child is born stateless. (3) Remove gender discrimination from national laws. (4) Prevent denial, loss or deprivation of nationality on discriminatory grounds. (5) Prevent statelessness in cases of state succession. (6) Grant protection status to stateless migrants and facilitate their nationalization. (7) Ensure birth registration for the prevention of statelessness. (8) Issue nationality documentation to those with entitlement to it. (9) Accede to the UN Statelessness Conventions. (10) Improve

---

22    For more information, see
      https://www.unhcr.org/media/global-action-plan-end-statelessness-2014-2024 (December
      26, 2023).

quantitative and qualitative data on stateless populations."

## 1.2 Nationality as proof of identity

Nationality has been interpreted as a component of fundamental human rights and as a form of proof of one's identity. However, over the past three decades, academic interpretations of the concept of "identity" have shifted. That is, whereas understandings of identity were once based on essentialist principles, they have now shifted to incorporate the principles of social constructionism and postmodernism (Cerulo, 1997). However, despite the abandonment of essential definitions and the rise of the social constructionist theory of identity in academia, it is still widely believed that citizens of a certain country share "essential" characteristics and qualities that are associated with that nationality, and it is assumed that these characteristics are genetic and, therefore, are "naturally" transmitted from one generation to the next. This essential understanding of "authentic" identity is based on the "we-ness" of a group perceived to share certain core characteristics. Moreover, this essentialist view sees it as "natural" for people to internalize a collective national identity.

Even when following a social constructionist perspective, however, it is still possible to identify people according to their country of origin or nationality and judge others' identities based on their roots, appearance, or name. In particular, as I indicated earlier in this chapter, people may unconsciously resort to this mode of thinking when meeting people for the first time at international conferences. Social workers can also fall victim to this thinking when working with immigrants and refugees from culturally and linguistically diverse backgrounds. However, this essentialist view ultimately reinforces the normative assumption that people should be strongly connected to their original country, culture, or region. This can marginalize the identities of people of mixed heritage and those who have migrated to various regions and countries. In many countries that do not allow dual or multiple citizenship, individuals must choose one nationality before reaching a certain age. This can have the effect of denying the plurality and diversity of individuals. It can also lead to a rejection of identities that are rooted in multiple cultural backgrounds. Finally, it can also unfairly force the individual to deny their attachment to the country that they were unable to claim citizenship for.

In addition to birthright citizenship, another method for acquiring citizenship is through naturalization. However, people from "stateless nations" (McGee & Barman, 2021), such as Kurd from Syria, who were even denied citizenship in Syria at birth, may be forced to migrate to other countries due to internal conflict. Kurds fled to countries bordering Syria to apply for asylum and seek refugee status. They have also sought to acquire citizenship by applying for naturalization. Since the beginning of the Syrian civil war in 2011, people living in a state of "double statelessness" (McGee & Barman, 2021) have found it difficult to prove that they are "stateless" when applying for asylum. In principle, asylum applications must be made in a country other than the country where one has citizenship; however, many Kurds from Syria lack the proper documentation to prove their country of nationality and, therefore, have been disqualified from the asylum application process. Should Syrian Kurds who applied for asylum in Germany and subsequently gained German citizenship attempt to "find" their identity in Germany, the country where they now have citizenship?

It is apparent that identity is not something that is decided solely by citizenship, one's country of origin, the language one is most fluent in, or what kind of foods one usually eats. It is also not determined solely by the group to which one belongs or the collective history shared by members of the group. Everyone should be able to choose how they identify, and national identity should not be forced on anyone. Shiobara (2017) points out that cultural globalization has resulted in an increase in the prevalence of cross-border identity; however, cultural cosmopolitanism should be predicated on the recognition that people's roots are hybrid, and no individual should be forced to abandon their cultural roots. Nationality is a fundamental human right that is necessary for obtaining a passport and proving one's identity, similar to an "ID card." However, it cannot function as the sole defining factor of one's identity. Although stateless people need to be granted citizenship, as it is a component of their basic human rights, they should not be forced to formulate an identity based on this citizenship. This is because individual identities are based on one's "lived experience" rather than one's citizenship. Moreover, identity itself is not defined by a single attribute or social position; rather, it is transformed through interactions with others.

## 1.3 Nationality as a tool for achieving a better life

In academic discussions, national identity is composed of two senses of belongingness: civic belongingness, which refers to the sense of being a citizen who makes up a nation, and ethnic belongingness, which refers to a sense of belonging to a certain ethnic group within a country (e.g. Lee, 2016; Sasaki, 2006; Tanada, 2019). Sasaki (2006, p. 129) studied Korean Japanese people residing in Japan and stated that "in recent years, an increasing number of people regard the acquisition of nationality as a mere formality, unrelated to the loss of ethnic consciousness" and pointed out that nationality is "a formal qualification that is separate from national identity." Another study reported that many respondents cited stability as a reason for seeking Japanese citizenship through naturalization. For example, respondents reported "being able to give my children Japanese citizenship" and "being able to carry a Japanese passport" as reasons for naturalization (Lee 2016, p. 121).

Obtaining citizenship as a route to a better life has become more common in recent years. A typical example of this is "birth tourism," which refers to travelling to a country that follows a *jus soil* citizenship policy. Indeed, pregnant women engage in "birth tours," spending a certain period of time before and after the birth of their child in a country that follows a *jus soil* policy so that their child can acquire citizenship in that country,[23] with the hopes that this citizenship will enable their child to build a better life and expand their future options. Disregarding questions regarding the morality and political implications of such tours, this chapter examines birth tours for the insight they provide regarding what Sasaki (2006) describes as "nationality as a qualification unrelated to national identity." People who build lives outside of the birth countries where they grew up, were educated, worked and spent their lives see their nationality not just as the source of

---

23    According to Mechling (2023), a birth tour from China to the United States costs between $30,000 and $100,000.

their cultural roots but also as a necessary tool for realizing a better life. Considering this situation, it may be necessary to deconstruct the essentialist discourse that has been produced around the topics of the nation-state, nationality and national identity and reconsider how nationality should be perceived given this reality.

# 2. The Dilemmas of Migrants' Social Integration and the Refugee Protection System

## 2.1 Complex structures of exclusion that transcend the dichotomy of "foreigners" and "nationals"

Nationality has a significant impact on people's lives. However, focusing solely on nationality does not explain all the factors impacting a person's social vulnerability and wellbeing. This is because it is not only nationality but also the various attributes, group categorizations and social positionings of people that can result in real-world discrimination and oppression, affecting people's overall wellbeing. That is, although nationality can solve problems, it can also create and maintain them.

To understand the situation of migrants in a country, the Migrant Integration Policy Index (MIPEX)[24], an indicator of the social integration of migrants, is employed. This indicator is used to compare the rights guaranteed to noncitizens and foreign nationals residing in 56 countries around the world. It also facilitates comparisons of the rights guaranteed for "foreigners" and "immigrants" in each country and the level of social integration achieved within eight policy areas, including labor market mobility, family reunion, education, health, political participation, permanent residence, access to nationality, and anti-discrimination. By referring to these indicators, it is possible to assess which countries make it easy for immigrants to acquire citizenship. On this index, New Zealand, Argentina, Brazil, Canada and the United States scored the highest while Saudi Arabia was at the bottom, with a score of zero. The report also found that 12 out of 56

---

24    See details at https://www.mipex.eu/what-is-mipex (February, 3rd 2024).

204

countries have not conformed to the international trend of granting dual citizenship to the children of immigrants (Solano & Huddleston, 2020).

Access to citizenship is included as an indicator of the social integration of immigrants because it is recognized that nationality is a core component of fundamental human rights and functions as a tool that migrants can use to achieve better and more stable lives in the country to which they have moved. However, as this paper has demonstrated, it is difficult to measure whether migrants feel subjectively integrated into society after acquiring citizenship and whether they see citizenship as proof of identity. In addition, it cannot be guaranteed that if an immigrant is able to acquire citizenship, they will be able to lead the same kind of life as a national who belongs to the social majority. For example, in the United States, where access to citizenship is considered relatively robust according to the MIPEX, second- and third-generation citizens with immigrant backgrounds are treated as an underclass and "systematically excluded from the image that US culture pretends to have, despite the fact that they are too powerfully culturally integrated" (Young, 2007, p. 56). The U.S. government attempted to construct a wall on the United States' border with Mexico to keep "illegal immigrants" out of the country. This political maneuver was notable not only for its overt exclusion of human beings but also for blurring of the lines between "migrants" and "citizens," where "large-scale cultural inclusion and systematic and structural exclusion are occurring simultaneously" (Young, 2007, p. 69). Young (2007) has pointed out that the social institutions mentioned by MIPEX and the mass media have become devices for sharing values for social integration while also structurally creating and maintaining a space for exclusion, a phenomenon that has been referred to as "social bulimia." While accessibility to citizenship can impact the social integration of immigrants, systems of structural exclusion can prevent supposedly integrated "ex-immigrants" from achieving better lives and improving their wellbeing.

## 2.2 Refugee protection systems: Nationality and border control

Citizenship in at least one country is an essential prerequisite when attempting to travel across borders. For example, holders of a UK passport can travel visa-free to 191 countries for 90 days and are reported to have the fourth most powerful passport in the world (Henly and Partners, 2023).[25] However, when entering the UK, only those with a passport issued by a country with a visa waiver agreement with the UK Government can enter the country without first applying for a visa.[26] This means that the scope and mobility of a person's international movements depend on the issuing country of their passport and the diplomatic relations between the issuing country and the destination country (Ogawa, 2023).

This fact was particularly evident when Afghans and Ukrainians attempted to evacuate to other countries. As of 2018, there were 146 countries that are parties to the Refugee Convention and member states have mechanisms in place to recognize people who flee from other countries and apply for asylum as refugees.[27] In August 2021, the Taliban took control over Kabul ahead of the deadline for the withdrawal of US troops and in February 2022, Russia launched a military invasion of Ukraine. Both events forced Afghans and Ukrainians, respectively, to flee their home countries and apply for asylum in other countries. According to the UNHCR (2023), as of the end of 2022, large numbers of people have fled from Syria (6.55 million), Ukraine (5.68 million), Afghanistan (5.66 million), Venezuela (5.45 million) and South Sudan (2.3 million) to seek refuge in other countries. Indeed, including the above five countries, refugees from just ten countries account for 87% of the total refugee population worldwide. Meanwhile, large numbers of refugees are being hosted in Turkey (3.57 million), Iran (3.43 million), Colombia (2.46 million), Germany (2.08 million) and Pakistan (1.74 million).

However, internally displaced persons (IDPs) actually outnumber refugees. The term IDPs refers to people fleeing from their home town while still remaining in their current country of residence. It is important to note

---

25 The passports issued by France, Germany, Italy, Spain, Japan, and Singapore are the most powerful and allow holders to travel to 194 out of 227 countries.

26 Until the Prime Minister, Keir Starmer, was elected in July 2024, the UK Government had attempted to transfer any people, including asylum seekers, who had entered the UK "illegally" without proper documentation to Rwanda (Yonekawa, 2024). This plan was introduced under the Boris administration in 2022, has been criticized, and has been under political debate worldwide.

27 For a list of ratifying, acceding, and successor states, see the UNHCR website. https://www.unhcr.org/jp/treaty_1951_1967_participant (Retrieved January, 30, 2024).

that according to the definition of "refugee," as established by the Refugee Convention, a person must be outside the country where they hold citizenship to apply for asylum. There are various reasons why IDPs are unable and unwilling to leave their current country of residence. However, given that a passport is always required when travelling across borders, passport issuance regulations and visa requirements regarding immigration to other countries can significantly impact an individual's ability to apply for asylum. According to the Henly Passport Index, which ranks passport strength according to the number of countries that can be travelled to visa-free, the Ukrainian passport ranks 32, with Ukrainian passport holders being able to travel to 148 out of 227 countries. The Afghani passport, meanwhile, ranks the lowest, with Afghani passport holders being able to travel to just 28 out of 227 countries as of 2023 (Henly and Partners, 2023). In other words, it is not even possible to apply for asylum in another country after legally leaving Afghanistan because a visa issued by the destination country is required in advance in most cases.

For example, the Japanese Government declined to issue even "short-term stay" visas to Afghans at the beginning of the political uprising in Afghanistan in 2021 (Ogawa, 2023). In contrast, since March 2022, when the Russian invasion of Ukraine began, the Japanese Government has been promptly issuing "short-term stay" visas to displaced persons from Ukraine, even if they had no acquaintances or relatives in Japan. Ogawa (2023, p. 20) pointed out that Japanese immigration strengthened border fortification by controlling the issuance of visas from third countries, such as Saudi Arabia, the United Arab Emirates and Pakistan. Moreover, Ogawa highlighted that this border control was dictated by racial hierarchies. Indeed, the country to which one had citizenship was used as a prerequisite to grant or deny entry into a country, even in life-threatening situations such as international migration due to war or persecution. It could also be said that the use of citizenship as a litmus test for entry may very well be a result of such geopolitical turmoil.

# 3.Intersectionality, or Deconstructing Categories

As the cases of the Hutus and Tutsis in Rwanda and the Serbs and Muslims in Bosnia demonstrate, throughout history, conflicts have occurred among groups of the same nationality due to discrimination based on race, ethnicity, tribe and religion. Moreover, some of these conflicts have even developed into genocides. Borders are artificially drawn boundaries and there is no guarantee that people of the same nationality will be able to work and live together in harmony. Even if a clear boundary is drawn around a group, there is no guarantee that the group shares "the same characteristics." Even if they share the same nationality, they will not necessarily share the same culture or language, nor will they necessarily interact with each other. Moreover, race, ethnicity and religion are not the only characteristics for formulating a group identity within a set boundary. It is also possible to categorize people by gender identity, sexual orientation, social class, occupation, education level and many more identity markers.

In 80% of cases, domestic violence victims are women. If a wife within an immigrant family is forced to flee her family, she is likely to lose her place in her current community. In addition, these women are often granted the right to stay in a country based on their status as the "family" of the working husbands, and therefore, they may be unable to remain in the country if they divorce their husbands. Even in cases where children are being abused, it is difficult to temporarily separate them from their families. The National Association of Social Workers has also pointed out that immigration laws prevent family visitation and family reunification and they noted that when family members have different immigration statuses or different nationalities, it can be difficult to make a complaint of domestic violence or abuse. Moreover, reports of employers exploiting immigrant workers can lead to "deportation" for workers, with the state ignoring demands for security and justice for immigrants (National Association of Social Workers, 2015).

Furthermore, while assisting and researching survivors of human trafficking in the United States and Japan, I have heard on multiple occasions that survivors are often reluctant to ask someone from their country to provide language interpretation because many feel ashamed at the thought of their experiences of victimization becoming known to someone from their own country. Moreover, many fear that their whereabouts may be revealed to "perpetrators" who also live within ethnic communities. Within every expat community, there is a further segmentation of sub-communities according to the method and timing of migration, class status and educational background, as well as region of origin and ethnicity. According to Biestek's seven principles of the Western-rooted social work relationship, the "principle of individualization" states that one should not judge a welfare service user's situation based on their group attributes, such as whether they are elderly or disabled or display symptoms of a disease, such as Alzheimer's disease. Therefore, it is important to view each person as an individual, even if they share the same "nationality" as others.

Recently, the concept of intersectionality has emerged as a method for analyzing the different forms of discrimination and oppression suffered by people of the same nationality, gender, race or ethnicity depending on the social status they are attributed in society. Indeed, it provides "[a] critical analytic framework that enables analysis of structural identities, including class, race, gender, sexuality, age and disability and the ways that they intersect and compound" (Caragata, 2023, p. 101). Intersectionality acknowledges and makes visible the intersection of different social positionalities that are interdependent and overlapping and occur within systems and structures of power (Caragata, 2022, p. 101). However, each individual's experience of oppression and the ways in which intersectionality is articulated also differ depending on the surrounding context (Ang et al., 2023, p. 5). Furthermore, even if the concept of intersectionality is applied to analyze the specific experiences of discrimination that occur at the intersection of multiple identity markers of the individual, this still involves essentialization based on identity categories. That is, while it is possible to analyze how power and social conditions have a structural impact on individuals, individual interpretations of these structures and attempts to respond to them can vary from person to person. How can we free ourselves from categorization? Is it possible to dismantle all categories?

# 4.Beyond Nationality and Categorizations

This chapter examined the definition of nationality, assessed its importance for people and examined how it can affect people's lives. This chapter also considered how identity categories, in addition to nationality, intertwine with each other to create oppressive structures, as well as how individuals experience these structures. For social workers to work with service users of different nationalities, it is important for them to understand how the concepts of "us" and "them" are defined, as well as how boundaries are drawn around categories of people (Sasaki, 2024). Additionally, it is important to understand that categorization by nationality has been used for the purposes of discrimination, nationalism and international politics. However, immigration control and refugee protection systems that are governed by international treaties around the world are also based on the premise of the "nation-state." Therefore, they cannot be easily dismantled. When engaging in social movements for transformation at the macro and meso levels, the issue of categorization may be effective in bringing people together and making them feel a sense of belonging, in turn creating a sense of "not being alone" as they work together. In accordance with the work of anti-oppressive social work, it is essential to make visible how the privileged categories to which the majority belong intersect to reinforce power structures while maintaining conditions of oppression that impact minorities. Subsequently, it is necessary to promote change to these structures themselves. However, if society pursues the immediate pigeonholing of individuals into categories based on various attributes and social positionalities, including nationality, then micro-level practices may render the strengths and individuality of each person invisible and hinder empowerment.

One approach that can mitigate the bothering of categorization is to understand how categorization creates power structures and structures that oppress minorities at the macro level. Subsequently, it is necessary to analyze the experiences of individuals in the environment and context that surrounds them, with the aim of transforming their individual relationships. This is exactly what social workers around the world are consciously and unconsciously attempting to achieve in their daily practices. From an academic perspective, simply asserting that all categories are socially constructed or advocating for the dismantling of all categories is not sufficient to promote social change and concrete solutions to the issues impacting people in the real world. Social workers are required to analyze how various categorizations affect the identities and behaviors of individuals in their daily lives and what specific challenges they pose. It is necessary for social workers to take concrete measures to resolve these challenges and to change society to facilitate them.

## Acknowledgements

This work was supported by JSPS KAKENHI (Grant Numbers JP20K02291 and 24K00338).

## References

Ang, S., Lynn-Ee Ho, E. & Yeoh, B. (Eds.). (2021). *Asian Migration and New Racism Beyond Colour and the "West."* Oxon and New York: Routledge.

Caragata, L. (2022). Seeing Low-Income Single Moms: Intersectionality Meets Struggles for an Anti-oppressive Practice. In Baines, D., Clark, N. & Bennett, B. (Eds.). *Doing Anti-oppressive Social Work: Rethinking Theory and Practice (4th edition)*. Manitoba: Fernwood Publishing.

Cerulo, K. A. (1997). Identity Construction: New Issues, New Directions. *Annual Review of Sociology*, 23. 385–409.

Henly and Partners. (2023). *These Are the World's Most (and Least) Powerful Passports in 2024*. Retrieved February 3rd, 2024 from https://www. henleyglobal.com/newsroom/press-releases/global-mobility-report-2024-january

Immigration Services Agency. (2023). 令和5年6月末現在における在留外国人数について. Retrieved December 26, 2023 from https://www.moj.go.jp/isa/publications/press/13_00036.html (in Japanese)

International Organization for Migration. (2022). Chapter 1: Report Overview: Technological, geopolitical and environmental transformations shaping our migration and mobility futures, *World Migration Report 2022*. Retrieved December 26, 2023 from https://publications.iom.int/books/world-migration-report-2022-chapter-1

Kim, W. (2016). マイクロアグレッション概念の射程. Institute of Ars Vivendi, Ritsumeikan University. *Hokokusho, 24*, 105–123. Retrieved from https://www.ritsumei-arsvi.org/uploads/center_reports/24/center_reports_24_08.pdf (in Japanese)

Lee, S. I. (2016). コリア系日本人の再定義：「帰化」制度の歴史的課題. In Komai, H. (E.S). & Sasaki, T. (Eds.). マルチ・エスニック・ジャパニーズ　○○系日本人の変

革力. Akashi Shoten. (in Japanese)

McGee, T. & Bahrman, H. (2021). Navigating Intersecting Statelessness: Syrian Kurds in Europe. Retrieved February 3, 2024 from https://www.statelessness.eu/updates/blog/navigating-intersecting-statelessness-syrian-kurds-europe

Mechling, L. (2023). A lot of these women had no idea what they got into: Inside the world of birth tourism. *The Guardian*. Retrieved February 3, 2024 from https://www.theguardian.com/tv-and-radio/2023/dec/11/birth-tourism-documentary-china-us-citizenship

Ministry of Education, Culture, Sports, Science, and Technology Japan. (2022). 日本語指導が必要な児童生徒の受入状況等に関する調査. Retrieved December 26, 2023 from https://www.e-stat.go.jp/stat-search/files?page=1&layout=datalist&toukei=00400305&tstat=000001016761&cycle=0&tclass1=000001171786&tclass2=000001171787&tclass3val=0 (in Japanese)

Ministry of Justice Civil Affairs Bureau. (2023). 国籍別帰化許可者数. Retrieved December 26, 2023 from https://www.moj.go.jp/content/001392230.pdf (in Japanese)

National Association of Social Workers. (2015). *Social Work Speaks* 2015–2017 10th edition. NASW Press.

Ogawa, R. (2023). Evacuation from Afghanistan and Racialized Border Control. *Migration Policy Review, 15*, 10–27.

Sasaki, A. (2024). Reconstructing the Narrative of "Because Japan Is an Island": Discussions of Immigration, Migration, and Refugee Policy. In Gaitanidis, I. & Pool, G. (Eds). *Teaching Japan: A Handbook* (pp.3-21). Tokyo: MHM Limited, and Amsterdam: Amsterdam University Press.

Sasaki, T. (2006). 日本の国籍制度とコリア系日本人. Akashi Shoten. (in Japanese)

Shiobara, Y. (2017). 分断と対話の社会学－グローバル社会を生きるための想像力. Keio University Press. (in Japanese)

Solano, G. & Huddleston, T. (2020). *Migrant Integration Policy Index 2020*. Retrieved February 3rd, 2024 from https://www.mipex.eu/what-is-mipex

Sue, D. W. & Spanierman, L. (2020). *Microaggressions in everyday life*. John Wiley & Sons.

Tanada, H. (2019). Lifestyle, Identity & Religious Practices of Muslims Living in Japan-The Cases of Muslims Naturalized as Japanese Nationals. *Annals of Japan Association for Middle East Studies, 35.* 153–175. (in

Japanese)

Universal Declaration of Human Rights, G.A. Res. 217 (III), *A, U*.N. Doc. A/ RES/217(III) (Dec. 10, 1948). Retrieved December 26, 2023 from https:// www.un.org/en/about-us/universal-declaration-of-human-rights

UN General Assembly, Convention Relating to the Status of Refugees. (July 28 1951). United Nations, Treaty Series, vol. 189, p. 137. Retrieved December 26, 2023 from https://www.refworld.org/docid/3be01b964. html

United Nations Convention on the Rights of the Child. (November 20, 1989). Retrieved December 26, 2023 from https://www.ohchr.org/en/ instruments-mechanisms/instruments/convention-rights-child

United Nations Department of Economic and Social Affairs Population Division. (2022). The 2022. Revision of World Population Prospects, Retrieved December 26, 2023 from https://population.un.org/wpp/

United Nations High Commissioners for Refugees. (2023). Global Trends Report 2022. Retrieved December 26, 2023 from https://www.unhcr.org/ global-trends-report-2022

Ventura, R. (Ed.). (2018). Made in Japan Stories of Japanese-Filipino Children. Manira: Ateneo de Manila University.

Wang, M. S. & Lin, C. H. (2023). Barriers to Health and Social Services for Unaccounted-For Female Migrant Workers and Their Undocumented Children with Precarious Status in Taiwan: An Exploratory Study of Stakeholder Perspectives, *International Journal of Environmental Research and Public Health*, 20. 956. Retrieved February 3rd, 2024 from https://doi. org/10.3390/ijerph20020956

Yonekawa, M. (2024). 不法入国者らをルワンダに移送するイギリスの計画が物議『ルワ ンダは安全』は本当か. *The Asahi Shimbun Globe+* (January 15, 2024). Retrieved March 13, 2024 from https://globe.asahi.com/article/15108107 (in Japanese)

Young, J. (2007). *The Vertigo of Late Modernity*. Sage. [translated by Kinoshita, C., Nakamura, Y. & Maruyama, M. (2019). 後期近代の眩暈―排除から過剰 包摂へ 新装版 ]. Seidosha. (in Japanese)

# Chapter Eight

## Foreign Aid and the National Interest

Takeshi Sato-Daimon

Following the end of World War II, international foreign aid efforts emerged to facilitate the reconstruction of countries destroyed by the war. War-devastated countries in Asia and Africa—many of which gained independence by the 1960s—became major recipients of official development assistance (ODA), the most common form of foreign aid provided to poor countries. Some ODA recipient countries have graduated from aid recipients to become aid providers. Moreover, traditional and new donors are increasingly experiencing difficulty reaching a consensus regarding a variety of factors related to aid policies, such as considerations for environmental protection and the terms of aid project financing and procurement. Traditional donors feel that new donors are challenging existing rules and guidelines, questioning even the basic definition and scope of ODA. New donors have also been perceived as using ODA to pursue their own national interests. This chapter addresses the link between foreign aid and national interest, asking whether donor countries assist other countries out of a motivation to pursue their own economic and political objectives.

## 1. What Motivates Countries to Provide Aid?

### 1.1 Overview of Official Development Assistance

Foreign aid began in the late 1940s, immediately following the end of World War II. Subsequently, intensifying postwar rivalries between the East and West in foreign assistance provided to allied countries, as aid was seen as an important tool for making recipient countries dependent on aid providers. In 1948, the United States enacted the Marshall Plan to assist Western European countries in reconstruction.[28]. Likewise, the Soviet Union assisted the planned economies of Eastern Europe. By the 1950s and 1960s, Western countries had begun to assist former colonies in Asia and Africa. Japan also began to extend ODA through the Overseas Economic Cooperation Fund in 1962.

In the post-World War II climate, there was a lack of policy coordination among major foreign aid donors. However, in the late 1960s, major donor countries established a framework to govern the terms of foreign aid. The Development Assistance Commission (DAC) of the Organisation for Economic Cooperation and Development (OECD) defined ODA as a form of publicly funded financial support with a "grant element" greater than 25%. A grant element is defined as "the difference between its face value and the sum of the present value of debt service to be made by the borrower, expressed as a percentage of the face value of the loan.[29]" Therefore, a loan with a grant element of 100% would be a "gift" or technical assistance.

Major bilateral ODA and other official flows (OOF) providers include the United States, Germany, France, the United Kingdom, and Japan (Table 8-1). Export credits are publicly guaranteed credits, and they are different from the private flow of money, as reported in Table 8-1 below.

For most recipient and new donor countries, the OECD-DAC definition of ODA is not binding, and therefore, recipient and donor countries do not distinguish between ODA and OOF. Both types of financial flows are generally more concessional than private financing and can fill in financial gaps of recipient countries through projects and programs, generally referred

---

28 Adopted by the US Congress in April 1948, the Marshall Plan was "[a]n Act to promote world peace and the general welfare, national interest, and foreign policy of the United States through economic, financial, and other measures necessary to the maintenance of conditions abroad in which free institutions may survive and consistent with the maintenance of the strength and stability of the United States."

29 World Bank website, https://thedocs.worldbank.org/en/doc/287062306faaab990e9ea7a5de-b0ace8-0410012017/original/grant_element_calculation_formula_2013.pdf (accessed December 20, 2023).

216

Table 8-1. ODA and OOF Net Disbursement (in millions of USD)

|  |  | 2019 | 2020 | 2021 | 2022 |
|---|---|---|---|---|---|
| US | ODA | 32,980.72 | 35,396.41 | 47,528.16 | 60,328.68 |
|  | OOF | 311.03 | 622.74 | 2,215.74 | 1,861.39 |
|  | Exp Credits | ▲ 693.00 | ▲ 332.29 | 18,221.27 | 3,987.92 |
|  | Private | 77,886.93 | ▲ 68.736.33 | 165,566.53 | 114,517.64 |
| Japan | ODA | 11,720.19 | 13,660.18 | 15,767.00 | 16,747.35 |
|  | OOF | ▲ 770.10 | 4,700.51 | 712.19 | ▲ 11.52 |
|  | Exp Credits | ▲ 1,029.55 | ▲ 5,216.96 | ▲ 690.96 | ▲ 2,675.61 |
|  | Private | 45,024.93 | 18,723.15 | 22,071.50 | 39,428.18 |
| UK | ODA | 19,344.60 | 19,253.43 | 16,277.78 | 15,761.32 |
|  | OOF | ▲ 400.46 | 146.76 | ▲ 131.84 | 298.02 |
|  | Exp Credits | n.a. | n.a. | n.a. | n.a. |
|  | Private | n.a. | n.a. | n.a. | n.a. |
| France | ODA | 11,984.15 | 16,013.14 | 16,721.92 | 17,558.93 |
|  | OOF | 248.29 | ▲ 400.84 | 37.34 | 146.21 |
|  | Exp Credits | n.a. | n.a. | n.a. | n.a. |
|  | Private | 9,618.27 | 5,108.83 | 2,276.49 | 7,959.83 |
| Gemany | ODA | 24,122.38 | 29,320.38 | 32,455.57 | 36,444.68 |
|  | OOF | 13.7 | 422.45 | 1,271.98 | 231.17 |
|  | Exp Credits | ▲ 1,947.72 | ▲ 1,222.21 | ▲ 1,259.38 | ▲ 1,373.27 |
|  | Private | 18,477.00 | 14,665.77 | 35,216.30 | 18,357.29 |

Source: OECD database

to as "intervention" by the OECD-DAC.[30]

Distinguishing between ODA and OOF in terms of grant element is, in fact, becoming increasingly irrelevant when evaluating development impacts, even for development agencies in OECD member countries. In this context, development agencies can be divided into two types—institutions specialized for technical assistance and grants and institutions with various lending and nonlending financial schemes, which are often called development financial institutions (DFIs).

Major present-day bilateral DFIs include the Agence Française de Dévelopement (AFD) of France and its subsidiary Proparco Group, which specifically targets private-sector development. The German agency Kreditanstalt für Wiederaufbau (KfW) also provides both ODA and OOF. The International Bank for Reconstruction and Development (IBRD) is the

---

30    OECD on "Evaluation Criteria," https://www.oecd.org/dac/evaluation/daccriteriaforevalu-atingdevelopmentassistance.htm (accessed 20 December 2023).

original institution founded pursuant to the Bretton Woods Agreement in July 1944, and it offers both ODA and OOF. Meanwhile, the International Finance Corporation (IFC), which is a member of the World Bank Group, specializes in private-sector development and offers OOF. The Asian Development Bank (ADB), Inter-American Development Bank (IDB), European Bank for Reconstruction and Development (EBRD), African Development Bank (AFDB), and Islamic Development Bank (ISDB) are regional DFIs offering both ODA and OOF.

In Japan, ODA is handled by the Japan International Cooperation Agency (JICA), whereas OOF is handled by the Japan Bank for International Cooperation (JBIC). Both the JICA and JBIC are major contributors to the objectives outlined in the Development Cooperation Charter, which was recently updated in Tokyo in June 2023. The charter states that "Japan will enhance synergies by organically combining various schemes of the government and its affiliated agencies and promote development cooperation in coordination with private funds." Agencies affiliated with the charter include the JICA, JBIC, Nippon Export and Investment Insurance (NEXI), and other OOF agencies. The underlying expectation is that contributors of ODA and OOF should work together in a complementary relationship rather than competing with one another.

Complementarity between ODA and OOF is largely not an issue in countries such as the United States, United Kingdom, or Sweden because, in these countries, ODA is always provided as a grant rather than a soft loan. The United States Agency for International Development (USAID), Swedish International Development Agency (SIDA) and the UK's Department for International Development (DFID) are the representative agencies active in this space. The DFID was established in 1997 when then-Prime Minister Tony Blair of the Labor Party was playing a leadership role in reaching agreements regarding various international development goals. These initiatives eventually evolved into the Millennium Development Goals (MDGs) and Sustainable Development Goals (SDGs), which were subsequently adopted by the United Nations General Assembly. However, when the Tories returned to power, the DFID was scrapped and integrated into the Foreign Office in 2020.

## 1.2 Linking foreign aid to national interest in the past and present

During the Cold War, foreign aid was often used as another mechanism for pursuing national interest by leading economic powers. According to Hans Morgenthau (1969), a founding father of the theory of political realism during this period, "[A] policy of foreign aid is no different from diplomatic or military policy or propaganda. They are all armoury of the nation" (p. 105). Liberal internationalists challenged the Cold War paradigm and saw foreign aid as a concerted effort to promote cooperation in an interdependent world. This view prevailed until around the early 2010s when new tensions emerged between the United States and China over economic and political issues.

Another influential theory of foreign aid during the Cold War era was the Marxian perspective represented by the Prebisch–Singer hypothesis "dependency,"[31] of which interpreted foreign aid as a tool used by powerful capitalist states and multilateral corporations to exploit poor nations on the periphery. Supporters of dependency theory, who generally oppose economic globalization, argue that foreign aid should be avoided. Recently, young leftists have shown renewed interest in this theory.

Since the 2010s, China has emerged as a challenger to the traditional aid paradigm and the OECD-DAC's control over determining aid guidelines and policies. Indeed, in recent years, China—whose national interests often conflict with those of European donors—has emerged as the top financer for foreign aid. In Southeast Asia, China has overtaken Japan as the top financier in the region, challenging Japanese national interests. Similar tensions have arisen between the United States and China over Latin American markets.

In the field of political science, competition often implies conflict; however, from the perspective of economics, conflict can also imply efficiency and the maximization of social welfare provisions and well-being. For economists, therefore, "aid competition" can help realize development outcomes in the most cost-effective manner because only a donor who makes the least costly offer can win an international competitive bid. However, while aid

---

31   The thesis is attributed to Prebisch (1950) and Singer (1950).

competition can reduce costs, aid confusion may occur when different donors engage in an uncoordinated race to the bottom, which may result in the quality of aid being sacrificed.

## 1.3 Foreign aid and national interest: The case of Japan

After World War II, Japan was mandated to help war victims in Asian countries as a condition of its independence; this marked the starting point for Japan's foreign aid policy. In San Francisco in 1951, Tokyo agreed to "assisting to compensate those countries for the cost of repairing the damages, by making available the services of the Japanese people in production salvaging and other work for the Allied Powers in question."[32]

Japan's foreign aid program, which had begun as war reparations, expanded to include developing countries, with Japan becoming one of the top donors by the early 1990s. At this time, Japan's foreign aid policy was characterized by a noninterventionist and noninterference stance, which is sometimes referred to as the "spirit of Bandung,"[33] a reference to a conference held in Bandung, Indonesia, in 1955.

By the end of the 1990s and early 2000s, a period marked by growing military conflict and political tensions in international relations, Japan had radically changed the direction of its foreign aid policies. Japanese ODA began to assist in the reconstruction of war-torn countries such as Timor-Leste, Afghanistan, Iraq, and Haiti.[34] In April 2023, the Japanese Government announced its plan to extend foreign aid to the militaries of like-minded countries, clarifying Tokyo's intention to link foreign policy with military objectives. In June 2023, Tokyo adopted the Development Cooperation Charter, marking its departure from a conventional request-based process to instead invest in infrastructure and compete more actively with China's Belt and Road Initiative.

---

32  Article 14 of the San Fransico Treaty.

33  One of the ten principles of the Bandung Conference includes "4. Abstention from intervention or interference in the internal affairs of another country."

34  See Daimon-Sato (2021) for a review of the military and economic cooperation of Japan.

## 1.4 Free and Open Indo-Pacific (FOIP) Initiative and the Abe Doctrine

Shinzo Abe intended to achieve reciprocity and parity among nations by increasing Japan's commitment to the international order and the rule of law. The FOIP, one of the legacies of the Abe Doctrine, sought to counterbalance an emerging hegemony in Asia, rejecting the rhetoric of Chinese leaders and what they called "core interests" to pursue territorial ambitions. Unlike his predecessors, Abe never avoided debates on any issue with any party.

The Abe Doctrine might be interpreted as more political realism than liberalism, although the distinction between the two ideological camps has recently become blurred. While Mearsheimer (2018) rejects "'liberal hegemony' [in which states fight] to protect human rights and spread liberal democracy around the world" (p. 152), Fukuyama (2022) justifies the use of force to achieve "liberal nationalism" because "liberal society does this by creating a powerful state but then constraining the state's power under the rule of law" (pp. 80–91).

During the Cold War, the United States and Japan, together with development finance institutions, continued to support illiberal democratic regimes—including most Asian countries up until they democratized in the 1980s—through economic and military assistance.

The Abe Doctrine recommended engagement with adversaries because such engagement, although capable of triggering diplomatic confrontation in the short term, was seen as necessary for achieving mutually beneficial international relationships in the long term. China and Japan, having commemorated the 50th anniversary of diplomatic normalization in 2022, must engage with one another diplomatically in order to avoid military confrontation and achieve a lasting state of equilibrium.

The Russian Invasion of Ukraine in 2022 has added additional urgency to achieving agenda items of the global community, including ensuring energy security (cf. European dependence on Russian natural gas), providing humanitarian assistance for Ukrainian refugees and economic and military assistance to Ukraine, and enforcing economic sanctions against Russia. The Group of 20 (G20) summit, which includes ministers of finance and the heads of central banks, met in Washington in April 2022. At this meeting, leaders could have adopted a more concrete joint economic recovery plan; their failure to do so demonstrates the deepening chasm between various nations over their stance on Russia.

The ongoing war in Ukraine has seemed to confirm the predictions of opponents of liberal democracy, as described by John Mearsheimer in his book *The Great Delusion*. Regarding the Ukrainian crisis, Mearsheimer states,

[T]he United States and its European allies share most of the responsibility for the crisis. The taproot of the trouble is NATO enlargement, the central element of a larger strategy to move Ukraine out of Russia's orbit and integrate it into the West. At the same time, the EU's expansion eastward and the West's backing of the pro-democracy movement in Ukraine—beginning with the Orange Revolution in 2004—were critical elements, too. (Mearsheimer, 2014, p. 1)

The debates generated by the COVID-19 pandemic, the lessons it has taught society, and its various effects seem to suggest one undeniable trend: Liberal institutions have suffered a loss of credibility at both the national and international levels. In the following sections, this essay discusses the complexity of international relations through the lens of China–Japan aid diplomacy.

# 2. Foreign Aid Competition and Cooperation

## 2.1 Recipient perspectives

The effectiveness of foreign aid critically depends on how policymakers in recipient nations utilize aid to translate intended policy goals into tangible outcomes (Bourguignon & Sunberg, 2007, p. 317). During the 1980s and early 1990s, low-income countries in sub-Saharan Africa received program loans from the International Monetary Fund (IMF) and the World Bank for so-called "structural adjustments." These loans were intended to introduce market mechanisms into state-controlled economies, and therefore, they can be understood as an application of the Washington Consensus.

In many cases, however, these structural adjustment programs did not achieve donors' intentions, largely because Washington economists tried to implement a uniform prescription for a variety of problems. Consequently, most recipient countries, which had already been poor, became highly indebted by the mid-1990s, when the Washington Consensus collapsed.

Western donors also sought to condition their foreign aid on achieving a democratic process of development. However, the results were mixed. Many countries in the Middle East achieved democracy following the Arab Spring of 2010. In most sub-Saharan African countries, however, Western foreign aid did not facilitate democratization. The COVID-19 crisis shattered people's fundamental faith in democratic principles as they watched as states with stricter control over their economies were able to more effectively deal with the crisis.

## 2.2 China's cooperation on international development

In 2015, Beijing established its own ODA-oriented agency known as the China International Development Cooperation Agency (CIDCA).[35] This agency was responsible for overseeing what was previously accomplished through a complex network of independent channels with the Ministry of Commerce and the Ministry of Foreign Affairs. The Chinese Export-Import Bank and Development Bank of China have continued their OOF operations.

One remarkable achievement of CIDCA was its ability to quickly supply countries worldwide with emergency medical aid, including vaccines, during the early stages of the COVID-19 pandemic. Indeed, the COVID-19 pandemic revealed the importance of avoiding the pitfalls of isolationist policies at times when countries and people are at risk of being left behind. China's approach could be referred to as a form of idealism that rejects the liberal view on which the mainstream consensus of economists is based

---

35    http://en.cidca.gov.cn/ (accessed December 20, 2023).

(Deudney & Ikenberry, 1999).[36] This way of thinking directly confronts the realist perspective that considers aid, trade, and investment to be a diplomatic tool to pursue the benefit of one's own country(Morgenthau, 1962, 1969).

Although different from the classic realism that was witnessed during the years of confrontation between the United States and the Soviet Union in the Cold War era, this neo-realism can be understood as a characteristic of the so-called "G-Zero" era, which is marked by trade competition between the United States and China, among other things. Building on international relationship theory—which focuses on regionality, identity, and social norms—constructivism has positioned itself within aid theory by promoting the eradication of poverty and SDGs as a high-level norm (Fukuda-Parr & Hume, 2011). From any perspective, aid can be considered a tool of diplomatic and political mediation.

There is little doubt that the post-pandemic balance of power regarding foreign aid will be influenced by China and that the positions of traditional aid powers will suffer retreats. Chinese authorities have been using foreign aid as an important diplomatic tool across the world with the goal of establishing and maintaining influence in recipient countries. Indeed, this is why many countries are facing important decisions about the extent to which they are willing to give up their democracy while using resources from China to accelerate economic recovery following the COVID-19 shock.

## 2.3 The aid complementarity hypothesis

Using a game-theoretical framework, Daimon-Sato (2021) presented a "win-win-win" hypothesis that painted a favorable picture of a grand coalition between China, India, and Japan. If there is no cooperation between these three countries, then it will be difficult to achieve mutually beneficial payoffs. However, if a coalition is formed between the three parties, then trilateral benefits will be obtained, with enforcement mechanisms used to achieve common economic interests.

---

36    Some have claimed that liberalism and liberal internationalism are capable of countering the threat posed by the pandemic (Mawdsely, 2012); however, an assessment of actual performance reveals that this assertion was exceedingly optimistic.

Previously, Panchamukhi (1983) provided a more formal definition of complementarity in the context of foreign aid. According to Panchamukhi, two entities are said to be complementary in any given activity when (a) the activity cannot be performed unless both entities are present, (b) the level of the activity cannot be maintained when the level of one of the entities changes; and (c) any increase or decrease in one entity necessarily implies some increase or decrease in the other entity when the level of the activity is also increased or decreased.

Using the conceptual framework, it is possible to define reciprocal complementarity as south–south cooperation, equal partner cooperation, or interdependence and one-sided complementarity as center–periphery relations (growth center versus supplier countries) or dependence. This analysis could be further subdivided into sectoral-level (input-output, inter-industry, or intra-industry) complementarities. It is also possible to extend this analysis to a multi-dimensional perspective that sees complementarities as resources (skilled labor capital), institutions, and hardware and software (infrastructure and management systems).

## 2.4 Aid complementarity in practice

In May 2022, I conducted an interview with a seasoned Chinese engineer in Dili, Timor-Leste. At the time, Beijing was extending OOF for the construction of Tibar Bay Port, a $500 million investment expected to serve as the country's largest international port, which was carried out on the basis of a public–private partnership led by the French firm Bolloré.[37] When the port was near completion in May 2022, we had the opportunity to engage in an informal hour-long conversation with a Chinese project manager from Shanghai Harbor Engineering.

The project manager, who had trained as a civil engineer in Japan, cheerfully welcomed us and voluntarily shared details about his international work experience. I was struck by his positive perspectives on the development of Timor-Leste, as such positivity is missing in the Japanese aid

---

37  Bolloré is a firm registered with the Paris Stock Exchange, and its shares are largely owned by the Bolloré family.

milieu. All Japanese aid professionals expressed skepticism, if not hostility, about China's presence in Timor-Leste.

This seasoned senior manager stated, "Our harbor project could *complement* a road financed by Japan in terms of gaining access to the capital city Dili. We should share the great opportunities for further development investment." Japanese skepticism was due to a setback whereby the construction of a major national road co-financed by Japan and the Asian Development Bank was awarded to the Shanghai Construction Group and Sinohydro Corporation, both of which are private corporations headquartered in China, despite Japan's expectation that a Japanese firm would win the bid.

This experience in Dili is a reminder that the complementarity of foreign aid can be observed at the grassroots level. It is easier to coordinate aid policies among practitioners than among top decision-makers because coordination produces practical benefits. However, top decision-makers, who are inevitably mandated to maximize national interest, see no benefit, and therefore, competition tends to prevail.

# 3. The Post-COVID-19 Development Paradigm[38]

## 3.1 The collapse of liberal capitalism and the search for a new form of capitalism

The system of international cooperation based on liberalism and free trade is represented by the IMF and World Bank—two institutions created by the countries victorious in World War II, particularly the United Kingdom and the United States—and the Bretton Woods system, which was created pursuant to the General Agreement on Tariffs and Trade (GATT), the predecessor to the World Trade Organization (WTO).

Since the 1970s, these institutions have become major players in the system of global liberalism. Within this system, the Summit of Developed Countries—which was launched by Germany, France, the United Kingdom,

---

38    This section is an updated summary of Daimon-Sato (2022), originally written in Japanese.

Japan, and the United States and later became the G7 Summit after the addition of Italy and Canada—became the driving force for liberalism. Emerging countries such as China and South Korea achieved strong economic growth and came to occupy important positions within the world economy. However, as a consequence of the Asian financial crisis in 1997, Indonesia, South Korea, and other Asian countries were pressured to comply with IMF recommendations and suffered serious economic damage. In Indonesia, the Suharto regime collapsed after being in power for 30 years. South Korea implemented structural economic reforms in response to what is referred to in South Korea as the "IMF crisis." Amidst these circumstances, 20 countries, including emerging countries, formed a group known as the "Finance Ministers and Central Bank Governors of G20 countries." In 2020, this group held eight meetings, including six Finance Ministers and Central Bank Governors' Meetings, one Finance Ministers' and Health, Labor and Welfare Ministers' Meeting, and one Summit Meeting focusing on COVID-19 countermeasures.

The COVID-19 pandemic challenged the assumption that the free-market model was sustainable and reliable. Paradoxically, political parties and media outlets that identify themselves as "liberal" endorsed restrictions on individual liberties by the state—restrictions that they would have rejected in the past. Conservatives, who should be ideologically at odds, began to make statements that sounded liberal in character, such as opposing government intervention and arguing for the right not to be vaccinated, creating a gap between liberals and conservatives.

During this period of questioning, interest in Marxism increased. Starting with Piketty's book *Capital in the Twenty-First Century* (2014), which heightened interest in the New Left, arguments for degrowth developed and gained support from the "generation left" (Latouche, 2020). Degrowth advocates are skeptical of SDGs and argue that they are a scam to enrich certain Western companies while causing environmental destruction. They claim that the SDGs are merely a means of protecting and concealing special interests.

Meanwhile, China has expressed a desire to provide leadership on international development goals, including SDGs and climate change. With the newly established CIDCA, China has rebelled against the development paradigms established by Western countries; however, in the field of SDGs, it has promoted cooperation coordinated primarily by the United Nations. China's power in Asia and Africa has been expanded to counter Western powers and the United States through south–south cooperation and "One Belt, One Road" policies. The COVID-19 pandemic led to the development of vaccine diplomacy, which further advanced the expansion of China's power, destabilizing the post-COVID-19 capitalist model.

## 3.2 Platform capitalism

The United States and the United Kingdom, which laid the foundation for the free trade system, have shifted away from international cooperation; meanwhile, China, which has challenged entrenched international paradigms, has begun challenging the conventional free capitalist system. Many investors appreciate the Chinese model, which is the only model that has recorded positive growth following the COVID-19 pandemic.

Some members of "generation left" support the state-capitalist model, which endorses the nationalization of property and large corporations and champions state intervention in private business. The neo-Marxist model of state capitalism posits that individual rights, such as freedom to conduct business and the right to privacy, run contrary to national interests and the social order and, therefore, should be restricted. In response to the COVID-19 pandemic, this model was effectively adopted not only in China but also in many other countries.

Robert Boyer is a member of the so-called "regulation school," which is based on the principle of coordination between markets and state institutions to facilitate solidarity within civil society. Boyer (2020) uses the concept of "platform capitalism" to explain how the transformation of the capitalist model was accelerated by the COVID-19 pandemic. Here, the term "platform" refers to Google, Apple, Facebook, Amazon, and Microsoft (GAFAM) in the United States and Chinese software programs and apps such as TikTok, Weibo, and WeChat. In China, GAFAM is not accessible, and information from the Western internet is blocked by a robust censorship infrastructure, which could be referred to as another "Great Wall." It is a modern version of the Berlin Wall, and it symbolizes the US–China confrontation.

For capitalism in the 21st century, information is a valuable asset. The intensification of the US–China confrontation can be seen as an axis of confrontation between US and Chinese platforms and their owners, which include private companies and political parties, such as the Chinese Communist Party. When a person is infected with COVID-19 in China, the authorities are able to ascertain details about that person, such as their location and even their bank balance. Consequently, buildings and areas throughout the country, including Hong Kong, were locked down when positive cases were identified.

Moreover, information hosted on GAFAM platforms that is inconvenient for important shareholders is automatically removed by artificial intelligence. One example is the frequent removal of YouTube videos that oppose vaccinations. This demonstrates that GAFAM funding sources are closely related to vaccine interests. On both sides of the Great Wall, information that is inconvenient for authority is censored.

In Europe, citizens who willingly got vaccinated rose up in violent opposition to mandatory vaccination passports. Although they recognized that vaccination is important for the safety of individuals and communities, some were skeptical of allowing authorities to collect information about individuals' health. European idealists believe that big data is a public good that should be managed by citizens (Boyer, 2020). The COVID-19 policy adopted by Sweden strongly reflects Europe's idealism, which is typified by a rejection of market supremacy.

## 3.3 SDGs reexamined

The SDGs are an expansion of the MDGs and consist of 17 goals and 169 numerical targets. The SDGs were adopted by the United Nations General Assembly in September 2015, the year that the MDGs ended. Within the open and participatory climate of policymaking, the lobby groups with the loudest voices can have a decisive influence, and therefore, populist policies tend to be adopted. MDGs have been criticized as examples of wishful thinking, with critics arguing that they lack specific policy tools and responsible entities. The SDGs have not overcome any of the structural deficiencies of the MDGs.

The first and most important of the eight goals set forth by the MDGs was poverty eradication, which has been achieved mainly in East and Southeast Asia; however, this was achieved using a growth strategy not recognized by the MDGs. In response to the withdrawal of infrastructure investments by the World Bank and European and US donors, countries in Asia, Africa, and Latin America accepted Chinese capital through the establishment of the Infrastructure Investment Bank (AIIB), headquartered in China, and loans from China.

To rebuild the world after the COVID-19 pandemic, SDGs must be reconstructed as a sustainable solution. The most pressing problem facing the SDGs at present is that the collection and reporting of indicators do not produce a benefit commensurate to the administrative burden they place on developing countries. There are no penalties enforced for not achieving the indicators, and there is also no reward for achieving them.

## 4. Concluding Remarks

National interest plays a significant role in shaping donors' approaches to foreign aid. First, participation in foreign aid is motivated by national economic interests. By helping spur economic growth in other countries, donors can also benefit. Second, this essay demonstrated that countries participate in foreign aid out of a motivation to strategically influence regional and global security. Third, humanitarian considerations, such as those that arose during the COVID-19 pandemic, are also related to a country's self-interest to exercise leadership.

The world survived COVID-19. However, the SDGs—which have been criticized by both liberals and conservatives and have not been able to provide effective solutions for the COVID-19 pandemic—must be fundamentally reviewed. In addition, companies and investors should play a greater role, a fact that has often been overlooked. Non-governmental organizations and volunteers have not had a meaningful impact on development initiatives. National and international organizations require time to gather opinions and develop comprehensive policies. Companies and investors have an advantage, as they can act quickly.

For an internationally coordinated regime to replace the current SDGs, ethical businesses based on resilient economic systems must become the new standard. This would ensure that in the event of a future pandemic, they will not make poor choices, such as isolating individuals, controlling information, or surprising human rights.

In the event that a highly virulent pandemic comparable to Ebola were to occur, there would be no mechanisms of resilience to help the international community collaborate and respond. During the COVID-19 pandemic, most countries implemented strict economic lockdowns. The SDGs confirmed that these are shallow solutions that are ineffective for responding to a pandemic. In Japan, states of emergency were repeatedly announced with no clear legal justification, eroding public confidence in the government and medical experts.

To return to the question asked at the outset, our analysis seems to confirm that when assisting other countries, donors are motivated by the pursuit of their own economic and political objectives; however, it is possible for competing donors and countries to mutually benefit if they agree to common goals. The SDGs are goals that have been commonly agreed on by international donors, both traditional and new. These donors are trying to overcome the limitations witnessed while working with the MDGs. The COVID-19 experience has highlighted the need to reexamine the basic premise of what the global community seeks to achieve.

# References

Boyer, R. (2020). *Les Capitalismes à l'épreuve de la Pandémie*. Paris: Le découverte.

Bourguignon, F. & Sundberg, M. (May 2007). If foreign aid helping? Aid effectiveness – Opening the black box. *American Economic Review, 97*(2), 316–321. https://doi.org/10.1257/aer.97.2.316

Daimon-Sato, T. (2021). Nexus of military and economic cooperation: Japanese challenges in Afghanistan and Iraq. *Journal of US–China Public Administration, 18*(1), 1–15. https://doi.org/10.17265/1548-6591/2021.01.001

Daimon-Sato, T. (2022). 資本主義経済とSDGs―豊かさの意味を問い直す [Economy reconsidered]. In Noda, M. (Ed.). SDGsを問い直す―ポスト / ウィズ・コロナと人間の安全保障. Kyoto: Horitu Bunka Sha. (in Japanese)

Deudney, D. & Ikenberry, G. J. (1999). The nature and sources of liberal international order. *Review of International Studies, 25*(2), 179–196. https://doi.org/10.1017/S0260210599001795

Fukuda-Parr, S. & Hulme, D. (2011). International norm dynamics and the "end of poverty": Understanding the Millennium Development Goals. *Global Governance, 17*(1), 17–36. https://doi.org/10.1163/19426720-01701002

Fukuyama, F. (May/June 2022). A country of their own: Liberalism needs the nation. *Foreign Affairs*, 80–91.

Lancaster, C. (2007). *Foreign Aid: Diplomacy, Development and Domestic Politics.* University of Chicago Press.

Latouche, S. (2020). *La décroissance*. Paris: Que sais-je.

Mersheimer, J. (2018). *The great delusion: Liberal dreams and international realities*. Yale University Press.

Mearsheimer, J. (2014). Why the Ukraine crisis is the West's fault: The liberal delusions that provoked put in. *Foreign Affairs, 1.*

Morgenthau, H. (1962). A political theory of foreign aid. *American Political Science Review, 56*(2), 301–309. https://doi.org/10.2307/1952366

Morgenthau, H. (1969). *A New Foreign Policy for the United States*. Frederick A. Praeger.

Panchamukhi, V. R. (1983). Complementarity and economic cooperation: A methodological discussion. *Foreign Trade Review, 18*(2), 5–18.

Piketty, T. (2014). *Capital in the 21st Century.* Harvard University Press.

Prebisch, R. (1950). The economic development of Latin America and its principal problems. *Economic Bulletin for Latin America, 7,* 1–12.

Singer, H. (1950). The distribution of gains between investing and borrowing countries, *American Economic Review, Papers & Proceedings, 40,* 473–485.

# Chapter Nine

## Mapping the Distribution of Social Workers and Social Work Schools

Masateru Higashida

This chapter explores the demographic distribution of social work-related data in the world using several databases and geographic information system (GIS) analysis. I use open data collected and published by international organizations and other stakeholders. This data includes estimates of the distributions of social workers and social work schools across the globe. ArcGIS Online, a web-based mapping software, was used for mapping the data. This chapter aims to visualize the "objective" and cross-sectional features of the data; therefore, I attempted to present the data analysis while limiting my own subjective interpretation. Nevertheless, I recognize that no researcher can conduct data analysis completely free of their own interpretations and social biases (Gergen, 2022). In addition, I faced several difficulties during the analysis and writing processes, particularly with respect to data collection. The results of the data analysis in this chapter remain exploratory, as reliable and valid data on social workers does not seem to exist for all countries in the world. Thus, it was impossible to verify the reliability of other data used in this paper.

There is significant controversy surrounding the question of which countries and territories to recognize when developing a comprehensive list of the world's countries. For example, as of April 2023, there were 193 recognized member states of the United Nations (UN). This does not include the Vatican, the Republic of Kosovo, the Cook Islands, Niue, Taiwan (Republic of China), Palestine (Provisional Authority of Palestine), Somaliland (Republic of Somaliland) and others. This chapter uses the UN's list of sovereign states for comparison with the number corresponding to the existing data; however, I remain neutral with regard to the jurisdictional claims of maps used in this chapter. For instance, the borders on the maps used in this paper were based on data from the GIS software, and this paper does not attempt to make any political claims about the legitimacy of specific borders.

234

# 1. Number and Distribution of Social Workers

Although there are somewhat conflicting claims about the number of social workers worldwide, it appears that the number is generally increasing. As of 2019, the International Federation of Social Workers (IFSW, 2021) claimed to represent more than 3 million social workers from 128 member countries. Just 3 years later, in their 2022 report (IFSW, 2023), the federation stated that it now represented more than 5 million social workers from 146 national associations. As of November 2022, the global population was estimated to be slightly over 8 billion people, and therefore, a rough estimation would indicate that there are approximately 6.25 social workers per 10,000 people globally. However, adequate and reliable data for estimating the global geographical distribution of social workers could not be collected during the study period. Accordingly, I planned to collect as much information as possible while adopting the aggregation method, mainly by areas of practice, states and organizations.[39][40]

The World Health Organization (WHO) has made available data specific to social workers working in the field of mental health. This data pertains to "[s]ocial workers working in mental health (per 100,000 population), including professionals working in private and public mental health facilities as well as private practice." Data regarding the number of social workers per 100,000 people globally are available (n = 100); therefore, I converted this ratio to per 10,000 population (see Figure 9-1 for distributions by country).[41] Overall, the number of social workers ranged from 0 (Cyprus) to 14.54 (Canada), with a median of 0.05. In addition, 9 countries had more than 0.50 social workers per 10,000 people (Canada, Monaco, Costa Rica, United States, Belgium, Panama, South Korea, Japan and Brazil), whereas 25 countries had less than 0.01 social worker (Iraq, Equatorial Guinea, Burundi, Senegal, India, Tanzania, Yemen, Togo, Madagascar, Eritrea, Ethiopia, Uganda, Niger,

---

39   The Minutes of 2002/2004 also mentioned that they represented 470,000 social workers from 78 countries (IFSW, 2012).

40   In April 2023, I contacted IFSW Secretariat regarding this issue, but I did not receive a response by the writing date.

41   Statistical processing of the ratio was impossible because basic data such as real number were not available.

Sierra Leone, Angola, Central African Republic, Republic of Congo, Ecuador, Zambia, Mozambique, Myanmar, Burkina Faso, Guinea, Chad and Guatemala).

Moreover, there is additional data that has been published by national and regional institutions. This begs the question as to whether aggregating all these data would result in an estimate for the world's social workers. For example, the Bureau of Labor Statistics (2022) in the United States estimated that 708,100 people—or 21.3 people per 10,000—were working as social workers in 2021; it was also anticipated that 74,700 new individuals per year would join the social work field. According to existing data, overall employment of social workers was forecasted to grow by 9% between 2021 and 2031, which was higher than the average for all occupations.

In the United Kingdom, the number of social workers has also been trending upward and is estimated to increase from 111,100 in 2010 to about 122,300 in 2022, which is roughly 18.1 people per 10,000 (Statista, 2022).

Figure 9-1. Mapping the WHO's Estimates for Social Workers Engaged in Mental Health

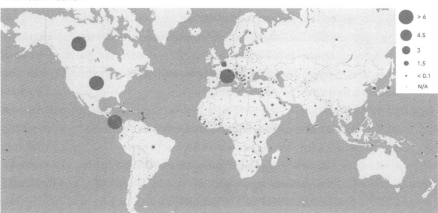

Note. The figure was created by the author using ArcGIS Online. Demographic data on social workers in the mental health field were used to create this map (WHO, 2019). Among the 100 countries selected by the WHO, the estimates of the number of social workers per 10,000 population are presented by country. Black dots (N/A) indicate the countries among the 193 UN member states that did not contribute data.

In Japan, 280,968 certified social workers were registered because of the national qualification system that was institutionalized in 1987. Consequently, there are now approximately 22.5 certified social workers per 10,000. In addition, there are approximately 100,000 nationally certified mental health social workers as well as 1,880,000 certified care workers, social welfare officers and civil welfare volunteers. Therefore, there is controversy over the question of who should be regarded as a "social worker" depending on the context.

Related data are also available for Southeast Asia and the surrounding region (see Table 9-1). Figure 9-2 shows the ratio of social workers per 10,000 people plotted for the following countries: Cambodia, Fiji, Indonesia, Kiribati, Lao People's Democratic Republic (Lao PDR), Malaysia, Mongolia, Myanmar, Papua New Guinea, the Philippines, Solomon Islands, Thailand, Timor-Leste, Vanuatu and Vietnam. With the exception of two countries for which

**Figure 9-2. Estimation of the Numbers of Social Workers Identified in Southeast and East Asia**

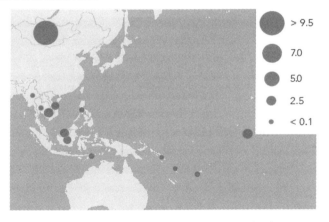

*Note.* The figure was created by the author using ArcGIS Online. The data were extracted from the UNICEF East Asia and the Pacific Regional Office (2019): Cambodia, Fiji, Indonesia, Kiribati, Lao People's Democratic Republic, Malaysia, Mongolia, Myanmar, Papua New Guinea, the Philippines, Solomon Islands, Thailand, Timor-Leste, Vanuatu and Vietnam. The approximate minimum underestimation and real value were derived by converting to the ratio per 10,000 people. However, as shown in Table 9-1, this data are based on statistics and do not necessarily represent the actual situation.

## Table 9-1. Estimations Regarding Social Workers in Southeast Asia and Surrounding Countries

| Country | Size and scope of social service workforce | Professionalization |
|---|---|---|
| Cambodia | Approximately 3,764 social workers, 33% of whom work for the national government and 67% work for provincial and local government. There is also an unknown number working for NGOs. | Established professional association; no code of ethics |
| Fiji | 57 working for the government, as well as an unknown number working for NGOs and FBOs | Established professional association; code of ethics |
| Indonesia | 45,000 in government and an unknown number at NGOs | Established professional association; code of ethics; law regarding professional social work currently in parliament |
| Kiribati | 31 in government and an unknown number at NGOs and FBOs | Not established |
| Lao People's Democratic Republic | Figure not available; anyone working in social welfare | Not established |
| Malaysia | 6,900, including 5,000 child protection officers | Established professional association; code of ethics; law regarding professional social work currently in parliament |
| Mongolia | 2,856 at central and local governments in the sectors of education, health and justice; there is also an unknown number at NGOs | Six established professional associations; code of ethics |
| Myanmar | An estimated 200, as well as an unknown number at NGOs | Not established |
| Papua New Guinea | Figures not available | Established professional association; code of ethics |
| Philippines | Figure not available; one estimate suggests 5,423 registered social workers in Department of Social Welfare and Development, not including health, education, justice sectors; plus, an unknown number at NGOs | Established professional association; code of ethics and practice standards; profession of social work mandated by law, with protected title; system of professional licensing |
| Solomon Islands | 13 in government and an unknown number at NGOs and FBOs | Not established |
| Thailand | 3,000 registered social workers, not including para-social workers; other paraprofessional and volunteer numbers not known; unknown number of social workers at NGOs | Established professional association; code of ethics; profession of social work mandated by law, with protected title, system of professional licensing |
| Timor-Leste | 90 in government and an unknown number at NGOs and FBOs | Not established |
| Vanuatu | 7 in Ministry of Justice and Community Services (other government, NGO and FBO numbers unknown) | Not established |
| Viet Nam | 16,424 in government and an unknown number in NGOs and FBOs; estimated demand for 58,033 in government social welfare | Established professional association; code of ethics; draft of decree on social work |

*Note.* Data were extracted from UNICEF East Asia and the Pacific Regional Office (2019: 99-103).

FBOs = Faith-based organizations; NGOs = Non-governmental organizations.

no data were included (Lao PDR and Papua New Guinea), Mongolia (9.52 social workers per 10,000 people) was the country with the highest rate, followed by Kiribati (2.82 social workers) and Cambodia (2.40 social workers). Meanwhile, seven countries (Myanmar, Solomon Islands, Vanuatu, Thailand, Philippines, Fiji and Timor-Leste) had less than one social worker per 10,000 people.

Figures on the number of community health workers were also shown. This is another example of the critical importance of the debate over who is considered a "social worker." Figure 9-3 shows a mapping of the true number of community health workers using numbers extracted from the most recent data collected by WHO (2023) on 98 different countries. The most recent period of data collection ranged from 2000 (Saint Vincent and the Grenadines) to 2021 (11 countries). It was difficult to calculate per capita, as only the frequency was shown. The number of social workers ranged from 0 (five countries: Guinea-Bissau, Malawi, Peru, Sri Lanka and Tuvalu) to more than 1 million (China and India), with a median of 1,859.

### Figure 9-3. Mapping of the Number of Community Health Workers

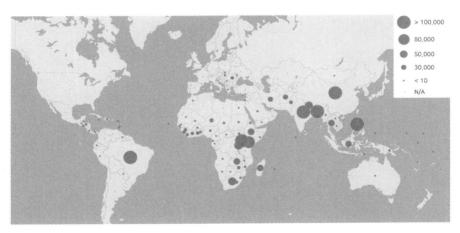

Note. The image was created by the author using ArcGIS Online. The data was sourced from the WHO (2023). Black dots (N/A) indicate countries and regions among the 193 member states of the United Nations that did not provide data.

## 2. Number and Distribution of Social Work Schools/Programs Identified by the International Association of Schools of Social Work

To estimate the number of social work schools globally, I used census data from the International Association of Schools of Social Work (IASSW; Rautenbach, 2021). According to the IASSW data, there were a total of 1,384 programs in 114 countries as of 2000. By 2010, there were 2,110 programs in 125 countries, and by the end of 2020, there were 3,572 programs in 159 countries. Due to the limitations of the methods, this data might not show the actual numbers and conditions of social work schools and programs; rather, the data covered only schools and programs which were identified by the IASSW. Therefore, in the case of some countries, these numbers may be considerably lower than the actual number. As some errors were observed in the open data, I adjusted the data and visualized the number of programs by

Figure 9-4. Mapping of the Number of Social Work Programs Identified by the IASSW Census

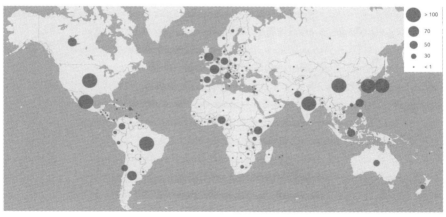

Note. The image was created by the author using ArcGIS Online. The raw data organized by Rautenbach (2021) was used. After deleting duplications, the data were calculated with modifications.

country (see Figure 9-4).[42] Overall seven countries had more than 100 programs (United States, Brazil, Japan, India, China, South Korea and Mexico), with the United States being the largest (714 programs). Meanwhile, countries with four or fewer programs accounted for the majority (51.9%) of the total.


## 3. Example: Relationship between Mental Health Social Workers and Social Work Schools

Figure 9-5 shows both the number of mental health social workers and the distribution of social work education programs in the Middle East and Africa. These figures are based on the same international data used above. As mentioned earlier, if there is no data for a specific country, it does not necessarily indicate that no data exists. That is, in some cases, data were available, but it was not possible to verify the accuracy of the data. Therefore, these figures should be considered material for discussion as visual data to capture cross-sectional trends.

I also explored the relationship between the estimated number of social workers in the mental health field and the number of social work schools identified by the IASSW. After excluding missing values from the obtained data (n = 73), the estimated number of social workers and the number of social work schools per population were log-transformed. The analysis showed a weak or modest – yet statistically significant ($p < 0.01$) – positive correlation between the two variables (r = .38).[43] This indicates that the relationship between the number of schools providing social work education and the number of social workers should be further explored.

---

42   For example, it is said that there are about 14 schools in Mongolia, but only two are shown.

43   Because this data is missing large amounts of important information, it is possible that there is bias in the data used.

Figure 9-5. Distribution of Mental Health Social Workers and Social Work Schools in the Middle East and Africa

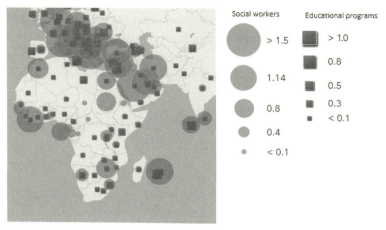

*Note.* The image was created by the author using ArcGIS Online. The data were retrieved from WHO (2019) and Rautenbach (2021). Since some data in the population ratio were 0, the logarithmic transformation was carried out after adding 1 to all real numbers.

# 4. Conclusions

This exploratory chapter illustrated the global distribution of social workers and social work schools. Because this chapter is intended to convey objective facts, I have abstained from interpreting the data. However, it is necessary to comment on data collection processes related to social work. As mentioned at the beginning of this chapter, the data needed for this study was not sufficiently organized, and its reliability could not be verified. Therefore, there are significant obstacles to producing a global picture of social work due to the difficulties related to defining "social workers" in each individual context. For example, the different types of practitioners considered to be social workers will likely vary by country: Buddhist social work as a case will be introduced in the next chapter. Therefore, the themes of this chapter must be continuously examined in future research.

# Acknowledgements

This work was supported by JSPS KAKENHI Grant Number JP23H00900.

# References

Gergen, K. J. (2022). *An Invitation to Social Construction: Co-creating the Future* (4th edition). SAGE.

International Federation of Social Workers (IFSW). (2012). *Minutes of the IFSW General Meeting 2004*. www.ifsw.org

International Federation of Social Workers (IFSW). (2021). *IFSW Statement on the Draft Convention on the Right to Development*. www.ifsw.org

International Federation of Social Workers (IFSW). (2023). *2022 End of Year Report*. www.ifsw.org

Rautenbach, J. V. (2021). *Global Directory of Schools of Social Work: Census 2020*. International Association of Schools of Social Work (IASSW).

Statista. (2022). *Estimated Number of Social Workers in the United Kingdom from 2010 to 2022*. https://www.statista.com/statistics/319253/number-of-social-workers-in-the-uk/

UNICEF East Asia and the Pacific Regional Office. (2019). *The Social Service Workforce in the East Asia and Pacific Region: Multi-country review.*

U.S. Bureau of Labor Statistics. (2022). *Community and Social Service.* https://www.bls.gov/ooh/community-and-social-service/social-workers.htm

World Health Organization, WHO. (2019). *The Global Health Observatory. Social Workers Working in Mental Health Sector (per 10,0000)*. https://www.who.int/data/gho/indicator-metadata-registry/imr-details/2959

World Health Organization, WHO. (2023). *Community Health Workers (number).* https://www.who.int/data/gho/data/indicators/indicator-details/GHO/community-health-workers-(number)

# Chapter Ten

## Buddhist Social Work

Josef Gohori

Akimoto (2017) proposed the concept of Buddhist social work as an organic and natural outcome of his critical consideration of the global definition of social work. Following a trajectory that leads "from Western-rooted social work to Buddhist social work," Akimoto has taken a unique approach to understanding Buddhist social work as one of forms to explore social work for all people. This claim refers to a certain disharmony towards the global definition of social work profession adopted in 2014 (ISSW, 2014). Suggesting a shift from Western-rooted professional social work might be considered an expression of objection against the definition that attempts to fit social work into an extremely narrow category. Therefore, this debate should be recognized as a discourse on the discipline of social work itself. Meanwhile, focusing on Buddhism as a representative cultural and social aspect that traverses boundaries between states and nations provides an international perspective. Moreover, by engaging in the overlap between Buddhist and indigenous social work, this debate is able to engage with a multilayered discourse. However, in this essay, we focus exclusively on the introduction of the concept of Buddhist social work into ongoing debates on social work more generally.

Building on Akimoto's work, Karma (2017), Herath (2017), and other scholars have identified several characteristics of Buddhist social work primarily from the perspective of Buddhist philosophy. In this chapter, we reflect on these characteristics while also clarifying the origin of Buddhist social work and its history of development.

244

# 1. A Brief History of Research Activities on Buddhist Social Work

The first attempts to reveal the potential of Buddhism in the field of social work were made in the early 2010s. During this initial stage, Tatsuru Akimoto initiated several projects that reconsidered the concept of social work within an Asian context. Between 2012 and 2015, a group of Vietnamese scholars led by Nguyen Hoi Loan worked with Vietnam National University to conduct a comparative study to identify the potential of Buddhism in the social work field (Sakamoto, 2014). In addition, Anuradha Wickramasinghe and other Sri Lankan practitioners highlighted several essential practice models in Sri Lanka, expanding the debate on functional alternatives (Sasaki, 2014). This led to the so-called "five-countries research" project, which included Sri Lanka, Thailand, Myanmar, Vietnam, and Nepal. This resulted in the creation of a solid base for proposing the ABC model (Akimoto, 2017). In order to systematically explore the potential for Buddhist social work in Asia, an international joint research project was conducted in 12 mainly Buddhist countries and regions. Based on field research, workshops, and symposia, a research book series entitled Exploring Buddhist Social Work was published. The series consists of 11 books published in both English and Japanese, resulting in 22 total books (2017–2024, Gakubunsha). The joint project was instrumental in the establishment of the Asian Buddhist Social Work Research Network, which has brought together around 150 scholars and practitioners from various countries. This network began publishing the International Journal of Buddhist Social Work in 2022, providing a new platform for scholarship on Buddhist social work.

Over the past decade, Buddhist social work has not only matured as a discipline. That is, the discipline as a whole is increasingly prioritizing the sharing and dissemination of research results and achievements.

## 2. Characteristics of Buddhist Social Work

This joint research project identified a significant number of activities hosted by Buddhist temples, Buddhists, Buddhist monks and nuns, and Buddhist NGOs in Asia. Activities focused on children, the elderly, and the poor, and they provided support and assistance for individuals, families, and communities, with many of the activities conforming with the core functions of social work. Meanwhile, some activities—such as educational and vocational programs, counseling, meditation, rehabilitation center services, hospice programs, and programs for chronic-ill patients, disabled persons, and HIV/AIDS patients—are understood within local contexts as a part of Buddhist social work. Moreover, these activities clearly traverse boundaries between disciplines, including medical care and education. Moreover, some activities, such as agricultural support, infrastructure building, and environmental programs, are clearly beyond the scope of what is generally recognized as related to social work. Indeed, this expanded scope of practice may be one of the defining features of Buddhist social work. All of the activities above are intended to support individual well-being and, therefore, should be recognized as an organic part of social work (Gohori, 2021a). This expanded understanding of the scope of activities included within the social work profession has been influenced and supported by a perspective that respects all sentient beings and considers humans and their environment to be interlinked. In Buddhism, the term *paticcasamuppāda*, meaning "dependent origination," refers to the interconnectedness of everything. That is, this term implies that all phenomena in the universe are interrelated and depend on one another. In this sense, human society (or culture) and the environment (or nature) are identical and indivisible. There are also examples from biology demonstrating that even our human bodies are composed of non-human microbiotas. Moreover, it is a scientifically proven fact that even the body of a single human is an aggregate of multiple interrelated human and non-human life. From the perspective *paticcasamuppāda*—which could be interpreted as meaning "everything matters"—it is clear that society could not exist as simply a "human society." Therefore, social work cannot focus exclusively on humans. Everything matters. This mindset is clearly different from the vertical hierarchy that has shaped the value system of Christian culture. Moreover, a logical analysis shows that it is also different from the client-centered approach, ecological approach, and other common theories in social work (Gohori, 2021b). This overlap between human society and the environment can be compared to Dominelli's concept of "green social work" (Dominelli, 2012); however, a unique characteristic of Buddhist social work is that it incorporates the Buddhist practice of not differentiating between different types of entities.

Therefore, it follows from this that Buddhist social work is underpinned by Buddhist teaching and that its ethical code strictly follows Buddhist principles.[44] This could be considered a common feature of faith-based organizations and activities with religious elements. However, some scholars have pointed out that some Buddhism-based elements, that shape the nature and basic theories and methods of Buddhist social work, are not only local attributes or accessories to something that could be called "universal social work." In Japan, for example, the concepts of social well-being and social networks include relationships with the deceased (continuing bonds) as an essential aspect of Buddhist social work (Klass, 1996; Gohori, 2016). Discussing her lived experience in Sri Lanka, Waruni (2021) describes how an understanding of responsibility and core elements such as human rights might be different in the Buddhist social work context. Somananda (2022)— who extracted social work-related theories and methods directly from original Buddhist scripts, or the so-called "Pali" canon—has produced pioneering works in the field.

However, arguably the most important characteristic of Buddhist social work is how it identifies the essential causes of the problems people encounter in their lives. Within Buddhist social work, the analysis and interpretation of the causes of social problems are strongly influenced by the Buddhist concept of *dukkha*, meaning "suffering." The Buddhist perspective on suffering begins by accepting the fact that it is impossible for a living being to avoid or eliminate the causes of suffering, such as death or illness. For this reason, some scholars have wrongly classified Buddhism as a nihilist belief system (Narada, 2022). However, the Buddhist interpretation of life is anything but nihilist. By accepting that some life events are inevitable, people

---

44    For comparison, the Five Precepts, also known as pañcasīla, are a basic code of ethics.

can understand that suffering originates from one's mental proliferations and conceptualization—not from life events. Based on the concept of *papañca*, meaning "conceptual proliferation," Buddhist social work utilizes a comprehensive approach, accounting for both the inside and outside and the materialistic and non-materialistic (spiritual) aspects of every matter.

In Buddhist social work activities, there are few trained social work professionals or people with qualifications equivalent to a social worker license. However, as Huong (2023) points out, the attitudes and patterns of behavior and communication of those who practice Buddhist social work follow the path of the bodhisattva. The concept of bodhisattva involves more than just adopting Buddhist virtues such as *karunā* (meaning "sympathetic joy") or *mettā* (meaning "loving-kindness"). Rather, the concept of bodhisattva is based on the teaching of compassion for the benefit of all sentient beings. Formal social work education (as an academic discipline and profession) emphasizes theories and methods, with a focus on *what* to do and *how* to do it. The education process of Buddhist social work, however, begins with a personal inner transformation of the provider of Buddhist social work provider.

Of course, there may be negative aspects to this approach. In Theravada Buddhism, the high social status of the clergy and gender biases are frequently cited as problems. In addition, disability and disease are sometimes interpreted by Buddhists as the result of having performed bad deeds in one's previous life. However, as Sirimanne (2015) has pointed out, many of these limitations are influenced more by local culture and social settings than Buddhist teachings. Nevertheless, it should be mentioned that this paper does not attempt to portray Buddhist society as perfect but rather as a form of social work. Moreover, as with any other form, it has its limitations and critical issues.

## 3. Conceptualization

As mentioned earlier, Akimoto proposed the ABC model to distinguish between (A) the "Western-rooted social work profession," (B) the modified (or indigenized) model of Western-rooted social work enriched by local (or indigenous) elements, and (C) the original (indigenous) model of social work. Definitions reflecting Akimoto's ABC model are as follows.

Below is the working definition of model C as adopted by members of the Asian Buddhist Social Work Research Network in 2017:

"Buddhist social work is human activities which help other people solve or alleviate life difficulties and problems, based on the Buddha-nature. Buddhist social work always finds causes to work on in both the material, or social arena, as well as in the human, or inner arena, working on both arenas in tandem. Its fundamental principles include compassion, loving kindness and mutual help, and interdependency and self-reliance. The central value is the Five Precepts. The ultimate goal is to achieve the wellbeing of all sentient beings and peace." (Akimoto, 2018, p. 3)

The working definition of model B as adopted in 2017 is as follows:

"Buddhist Social Work is the social work based on the Buddhist philosophy. It helps individuals, families, groups and communities enhance social functions, and promote their wellbeing and peace, and human happiness and harmony. It is an academic inter-discipline and profession. Buddhist Social Work professionals will demonstrate his/her knowledge and skills, values guided by the principle of Buddha-nature." (Akimoto, 2018, p. 3)

With respect to both definitions[45], there are some issues that must be considered. As with any working definition, both definitions are far from being finalized; however, there are important objections. Regarding model C, it is not clear if it is a definition of Buddhism itself or a definition of Buddhist social work (cf. Akimoto, 2017: 31–32). If asked to name the core characteristics of Buddhism as a philosophy, teaching, or way of life, most Buddhist scholars would agree that all or almost all parts of the above definition should be included. Even if the definition is too narrow to comprehensively convey all aspects of Buddhism, it still refers directly to its

---

45    It must be noted that the author of this paper was involved in these discussions.

249

component parts (Sobitha, 2023). Therefore, such a definition appears vague. It might be difficult to distinguish Buddhism from charity activities based on Buddhism (or provided by Buddhists) and from the well-known concept of "engaged Buddhism" (or "socially engaged Buddhism").

Meanwhile, the definition from model B could be interpreted as simply an extension of the global definition of social work. The statement that Buddhist social work is a form of social work implies that there is a universally accepted concept of social work. Moreover, having limited its scope to an academic discipline and profession, there is doubt whether this model would even be able to reflect and apply the characteristic features of Buddhist social work we have introduced in the previous section.

## 4. Conclusion

When addressing social work in the context of a specific religion, there are multiple options regarding how to proceed with discussions and place the topic into context. The first is a focus on faith-based organizations. The second involves addressing the relationship between religion/spirituality and social work. The next approach reflects the indigenous forms of social work-related activities in which religion indisputably plays an important role. This text attempted to introduce Buddhist social work and its characteristics and features; therefore, I would like to stop at this point in order not to open a debate on faith-based organizations or spirituality. However, Buddhist social work might show us how to understand this one form of social work.

# References

Akimoto, T. (2017). The globalization of Western-rooted professional social work and exploration of Buddhist social work. In Gohori, J., Akimoto, T., Ishikawa, T., Loan, N.H., Onopas, S. & Sangbo, K. (Eds.). *From Western-rooted Professional Social Work to Buddhist Social Work* (pp.3–41). Tokyo: Gakubunsha.

Akimoto, T. (2017). ABC model of Buddhist social work. In Gohori, J., Akimoto, T., Ishikawa, T., Loan, N. H., Onopas, S. & Sangbo, K. (Eds). *From Western-rooted Professional Social Work to Buddhist Social Work* (pp.22–25). Tokyo: Gakubunsha.

Akimoto, T. & Hattori, M. (Eds.). (2018). *Working Definition and Current Curricula of Buddhist Social Work*. Faculty of Sociology, USSH-VNU, and ARIISW.

Akimoto, T., Fujimori, Y., Gohori, J. & Matsuo, K. (2020). Objection to Western-rooted professional social work. To make social work something truly of the world: Indigenization is not the answer. Gohori, J. (Ed.). *The Journey of Buddhist Social Work: Exploring the Potential of Buddhism in Asian Social Work* (pp.65–68). ARIISW.

Dominelli, L. (2012). *Green Social Work*. Cambridge: Polity.

Fujimori, Y. (Ed.). (2020). 東日本大震災を契機とした、地域社会・社会福祉協議会と宗教施設（仏教寺院・神社等）との連携に関するアンケート調査. ARIISW. (in Japanese)

Gohori, J. (2016). 生者と死者を結ぶネットワーク〜日本的死生観に基づく生き方に関する考察 [The network between the living and the dead]. Joetsu: Joetsu University of Education Press. (in Japanese)

Gohori, J. (2019). On religion and social work. In Tran Nhan Tong Institute. (Ed.). *Social Assistance Activities of Contemporary Buddhism* (pp.107–114). Hanoi: Vietnam National University Press.

Gohori, J. (2021a). Cultural background of social work: Exploring the Buddhist social work. In Tulshi Kumar Das et al. (Eds.). *Social Work and Sustainable Social Development* (pp.63–69). Sylhet: Shahjal University Press.

Gohori, J. (2021b). Beyond the comparative study: An attempt to touch the essence of Buddhist social work. In Akimoto, T. & Someya, Y. (Eds.). *What Buddhist Social Work Can do While Western-rooted Professional Social*

*Work Cannot* (pp.xiii–xvii). ARIISW.

Gohori, J., Akimoto, T., Ishikawa, T., Loan, N. H., Onopas, S. & Sangbo, K. (Eds.). (2017). *From Western-rooted Professional Social Work to Buddhist Social Work. Exploring Buddhist Social Work.* Tokyo: Gakubunsha.

Gohori, J. & Someya, Y. (Eds.). (2021). *Social Work Academics Resisting the Globalization of Western-rooted Social Work Decolonization, Indigenization, Spirituality, and Buddhist Social Work.* ARIISW.

Herath, H. M. D. R. (2017). Buddhist social work: Theory and practice. In Gohori, J., Akimoto, T., Ishikawa, T., Loan, N. H., Onopas, S. & Sangbo, K. (Eds.). *From Western-rooted Professional Social Work to Buddhist Social Work* (pp.46–56). Tokyo: Gakubunsha.

Huong, N. (2023). What is a true Buddhist social worker? *International Journal of Buddhist Social Work, 2,* 78–89.

IFSW & IASSW. (2014). Global Definition of the Social Work Profession. Retrieved February 4, 2024, from https://www.ifsw.org/what-is-social-work/global-definition-of-social-work/.

Karma, S. (2017). Social welfare by Buddhist monasteries in Nepal. In Gohori, J., Akimoto, T., Ishikawa, T., Loan, N. H., Onopas, S. & Sangbo, K. (Eds.). *From Western-rooted Professional Social Work to Buddhist Social Work* (pp.57–65). Tokyo: Gakubunsha.

Kikuchi, Y. (Ed.). (2015). *Buddhist "social work" activities in Asia.* (Headed by Akimoto, T.). Asian Center for Social Work Research (ACSWR), Shukutoku University.

Klass, D. (1996). *Continuing Bonds: New Understandings of Grief (Death education, aging and health care).* Routledge.

Loan, N. H. (2020). Comparing Western-rooted social work and Buddhist social work in providing psychotherapy/counselling for people with mental problems in Vietnam. In Akimoto. T. & Someya, Y. (Eds.). *What Buddhist Social Work Can Do While Western-rooted Professional Social Work Cannot.* ARIISW.

Loan, N. H. (2022). Buddhist social work: Questioning the professionalism. *International Journal of Buddhist Social Work, 1,* 70–72.

Narada, P. (2020). Sri Lankan monk's social work process while disproving Weber's statement as Buddhism is an asocial religion. In Akimoto, T. (Ed.). *Buddhist Social Work in Sri Lanka: Past and Present* (pp.153–168).

Tokyo: Gakubunsha.

Oyut-Erdene, N. (2022). Buddhist social work: Questioning the professionalism. *International Journal of Buddhist Social Work, 1,* 70–72.

Sasaki, A. (Ed.). (2014). *(Professional) Social Work and its Functional Alternatives.* Asian Center for Welfare in Society (ACWelS), Japan College of Social Work, and APASWE.

Sakamoto, E. (Ed.). (2014). *The Roles of Buddhism in Social Work: Vietnam and Japan Comparative Research* (Headed by Akimoto, T.). Shukutoku University, USSH-VNU, ACWelS-JCSW, and APASWE.

Sirimanne, C. (2016). Buddhism and women: The Dhamma has no gender. *International Journal of Women's Studies, 18(1),* 273–292.

Sobitha, O. (2023). How Buddhist teachings encourage social welfare and altruism. In Gohori, J. (Ed.). *Reviewing Buddhist Social Work Through the Lens of History, Education, and Practice* (pp. 1–11). ARIISW.

Somananda, O. (2022). *An analytical study on applicability of teachings in Buddhism for the development of Buddhist social work education.* Doctoral thesis, Shukutoku University. (unpublished)

Waruni, T. (2020). A survey analysis on a more effective model of social work for Sri Lanka with reference to selected WPSW and BSW institutions operated in Sri Lanka. In Akimoto. T., Someya, Y. (Eds.). *What Buddhist Social Work Can Do While Western-rooted Professional Social Work Cannot.* ARIISW.

# Postface

Looking back on the journey we have undergone in the pursuit of new theories of international social work, we are filled with immense gratitude. It took years from the conception of the first edition to the publication of this extended second edition, the discussions, dialogues, and exchanges that took place over that time undoubtedly enriched this book's content. Once again, we express our deepest gratitude to all who have interacted and cooperated with us on this journey and for the connections that we have made.

On February 27, 2024, the first edition (Part I of this edition) was presented at the 8th International Academic Forum, International Social Work Beyond its Centennial Anniversary Theory Debate (Disappearance or Expansion, Reform or New Construction?), which was organized by the Asian Research Institute for International Social Work, with the support of the Japanese Association for Social Work Education. At this forum, we invited Professor Emeritus Lynne Moore Healy (University of Connecticut) and Professor Manohar Pawar (Charles Sturt University), who are both world-renowned researchers in international social work and whose work is mentioned in Chapter 1, to give lectures on the current state and future prospects of theories of international social work. The forum and our research exchanges gave us confidence that the content and perspectives of this book can enable further development of these topics among those who are passionate about the evolution of international social work.

A series of coincidences have brought us to a significant milestone. On April 6, 2024, at the Joint World Conference on Social Work, Education and Social Development (SWSD2024) held in Panama, Dr. Tatsuru Akimoto was awarded the Katherine Kendall Award,[1] established to honor Dr. Katherine A. Kendall (1910-2010), Honorary President of the International Association of Schools of Social Work, who made significant contributions to the internationalization of social work education. This award is significant not only in its reflection of individual achievements but also in its emphasis on

---

1  The transcript of his keynote lecture, entitled "International Social Work (ISW) Beyond Its Centennial Anniversary: ISW of Social Work (SW) in the Third Stage, Western-rooted SW, Buddhist SW, and SW of All", at the SWSD2024 conference is available at the following link: https://www.shukutoku.ac.jp/en/about/facilities/asiancenter.html

the collective importance of having and maintaining an international perspective in social work. In other words, it is related to the publication of this book.

The publication of this expanded edition of this book is important both for the present, when the need to understand international affairs comprehensively is greater than ever, but also for the future. It brings together multiple perspectives and insights and poses various questions that undoubtedly remain open for the future.

We look forward to making further updates to the expanded edition of this book, believing that the continuous exploration and development of international social work theory is only just beginning. We sincerely hope that this book will provoke lively discussion across all social work communities, but that is just the first step. In the future, we hope that all aspects of social work education, practice, and research will incorporate an international perspective, that is, a broader way of viewing matters. As encapsulated by the new definition presented in Chapter 3, we believe that social work itself will be enriched by incorporating the new perspectives of this book.

In conclusion, we express again our heartfelt thanks to everyone who contributed to the realization of this book project, and it would give us great joy if our readers would participate in ongoing dialogue on the future of international social work. We hope to realize international social work for everyone all around the world!

Masateru Higashida

# Index

## A

ABC Model in Buddhist social work 123, 245, 248-9
Abe Doctrine 221
access to nationality 204
activities 31, 58, 90
actual being 114
actual existence 116
affinity 126-7, 130, 161, 165
African Development Bank (AFDB) 218
Age of Enlightenment 189
Agence Française de Dévelopement (AFD) 217
Ahmadi, N. 35, 38
aid and assistance 31, 91, 139
aid competition 219
aid policies 220, 226
*Ainu* 94
alienated borderlands 170
all humans are brothers 185
all people(s) of all countries 16, 19, 94, 121, 125, 128-30
altruism 73
America First 185
American imperialism 28
American Revolutionary War 186
Americans with Disabilities Act (ADA) 64, 68, 118
ancestral history 182
Anderson, B. 181
Anglo-American 172
Anglo-Saxon 111, 146
anthropology 170
anti-discrimination 204
Appiah, Kwame Anthony 185
Arab Spring 223
ArcGIS Online 234, 236-7, 239-40, 242
artificial intelligence 229
Ashikaga, Y. 66, 71-3, 77

Asian and Pacific Association for Social Work Education (APASWE) 25, 27-8, 69
Asian Buddhist Social Work Research Network 245, 249
Asian Center for Welfare Society (ACWelS) 119
Asian Development Bank (ADB) 218, 226
Asian financial crisis 227
Askeland, G.A. 22, 38
Association of South-East Asian Nations (ASEAN) 77, 101
asylum 202, 206-7
authentic 22, 23, 146, 197, 201
authority of royal 181
autonomous entities 184
autonomy in self-government 169

## B

backlash 191
Bandung Conference 220
Berlin Conference 173
Berlin Wall 174, 228
bilateral 182, 216-7
birth outside hospitals and midwifery facilities 199, 200
birth tours 203
Biestek's seven principles of the Western-rooted social work 209
black box 108, 121, 124, 126
blank world map 139, 140, 147, 153
bodhisattva 248
Bodin, J. 21, 92
Boehm, W 31
Bolloré 225
boomerang 112, 113, 116, 125
border issues 175
border studies 168, 170, 176
Borderland Studies 170
borderless space 174

borderlessness 174
boundary-making 171
bourgeois revolution 103
Boyer, Robert 228-9
Bretton Woods Agreement/system 218, 226
Brown, J. 69
Buddha-nature 249
Buddhist countries and regions 245
Buddhist philosophy 244, 249
Buddhist principles 247
Buddhist social work 10, 12, 94, 99, 121-4, 127, 242, 244-50
buffer-line 172

# C

*Capital in the Twenty-First Century* 227
categories of functions 90, 128
categorization 10, 204, 209-11
categorized activities 45-6, 50
Catholic(s) 172
centrality of the nation-state 190
centralized political entity 179
certified care workers 237
certified mental health social workers 237
charity 124, 161, 250
chiefdoms 179
child protection 176, 199, 238
China International Development Cooperation Agency (CIDCA) 223, 227
China's Belt and Road Initiative 220
Chinese Communist Party 229
Chinese Export-Import Bank 223
Christian culture 246
Christian missionaries 173
Christian NGO 68
Christian sects 172
Cicero 189
citizen of the world 189
citizenship 10, 111, 189, 197-9, 200, 202-5, 207
city-states (polis) 189, 171, 172
civic belongingness 203
civil protection 188
civil society 228
civil war(s) 176, 202
civil welfare volunteer 237
civilization 119, 186

civilizing mission 186
class 78, 111, 143-4, 153, 187, 208-9
client-centered approach 247
climate change 15, 41, 176, 190, 193, 227
coexistent 97, 161
coexistent borderlands 170
Cold War 174, 188, 190, 219, 221, 224
collaboration among professional social workers 50
collaborations 34, 110, 122
collective history 202
collective identity 180, 181
collective imagination 181, 194
collective response 193
collective sense of national identity 179, 198, 201
collective well-being of humanity 193
collegiality 30
colonial boundary lines 173
colonial population(s) 186
colonial power 27
colonial rule 103
colonialism 31, 46, 118, 186, 187
Colonization 94, 171, 173, 186
combined definition 96
common goals 35, 231
comparative analysis 31, 91, 137, 194
comparative social policy 30, 32
comparative study 31, 45, 139, 245
compassion 124, 248-9
compound eyes 16, 21, 89, 93, 126, 138, 144, 176
Conference (1928) the first international social work conference in Paris 24
conflict prevention 35
constituency 16, 89, 109, 125-8
constituents 103, 109
constructionist paradigm 181
container but also a wall 73
contemporary era 191
contours of our global society 194
Convention on the Rights of Persons with Disabilities 118
Convention on the Rights of the Child 118, 198
conventional free capitalist system 228
conventional perception 181
conventional request-based process 220

257

Cooperative for Assistance and Relief Everywhere International (CARE) 66
cosmopolitan 79, 129, 185, 189-90, 193
cosmopolitanism 10, 24, 59, 76, 162, 179, 184-5, 189, 190, 192-4, 202
*cosmos* 184
Council on Social Work Education (CSWE) 29
counter-reaction 191
country of origin 199, 202
country-by-country social work 20
COVID-19 41, 184, 222-4, 227-31
Cox, D. 22, 35-8, 44, 47, 99
crew member of the spaceship Planet Earth 142
cross cultural perspective 45
cross-border 169, 170, 187, 193
cross-cultural contact 63, 65, 67, 69, 81
cross-cultural counselling 46, 65
cross-cultural social work 65, 69, 137
cross-cultural understanding 30
cross-cultural understanding and education 192
cross-national 41, 46
cross-sectional 234, 241
cultivation of multicultural understanding 182
cultural boundaries 29, 108
cultural globalization 202
cultural identities 184, 186
cultural imperialism 31
cultural inclusion 205
cultural perspective 46

# D

deceased (continuing bonds) 247
democracy 21, 35, 45, 47, 88, 91, 163, 221-4
denying the plurality and diversity of individuals 201
Department for International Development (DFID) 218
deterritorialization 175
developed countries 28, 80, 99, 118, 120, 192, 226
developing countries 31, 66-7, 69, 99, 118, 159, 230
development agencies 217

Development Assistant Commission (DAC) 216
Development Bank of China 223
Development Cooperation Charter 220
development financial institutions (DFIs) 217
development of international social work 42, 44, 46-7, 59, 66-7, 79, 86-8, 98
development of social work/social welfare 50-1, 74, 87, 89, 90, 93-4, 98, 113, 125, 131, 163
developmental assistance 66
developmental stage 43, 75, 81
dialectically 35-6, 40
difficulties and problems in people's lives 108-9
digital technology 193
dignity of humanity 184
Diogenes 189
disability 209, 248
disappearance of international social work 50
disaster 26-7, 43, 45, 66, 91, 138, 176, 193
discrete nation-state 193
discrimination 209-10, 155, 159, 199, 200, 204, 208-10
discriminatory ground 200
displaced persons 206-7
disseminating social work 43
dissemination of social work 28
Dissolution of the Soviet Union 174
distressed minority groups 26-7, 43, 138
DNA molecule 124
domestic interference 120
domestic practice and advocacy 33
domestic social work (practice) 20, 39, 68-9, 70, 104
domestic violence 34, 208
Dominelli, L. 41, 247
double statelessness 202
dual citizenship 205
dual or multiple citizenship 199, 201
*dukkha* 247

# E

Earthians 111
Eastern Europe 216

East-West relations (relationship)  28, 44,
    46-7
ecological approach  37, 247
ecology  35, 37, 47
economic expansion  15, 80
economic immigration  191
economic powers  219
educational expansion  192
egocentrism  138, 146, 153
elderly care  199
elite and the superiority of  146
emergency relief activities  66
Encyclopedia of Social Work  66, 71
enduring allure of national identity  191
engaged Buddhism  250
English-medium country  17
English-speaking  15, 52, 163
environment (or nature)  38, 65, 156, 247
environment protection  78, 192, 215
environmental degradation  193
equal partner cooperation  225
equality  49, 73, 76, 187
erasure of national borders  79, 129
essence of international social work  17, 80,
    137
essentialist discourse  204
ethical business  231
ethical guidelines  36
ethical practice  39
ethics  21, 31, 47, 238
ethics and governance  190
Ethnic belongingness  200
ethnic boundaries  182
ethnic group(s)  100, 102, 180-1, 193, 200
ethnic heritage  196
ethnocentrism  138, 192
ethnosymbolism  181
ethos  184, 185
EU (European Union)  77-8, 178, 222
Eurasia  146, 176
European powers  173, 179, 186
European countries  28, 157
everything matters  246
evolution of national consciousness  181
exchange of information, knowledge, ideas,
    skills, and model  25, 43, 63, 65
exploitation  173, 199
eyes (views) from the outside  93

# F

Falk, D.  32, 35
false narratives  191
family reunification  208
family reunion  204
family visitation  208
faith-based organization  238, 247, 250
feudal system  172
filtration-sites  172
final definition of the new international
    social work  17
Finance Ministers and Central Bank
    Governors of G20 countries  221, 227
Five Buddhist Commandments/Five
    Precepts/five categories  124, 247, 249
folk or ethnic group  102
forced migration  176
foreign affairs  63, 65, 70, 78, 81, 138-9
foreign aid  215-6, 219, 220, 222-6, 230
foreign policy  216, 220
foreign workers  65, 77
foreigners  65, 72, 155, 158, 174, 197, 204
fortification of international partnerships
    192
foster care  199
fostering empathy  193
four dimensions of action  33
Fourteen Points  173
Fourth (4th) International Academic Forum
    on Buddhist Social Work  124
fourth major practice method  30
Free and Open Indo-Pacific (FOIP)  221
free-market model  227
French Revolution  186
Friedlander, W. A.  71, 110
frontiers  71, 171-3
Fujimori, Y.  12
*Fukushi*  58, 74
Fukuyama, F.  221
functional alternative  245
functional definition  32, 33, 37, 45, 47, 50-1,
    95, 96
function-focused definition  52

# G

game-theoretical framework  224

Gellner, Ernest 180, 181
gender 111, 143, 176, 200, 208-9, 248
gender discrimination 200
genealogies 171
General Agreement of Tariffs and Trade (GATT) 226
general welfare 216
generation left 227-8
genocide(s) 148, 208
geographic information system (GIS) 234
geography 170
geopolitical order 169
given country 198
Global Action Plan to End Statelessness (the) 200
Global Agenda for Social Work and Social Development 36
global citizenship 189
global coexistence 194
global cross-border social issues 176
Global Definition of Social Work Profession 36, 94, 99, 108, 244, 250
global economy 190
global economy's interconnectedness 193
global financial organization 32
global in nature 193
global integration 191
global issues 30
global justice 190
global markets 193
global order 183
global profession 15, 88, 92, 120
global social issues 15, 41
global social work 42, 101
global values 182
global eyes 48, 91
global lenses 48, 91
globalization International Social Work in 23, 130
globalization international social work under 40, 51, 88, 95-8, 106, 120, 131
globalization of practice 36, 38
globalization of social issues and problems 23, 34, 38, 88
globalization of social work 23, 38, 41-2, 51, 97, 120, 122, 129, 131
globalization of standards 38-9
globalization of the realities 38

globalization of Western-rooted (professional) social work 15, 17, 88, 98, 120, 122
globalized ('local') practice 97
globalized 'local' social work 51, 97
globalized social system 34
globalized society 198
Gohori, J. 99, 124, 247
Goldman, B.W. 30
good (national) citizen 117, 142
good domestic social welfare 79
good international man/woman 142
good international[ly-minded] citizen 117
good internationalized state 79
good nation state 79
goodwill 43, 45, 124
Google, Apple, Facebook, Amazon, and Microsoft (GAFAM) 228-9
governance structures 192
Great Wall 228-9
Greater East Asia Co-prosperity Sphere 186
green social work 247
Group of 20 (G20) 221, 227
Gutenberg's printing press 186
G-Zero era 224

# H

habitation of the Earth 185
Han race 111
*Handbook of International Social Work* 22
Haug, E. 35-6, 38, 40, 44, 47
Healy, L. M. 17, 22, 24, 29, 30, 31, 33, 35-9, 42, 44, 47, 67, 99, 101, 176, 254
Henly Passport Index 207
Herath, H. M. D. R. 244
Hindu social work 94
historical reinterpretation 187
Hobsbawm, Eric 181
Hokenstad, M. C. 22
Holy Roman Empire 172
home country(ies) 10, 34, 64, 91, 108, 200
homogeneous group identity 180
host country(ies) 191
Huegler, N. 17, 22, 24-5, 27, 32, 37, 39, 40-2, 100
Hugman, R. 22, 34-6
human civilization 179, 194

260

human dignity 33, 37, 185, 189
human existence 176
human interaction 185, 194
human minimum 73
human perceptions and imaginations 194
human relationships 194
human rights 16, 21, 32-3, 35, 36-8, 40, 45,
    47, 50-1, 59, 71-3, 88, 91, 95, 108, 110, 127,
    130, 163, 185, 188, 193, 201, 202, 205, 221
human security 183-4, 188
human society (of culture) 246
human trafficking 176, 208
humanism 124, 189
humanitarian assistance 144, 221
humanitarian considerations 192, 230
humanity 184-5, 189, 190, 193-4
Huong, N. 248

# I

ID card 202
Idea (idee) 19, 111
ideal type 114, 128, 131
Idealtypus 112, 114
identity 10, 123, 170, 172, 176, 179, 180, 181,
    186, 191-2, 198, 201-5, 208-10, 224
ideological framework 182
ignorance and innocence 138, 147
imagined communities 181
IMF crisis 227
immigrant(s) 15, 26, 32, 45, 91, 138, 175,
    191, 201, 204-5, 208
immigration 175, 191, 197, 199, 207, 208
immigration control(s) 210
imperial families 181
imperial rule 186
imperialism 28, 31, 45-7, 49, 118, 120, 186
independence 28, 173-4, 180, 186-7, 215, 220
independence of former colonies 44, 46
independent entity 93, 104, 123, 128
independent entity out of the sovereignty 16
indigenous people 94, 186
indigenous people/invaders 143
'indigenous' 'social work' 123
individual dignity 193
inductive construction 86
Industrial Revolution 187
industrialization 99, 161, 162, 180

Infrastructure Investment Bank (AIIB) 230
inherently antagonistic 192
in-person interactions of pre-modern tribal
    societies 181
integrated community 184
Integration Policy Index (MIPEX) 204-5
Inter-American Development Bank (IDB)
    218
interconnectedness 191-3, 246
interdependence 32, 47, 182, 189, 190
interdependence and one-sided
    complementarity as center-periphery
    relations 225
interdependent borderlands 170
interdependent, coexistent system 116
intergovernmental organizations 27, 29, 63,
    67
intergovernmental social welfare 30
internal conflict 202
internal integration 180
internally displaced persons (IDPs) 206, 207
inter-nation collaboration 192
international action 33
international adoption(s) 33, 128, 138, 175
international agencies 31
International Association of Schools of
    Social Work (IASSW) 24, 28, 30, 36, 52,
    66, 69, 70, 94, 99, 108, 122, 137, 150, 240
International Bank for Reconstruction and
    Development (IBRD) 217
international comparative analysis
    (perspective, research, studies) 46, 63-4,
    67, 69, 81
international comparison 15, 137
International Convention on Human Rights
    72, 75
international cooperation 24-6, 43, 63, 66,
    73, 81, 138, 182, 187-8, 191, 226, 228
International Council on Social Welfare
    (ICSW) 24, 66, 70, 137
international development agencies 34
international development work 34
international disintegration 73
international events 32, 39
International Federation of Social Workers
    (IFSW) 25, 36, 52, 66, 70, 94, 108, 126-7,
    137, 235
International Finance Corporation (IFC) 218

international foreign aid 215
international friendship programs 65
International Journal of Buddhist Social
  Work 245
International Labour Organization (ILO)
  27, 43, 45, 66, 105, 128, 138
international lens 39
International Migration Services 24
International Monetary Fund (IMF) 222,
  226-7
international nongovernmental
  organizations (INGOs) 27, 45, 89
International Organization of Migration
  (IOM) 197
international organizations 27, 34, 50, 66,
  77, 90, 91, 182, 188, 190, 193, 200, 230, 234
international peace movement 187-8
international perspective 31, 39, 41, 45-6,
  65, 189, 244, 255
international policy development and
  advocacy 33-4
international politics 170, 210
international practice 30, 32-4, 41
international professional organizations 24
international relations 62, 65, 170, 172, 190,
  198, 220-2, 224
international social case work 26, 138
international social welfare 9, 65-6
international social welfare/work 62
International Social Work 20, 21, 23, 25-6,
  63, 87, 89, 90, 107-10, 112-22, 124-32,
  137-40, 142-4, 146-8, 150-1, 153, 161-3,
  165, 254
international social work (A) 19, 104-5, 112,
  117, 128, 131, 164
international social work (B) 19, 104-5, 108,
  112, 128, 131, 164
International Social Work´(dash) 20, 114-5,
  121-2, 129, 131
international/collaboration 63, 66, 81
"international" social work 23, 29, 43, 46,
  90, 92, 128, 138
internationalism 10, 24, 41, 59, 73, 162, 179,
  182-3, 187-8, 190-4, 224
internationalization at home 65, 70, 81
internationalization of social work 116-7
internationalization/globalization 23, 88,
  90, 94, 120, 122, 130-1

international-related activities 16, 91
interpersonal contact 181
intersectionality 209
intersections 175
inter-state relations 176
intertwine 210
Inuit 94, 165
Ioakimidis, V. 41
Islamic Development Bank (ISDB) 218
Islamic social work 94, 121, 127

# J

Japan Bank for International Cooperation
  (JBIC) 218
Japan Communication Continent 150
Japan International Cooperation Agency
  (JICA) 62, 66-7, 218
Jebb, E. 24-5, 43-4, 90
JICA Sadako Ogata Peace and Development
  Institute 184
Johnson, H. W. 24-5, 44
journey seeking commonalities 143
journey seeking differences 143
jus sanguinis 199
jus soli 199, 203

# K

Kagami, M. 77
Kant, Immanuel 184-5, 189
Kantian thought 111
Kimberly, M.D. 30
Kipling, Rudyard 186
Kojima, Y. 62, 64, 67, 71, 72
Korean Japanese 203
kosmopolites 184, 189
Kreditanstalt für Wiederaufbau (KfW) 217
Kurd 202

# L

labor market 204
labor protections 188
language 19, 52-3, 58-9, 60, 74, 100, 102-3,
  111, 158-60, 180-1, 186-7, 196-7, 202, 208
language issue 74, 162
language of nationalism 186

language policy reform  187
Lavalette, M.  41
Lawrence, S.  39
League of Nations  26-7, 43, 138, 187
League's Health Organization  26
Lee, S.I.  203
liberal internationalism  219, 224
liberal nationalism  221
Lin, C. H.  200
lineage  180, 182
linear flow  27, 31
linguistic homogeneity  196
linguistic(s)  170, 173, 196-7, 201
Link, R.  22, 39
lived experience  175, 202, 247
Loan, N. H.  245
local social work  20, 32, 38-9, 45, 48, 50-1, 97-8, 104
local practice  39, 51, 97
Longo, M.  170-2, 174-6
Lorenz, W.  38
love  124, 153
Lyons, K.  40-2

# M

mainstream international social work  15, 90, 94-5, 119
mainstream model  88, 90-1, 92-3, 98, 132
mainstream social work  21, 86, 94, 128, 164
maneuver  205
Maori  94
marginalize the identities of people of mixed heritage  201
Marshall Plan  215-6
Marx, K.  21, 92
Marxian perspective  219
mass media  76, 181, 205
Matsuo, K.  28, 69, 119
Mearsheimer, J.  221-2
Médecins sans Frontières  66
*metta*  248
microaggressions  196
Middle Ages  172
Midgley, J.  31
midwifery facilities  199, 200
military policy  219
Millennium Development Goals (MDGs)

218, 229-31
minority  26-7, 43, 45, 94, 138
missionary work  15, 25, 43
mobility  204, 206
modern Western thought  59
modernity  180-1
modernization  180
modified (or indigenized) model of Western-rooted social work  249
Morgenthau, Hans  219, 224
multi- (national) corporations  77, 142
Multi-actor approach  183
multicultural coexistence  192
multicultural education  192
multi-cultural social work  69
multi-cultural understanding  182
multiculturalism  15, 192
multifaceted  10, 126, 129, 171, 176, 180, 182, 191
Multilayered discourse  244
multiple (points of) view  10, 16, 21, 93
mutual dependency  77
Myrdal, G.  71-3, 78, 92
mythologized  172

# N

Nagy, G.  32, 35
narrative of nationalism  186
narrow (or specific) definition and broad (or general) definition  29
nation (definition)  102, 180
National Association of Social Workers (NASW)  25, 66, 67, 70, 71
national borders  16, 19, 34, 39, 49, 50, 78, 86, 88-9, 90, 92, 94, 101, 104, 106, 108-12, 116, 122-4, 128-9, 131, 138, 143, 153, 162, 170, 173-5, 184-5, 187-91
national boundaries  20, 30, 77-9, 81, 101, 138-9, 142-4, 154-9, 185, 193
national consciousness  181
national egoism  73
national interest(s)  76-8, 80-1, 115, 122, 162, 170, 185, 190, 215, 219, 228
national interests predominate  185
national licensing/certificate program  123
national minimum  73
national self-determination  180

263

national social work 16, 19, 20, 113-6, 118, 120-2, 126-32
national survival and prosperity 192
nationalism 10, 24, 59, 73, 75-6, 80-1, 103, 155, 162, 180-2, 185-7, 189-92, 198, 210, 221
nationality 10, 77-8, 80, 111, 196, 197-205, 208-10
nation-state (definition) 76, 143, 169, 174, 179-184, 190, 192-3, 204, 210
native people 94
natural disasters 66, 193
naturalization 197, 202-3
navigating global landscape 192
neoliberal agenda 190
neo-Marxist model 228
neo-realism 224
new construction 22-3, 86, 132, 254
new imperialism 28
new international social work 15-7, 95, 161, 163
newly-constructed International Social Work 161
Nippon Export and Investment Insurance (NEXI) 218
no killing 124
no stealing 124
noncitizens 204
non-English-speaking country 52-3, 59, 60
non-governmental organizations (NGOs) 28, 32, 52, 66, 68, 70, 75-6, 78, 94, 111, 121, 127-8, 130, 146, 238, 246
non-human microbiotas 246
non-materialistic (spiritual) aspects 248
non-Western world 15, 97, 122, 163
norm 20-1, 58-9, 61, 71, 76-7, 81, 87, 95, 126-7, 154, 174, 224
North- (and) South relation (relationship) 23, 43, 45, 49, 50, 63, 81, 137, 146
North American Agreement on Labor Cooperation (NAALC) 77
North American Free Trade Agreement (NAFTA) 77
North-South problem 27, 28, 44, 46

# O

official development assistance (ODA) 10, 28, 71, 215-6
Ogata, Sadako 183
Ogawa, R. 206-7
Ohno, K. 119
Okada, T. (Toru) 64, 67
Okada, T. (Totaro) 65, 71, 72-3, 77
Olympics 187
One Belt, One Road 228
One-Third World 143
online communities 193
oppression 204, 209-10
oppressive structures 210
organic part of social work 246
Organisation for Economic Cooperation and Development (OECD) 216
origin of social work 131
original (indigenous) model of social work 249
other official flows (OOF) 216-8, 223, 225
other types of social work 16, 121, 130
Overseas Economic Cooperation Fund 216

# P

Pali canon 247
pañcasīla 247
Panchamukhi, V.R. 225
pandemic(s) 15, 41, 184, 222-4, 227, 228, 230-1
*papañca* 248
Paris Stock Exchange 225
participatory media platforms 193
passport(s) 78, 142, 196, 202-3, 205-7, 229
*paticcasamuppada* 246
patriotism 191
Pawar, M. 17, 22, 24-5, 27, 32, 35-42, 44, 99, 100, 254
Payne, M. 22, 38
peace 26, 35, 130, 154, 172, 173, 183, 187-8, 216, 249
Peace of Westphalia 172-3, 179
Pederson, P. 29, 100-1, 108
people from "stateless nations" 202
perception 21, 58, 109, 139, 148, 156, 181, 194

Period I 42-3, 47, 88, 90
Period II 42, 46-7, 49, 88, 90, 139
Period III 42, 47-9, 51, 88, 91, 139
peripherals 97, 119, 123, 129, 169, 175
permanent residence 204
person standing watch 94
personal inner transformation 248
Peters' Projection 146
Phase I 87, 90, 92
Phase II 29, 47, 49, 87, 90, 92
Phase III 90, 92
Phase IV 90-1, 93, 96
philanthropy 124
Philippines-American War 186
philosophy 19, 109, 111, 114, 126-7, 129, 189, 244, 249
Piketty, T. 227
Pinker, R. 71-3, 78, 92, 143
pivotal ideology 191
pivotal role 182
Pizer, H.F. 69
placation measures 28
platform capitalism 228
Plato 21, 92
Platonic thought 111
pluralism 185
point of reference, approach 58
*polites* 184
political aggression 15
political opinions 200
political participation 204
populism 191
post-Cold War era 190
post-colonial era 186
post-COVID-19 capitalist model 228
postindustrial society 99
postmodern point of view 38
post-pandemic 224
post-truth era 191
Post-World War II 216
poverty 49, 65, 68, 70, 118, 155, 176, 183, 224, 230
poverty alleviation 80
poverty reduction 192
power difference 47, 49
power dynamics 180
power of nationalism 191
practice related to overseas 50

practice-based definition 33
Prebisch-Singer hypothesis 219
pre-industrial society 99
pre-modern Europe 172
pre-modern 179-81
prevalence of cross border identity 202
preventive measures against socialist revolution 28
principle of birthright citizenship 199, 202
principle of social constructionism and postmodernism 181, 201
principles of national sovereignty 186
private-sector development 217, 218
professional building 36
professional colonialism 120
professional imperialism 47, 49
professional social work organizations 27
professionalization 31, 123, 125, 130, 238
promotion of the profession 45, 47, 91
propaganda 219
propagation of nationalism 191
Proparco Group 217
Protestant(s) 172
public health issues 176

## Q

quantitative and qualitative data 201

## R

race 100, 102-3, 111, 155, 200, 208, 209, 220
Ramanathan, C. S. 39
Ranger, Terence 188
Rautenbach, J. 240, 242
reconciliation of environmental protection with economic growth 192
Red Cross 24, 43, 52, 66, 90, 105, 138
redefinition 161
reformist approach 28
refugee 29, 32-3, 65, 70-1, 77, 175, 200-2, 206-7, 221
Refugee Convention 206-7
refugee protection 210
refugee studies 198
regional 23, 25, 103, 126, 174, 185, 188, 218, 230, 236

265

regional associations  28
regionality  224
regulation school  228
rejection of identities  201
religion  76, 111, 143, 153, 158-9, 200, 208, 250
religious  25, 43, 94, 157, 172-3, 179, 188, 247
Renaissance  189
resistance movement  186
resolutions and declarations  72
right from birth to a name (the)  198
right of hospitality  184
rights of minorities  188
right to acquire a nationality  198
*Rinen*  19, 54, 111
Rohingya  200
roles and functions of international social work  41, 51, 97
Roman Empire  172, 189
Romanyshyn, J.M.  66
Rosen, Michael  189
Rousseau, J-J.  21, 92
Russian Invasion of Ukraine  207, 221

# S

Safeguarding individuals  183, 185
Sakamoto, E.  99, 245
Sanders, D.  29, 67, 100-1, 108
Sangbo, Karma  244
Sasaki, A.  99, 203, 210, 245
Save the Children  24, 43, 52, 90, 105
Schengen Convention  142
Scramble for Africa  173
seek refugee status  202
self-determination rights  175
self-sufficient, closed system  116
Sen, Amartya  183
sexuality  209
*shakai-fukushi*  61
Shanghai Construction Group  226
Shiobara, Y.  202
short-term stay  207
Sino centrism  146
Sirimanne, C.  248
sister city program  65
skepticism  226

small island country  146, 153, 156
Smith, Antony  180-1, 184
social bulimia  205
social care  124
social constructivism  170
social development  35-7, 58, 74, 188
social integration  204-5
social justice  19, 21, 35-6, 38, 45, 47, 50, 71, 88, 91, 95, 108, 110, 163
social media  191
social norms  224
social problems  28, 38, 39, 40, 50, 247
social strata  143
social welfare officer(s)  237
social welfare policy(ies)  33, 50, 64-5, 180
social welfare situation  15, 63, 64
social work = professional social work  99
social work = Western-rooted professional social work  108, 130, 161
social work and social workers  96, 162
social work as a whole  16, 95, 98, 105, 108, 126
social work by country  20, 94, 104
social work by government(s)  123
social work colonialism  31, 49
social work imperialism  120
social work internationalism  41
social work needs  39, 161
*Social Work Year Book*  43, 66-7, 71
social work's capacity  37
social work-developed countries  43, 52
socialism vs. capitalism  28
socially disadvantaged  71
social-work-less developed countries  52
sociology  62, 103, 170, 172, 198
socio-political contexts  181, 191
soft loan  218
solidarity  78, 184, 187, 190, 228
Somananda, O.  247
south-south cooperation  225, 228
sovereign country(ies)  16
sovereign nation(s)  16, 92, 100, 103-4, 108, 112, 122, 131, 161-2, 180
sovereignty  16, 89, 93, 102-3, 112, 113, 117, 123, 131, 162, 169, 172-3, 179, 182, 186, 188, 190, 192
spaceship Earth  142, 194
Spanierman, Lisa  196

spin-off 112-3, 125
Spinoza, B. 21, 92
spirit of Bandung 220
Spirituality 250
Stage I 98
Stage II 98
Stage III 98, 113, 125
standardizing language 186
state social work 20, 104, 123, 125, 127
state-capitalist model 228
stateless children 198-200
stateless people 175, 199-202
States Parties 198
Stein, H. 29
Stoic 189
Sue, Derald Wing 196
Suharto regime 227
Sun Wu-K'ung 163
supra-national 41
Supranationalism 174
Sustainable Development Goals (SDGs)
192, 218, 227
Swedish International Development Agency
(SIDA) 218

# T

Taliban 206
Tanada, H. 203
target population 36, 86, 109
technical assistance 216-7
Telegeography 150
Ten Christian Commandments 124
*The Invention of Tradition* 181
theory of the state model 88, 92, 98, 132
theory of the State 9, 21, 59, 86, 101, 129, 163
Theravada Buddhism 248
Thirty Years' War 172, 179
Thomas, R. 22, 176
TikTok 228
tool for realizing a better life 198, 204
torch 122, 131
Tories 218
Traditional nation-state system 174
trafficking 176, 208
trans- or inter-governmental organizations
127
transboundary perspective 193

transfer of information, knowledge, ideas,
skills, and model 50
transformation 173, 187, 190, 194, 210, 228,
242, 248
transgressions 176
transnational fostering 39
transnational organizations 138
transnational social fields 174
transnationalism 192
Treaty of Tordesillas 173
tribes 143
Two-Thirds World 63, 66, 137, 143
typical characteristics 197

# U

UN Security Council ("P5") 183
UN Statelessness Convention 200
UN World Food Program 188
undeveloped countries 28
undocumented migrants 199
UNICEF East Asia and the Pacific Regional
Office 237-8
unidirectional 31, 45-50
unidirectional relationship 47
unipolar theory 120
United Nation Hight Commissioners for
Refugees (UNHCR) 199, 200, 206
United Nations 16, 27-9, 34, 52, 59, 63, 66-7,
70-2, 75-8, 89, 94, 109-11, 115-6, 122, 129,
163, 182-3, 188, 197, 228, 234, 236, 239
United Nations Children's (Emergency)
Fund (UNICEF) 52, 66, 188, 237
United Nations Development Program 188
United Nations Development Program's
Human Development Report 183
United Nations Educational, Scientific and
Cultural Organization (UNESCO) 126-7,
188
United Nations General Assembly 218, 229
United Nations High Commissioner for
Refugees 188, 199
United Nations Population Fund (UNFPA)
148
United State Agency for International
Development (USAID) 218
United States Children's Bureau 66
universal capacity 184

267

Universal Declaration of Human Rights 72, 115, 182, 188, 198
universal human rights 185, 193
universal legal framework 185
universal social work 247
universalism 185
unregistered children 200

# V

value (judgmental) factor 163
value = human rights and social justice 40
value elements 51, 95
value-driven action 37
value-focused definition 37, 45, 47, 50, 96
various (other) types of social work 16, 121, 130
Vasudevan, V. 52
very modern era 185
view from the outside 16, 21, 163
viewing others as members of an extended family 194
virtual spaces 193
visa waiver 206
voluntary work without expecting returns 124
vulnerability 204

# W

Wang, M.S. 200
war orphans 65
war sufferers 26, 138
Warren, G. 24, 26, 33, 43-4, 67, 90, 139
Waruni, T. 247
Washington Consensus 223
way of viewing matters 16, 19, 21, 58, 59, 61, 71, 75-7, 80-1, 86, 89, 93, 95, 98, 109-10, 112, 120, 124, 126-7, 143-4, 163, 255
Webb, S. A. 41-2
WeChat 228
Weibo 228
welfare state(s) 21, 59, 73-4, 76, 81, 89, 92-3, 123, 125, 129, 138, 143, 163
welfare world 21, 54, 59, 61, 73-9, 81, 89, 92, 129, 163
wellbeing 36-7, 74, 89, 93, 104-5, 108, 126, 161, 204-5, 249

wellbeing of all sentient beings 249
well-being; human 33, 37, 58, 105, 109, 110, 126, 138, 143, 193, 219, 246, 247
well-being; social 247
we-ness 201
Western countries 27, 216, 228
Western European countries 27, 215
Western or Northern powers 28
Western theories 142, 176
Westernization 120, 129
Westernizing indigenous people 186
Western-rooted professional social work 9, 16-7, 36, 51, 52, 74, 96-100, 108-10, 113, 120, 122, 124, 126-7, 129, 130, 132, 161, 163, 165, 244
Westphalian systems 172, 190
white man's burden 186
Wickramasinghe, A. 245
Wilson, Woodrow 173
win-win-win hypothesis 224
women and gender 176
women's rights movement 187
workers' rights movement 187
working committee, CSWE's 29
working conditions 105, 199
World Bank 216, 218, 222, 226, 230
world citizen 118, 129, 142
world citizenship 184
World Cup 187
World Health Organization (WHO) 66, 128, 235-6, 239, 242
world state 79, 122
World Trade Organization (WTO) 226
World War I 25, 103, 173, 187
World War II 28, 103, 138-9, 158, 173, 182, 188-9, 215-6, 220, 226
world welfare 79

# X

Xu, Q. 22, 24

# Y

Yamato race 111
yardstick 21, 109-10, 115, 118, 122-4, 126-7, 129
Young, J. 205

# Z

Zionism 146
Zomia 175

# International Social Work
## of All People in the Whole World
## A New Construction
### Second Edition

2024 年 10 月 31 日　初版第 1 刷発行

編著
東田全央
秋元　樹
松尾加奈

デザイン
坂野公一＋節丸朝子
（welle design）

発行者
淑徳大学アジア国際社会福祉研究所

制作・発売
株式会社 旬報社
〒 162-0041 東京都新宿区早稲田鶴巻町 544
TEL 03-5579-8973　FAX 03-5579-8975
ホームページ https://www.junposha.com/

印刷・製本
中央精版印刷株式会社

© Masateru Higashida et al. 2024, Printed in Japan
ISBN978-4-8451-1955-4